G000165584

Reflections in a Chalice

The Memoirs of a Practical Priest

by

Brian Lucas

To Ann

with my very best wishes.

Brian Lucas

Published by Adastral Books

Published by Adastral Books
'Pen-y-coed'
6 Arnhem Drive
Caythorpe
Grantham
Lincolnshire
NG32 3DQ

brian.lucas@savageclub.com

2 4 6 8 10 9 7 5 3 1

First published 2011

© Brian H Lucas

The moral right of the author has been asserted.

All rights reserved. No part of this publication may be reproduced or transmitted in any form or by any means, electronic or mechanical, including photocopying, recording or any information storage and retrieval system, without permission in writing from the copyright holder.

Every effort has been made to trace the copyright sources of the photographs used. The publisher would be pleased to hear of any outstanding copyright permission in order that due acknowledgment might be made in any future edition.

Copyright acknowledgements

Black and White photographs in the text:
Page 19.   An Enemy of the People: Gables Studio, Lampeter
Page 23.   St Stephen's House Group: This photograph has been reproduced by kind permission of Gillman & Soame photographers.
Page 88. Escorting SS Uganda to Cyprus: No.84 Squadron.
Page 108. Handley Page Victor aircraft in flight: No.55 Squadron

Photographs in the Second Colour Section:
With His Holiness the Pope: L'Osservatore Romano
Savage Club Founders' Dinner: The Savage Club

ISBN 978-0-9567588-0-4

Printed in the United Kingdom by
CPI Antony Rowe
Chippenham, Wiltshire, SN14 6LH

For my family.

CONTENTS

ACKNOWLEDGEMENTS

For the past few years a former parishioner, Mrs Sheila Biggs, has been urging me to write my memoirs; she wanted to remember the many amusing anecdotes I had related to her. At her prompting I began to write this book at the beginning of 2010. Sadly, Sheila has died before it will appear in print, but she was the driving force behind this publication. May she rest in peace.

Throughout the writing and preparation of this book I have relied a great deal on a brother Savage as my mentor. Dr Eric Midwinter, OBE, a social historian and a co-founder of the University of the Third Age, who was for ten years the Visiting Professor of Education at the University of Exeter, and whose entry in Who's Who occupies a quarter of a page, has read every chapter as it was written, and has acted as a critical friend at each stage. The shape of the book is due in great measure to Eric's incisive comment and wise guidance. The errors and any inaccuracies are all my own.

I am grateful to Marshal of the Royal Air Force Sir Michael Beetham GCB CBE for jeopardising his good name by writing the Foreword. Sir Michael has been a good friend over the years and the Royal Air Force, and the nation, is indebted to him for his leadership and wisdom in the world of aviation.

I acknowledge freely the debt I owe to my wife for supporting my ministry and, at the same time, running our home and raising our family. She is by my side throughout the pages of this book.

Finally, my gratitude is due to my younger son, Simon, for his skill in editing this book and preparing it for printing. I also thank Robin Elliott, the Prepress Analyst at CPI Antony Rowe, who designed the cover as well as having oversight of the printing.

BHL
All Saints Day, 2010.

FOREWORD

by

Marshal of the Royal Air Force Sir Michael Beetham,
GCB, CBE, DFC, AFC, DL, FRAeS

This is a remarkable book because it is written by a remarkable man. Brian Lucas was born in the steel town of Port Talbot, on the South Wales coast, where he was educated at the local Grammar School. When he was ordained he was appointed to Llandaff Cathedral in Cardiff, under a dynamic dean, which gave him the confidence he needed in abundance in his next job, which was to build a new church between a pub and a fire station on a housing estate. Three years later it was finished, and when the church was consecrated in 1970, his love of flying moved him to accept a commission in the Chaplains' Branch of the Royal Air Force.

In six years he had completed two significant pieces of work, which displayed his appetite for getting things done. It also demonstrates his clarity of vision for the overall aim and his eye for detail, both of which he would require in the years ahead, when the Royal Air Force faced enormous challenges in restructuring. When he was appointed Chaplain-in-Chief of the Royal Air Force in 1991, it was a time of 'down-sizing' in the armed forces, and he feared that service men and women were being 'costed not valued', a theme he preached time and again.

He is a very effective preacher, and held the veterans of Bomber Command enthralled at the service, in a packed St Clement Danes Church, prior to the unveiling of a statue of Sir Arthur Harris by Her Majesty Queen Elizabeth The Queen Mother, causing the congregation to laugh out loud at his anecdotes. A friend of his, a Roman Catholic chaplain, has described his chief memory of Brian as, "one of laughter, and not just your common or garden laughter, but the stomach-hurting rolling-on-the-floor variety. We have burned gallons of midnight oil together ranging widely over history, theology, poetry, beauty and even on a couple of occasions have actually solved the riddle of the Universe, which, alas, escaped us both the morning after!"

His first tour of duty was with a maritime reconnaissance squadron in Cornwall operating first Shackleton and later the new Nimrod aircraft. Joining the crews on patrol for long hours over the Western Approaches he was in his element as a priest among men. His passion for aviation shines through nearly every page of the book with a boyish enthusiasm. He was never happier than when he was visiting RAF units and moving among the people he served as Archdeacon.

This book is chiefly remarkable because it sheds light on the enormous amount of pastoral activity being carried out on a daily basis in the hangars and workshops of the Royal Air Force, much of which is unseen and unsung. It is my belief that it is a good song, and Brian Lucas sings it well.

Michael Beetham
October 2010
Norfolk

CHAPTER ONE:

The Early Years

On a chilly evening in January 1940 some of her cousins and friends surrounded my mother's bed at "Pen-y-coed" in George Street, laughing and joking until tears streamed, when the midwife arrived and ordered them out. A few hours later Brian Humphrey Lucas was born. I was brought up in that house in Port Talbot, South Wales, in a loving and supportive church family. I learned the Christian faith on my mother's knee. My parents didn't make a show over their worship, but my father sang bass in St Theodore's Church choir and my mother took me to the Sunday morning Sung Eucharist from an early age.

My earliest memory, when I was about three years old, was of angels singing as I crept into bed alongside my Mum in the morning. It was a soft, ululating murmur, almost like sighing. As far as I could tell, the sound came from near the Plaza Cinema about half a mile away, but when I grew older I traced the sound to the gas meter in the front lounge below the bedroom. My next certain recollection is the sight from Pen-y-Cae Road of a red glow over Swansea, across the bay, as the town burned after a ferocious bombing raid in 1944.

Edith Mary Owen, my mother, was a Silver Service Waitress, first in the Esplanade Hotel, Porthcawl, and later in the Grand Hotel, Port Talbot. I can remember her demonstrating how to replace a soiled dining room table cloth, fully set out with cutlery and glassware for six diners, without revealing an inch of table-top. It was done by feeding the clean linen under the wine-stained cloth, moving the cutlery etcetera as it crept over the table, ending with a clean tablecloth in place and a rolled-up soiled cloth in her hand. It was a skilful task, which few hotels can boast today. She met my father when she began to attend his dances as she was an elegant and competent dancer. Before the war, my father, who was a fine ballroom dancer, had set up an evening Dancing Academy complete with a small dance band, and arranged dances when his work permitted. They married in St Theodore's Church, Port Talbot, on Easter Day 1939. As a young boy I could not understand why my older cousin Audrey was in the wedding photograph as a flower girl, while I was nowhere to be seen; it was most unfair.

My father, Frederick George Humphrey Lucas, was a Master Printer having served his apprenticeship with Mr Sid Corr, a local printer, and in Birmingham. In 1939 he ran a printing works single-handed in King Street, Port Talbot, employing a compositor on a casual basis. It was in effect an extensive garden shed which was packed with machinery and type-cases. As it was a wooden structure all the machinery was worked by hand. The huge poster press, which occupied nearly all the length of one side of the building, was turned by a handle attached to a flywheel reaching to his shoulder. When I was older, and the busy Christmas Pantomime season was imminent, with its demand for advertising posters, I would take turns with my grandfather in turning the wheel while Dad fed the paper and inked the big rollers without stopping production, unless I lost concentration and the handle lifted me right over the top of the flywheel. His stationery store and office occupied a room in the house itself.

During the Second World War several occupations essential to the war effort were 'reserved' from conscription to the armed forces. The printing trade was one such occupation, so my father did his 'bit' first by joining the Home Guard, and then by joining the British Transport Police as a constable. During the heavy raids on Swansea he was moved to the Swansea Docks. If he was on the early shift he

My father & mother at Hereford, 1937

would leave our house in George Street at 4.30 in the morning, cycle to Briton Ferry where he would rouse the ferryman to row him across the River Neath. He would then continue his journey along Jersey Marine road to arrive at the docks by six o'clock. At two o'clock he would cycle home along the same route. I was aware of my mother's anxiety for him, though she never showed it in front of me, and after lunch I would position myself in the bay window of the living-room with a view of the garden gate and wait with mounting worry until he appeared pushing his bike up the garden path, and my world was safe again. On Fridays my anxiety was tinged with excitement, for he bought a comic for me on his way home. After a hurried lunch, he would be off again to his printing works to catch up on the backlog, returning home mid evening ready for supper, sleep and another early start.

Later in the war he was transferred to Port Talbot Docks, which made life easier for him. In 1944 I was startled one morning to see a long line of US Army vehicles of all description lining the streets around my home. Together with my friends I learned the phrase, "Any gum, Chum?" And as we went from truck to truck we soon amassed quite a store of American chewing gum. I impressed one GI by explaining that the film actor Ray Milland was my father's first cousin; he gave me a dime, which I still have. My father told me that when he went on duty at the dock entrance at noon that day he was met by the sight of his colleague controlling a long line of American trucks, tank transporters, fuel tankers, Jeeps and weird vehicles designed for specific tasks. They were embarking on ships berthed at every quay, and when asked how long this had been going on he had the reply, "Since 6 o'clock this morning." The embarkation lasted for thirty-six hours; at each high tide the ships sailed out to be replaced by others. No-one knew then what all this was about, but the destination of this armada was Normandy. Out in Swansea Bay was observed the shape of what became known as a Mulberry Harbour being towed from Swansea Docks.

Into this mad-cap world my sister, Barbara, was born in 1944, but as babies didn't do anything interesting, her birth made little impact on me then. It was only when she was old enough to have a doll's pram that I would remove the doll, insert Barbara, and race about the garden with it, to her great delight and my mother's terror.

As 1945 was about to come to an end, I was allowed to put on my dressing-gown and go downstairs into the back yard with Mum and Dad to "see in" the New Year. Just as I was wondering what the fuss was about, I heard a ship in the docks sound its whistle, and as Big Ben struck midnight on the wireless, all the ships began to sound off with whistles and hoots, and whoops from the warships in port. Then the St Theodore's church bell started ringing and a train passing through the station sounded a shrill blast; before midnight had passed there was the sound of pandemonium in the air and I found myself shouting with glee at the noise.

I started at the Central Infants School that year and, allegedly, dragged my teacher, Miss Ware, around the classroom in an attempt to escape; I declared that I had now been to school and that was an end of the matter. I cannot remember that and was very fond of the patient and gentle Miss Ware. I can remember to this day the classroom smell of plasticene clay and milk; and I remember Pimpo, a toy clown on a round base which allowed it to roll about when pushed.

After the war our house was always full of laughter, especially in the weeks before Christmas, when my father would have a barrel of beer delivered, which he would set up in the cold pantry off the scullery. For some reason known only to him, the pantry became "The Harp & Mallet" for the festive season. My father, my uncles, with my mother and her cousin, Rene, would spend entire evenings conversing quietly until an outrageous gale of laughter would erupt; or they would start singing in harmony the hymn tunes that only the Welsh can compose. My sister and I, long since banished to bed, would sit on the stairs listening to the jollity, until the opening of the lounge door would send us scurrying like mice to our bedrooms. We would observe from the front bedroom window Uncle Fred departing with bags of Christmas presents for his children hanging from the handlebars of his bicycle, laughing as he weaved his way down the street, my other uncles and my father trying to keep him upright as he went, and my mother fearing for her brother's life.

One of my uncles visited very infrequently and I asked my mother one day why Uncle Bill was different from my other uncles. She cuddled me so that I couldn't see her tears, but I felt them splash on my head as she explained that he had been a prisoner of war in Burma and when he came home after the war she didn't recognise her own brother. I liked my Uncle Bill but even as a boy of seven I recognised emotional scar tissue—although I didn't call it that. He never ever talked about the war, and he never attended parades on Remembrance Sunday, on the contrary, they were anathema to him.

On Sunday mornings after church my father would take Barbara and me for a walk while Mum prepared the lunch. The usual destination was the Dyffryn steam locomotive depot in Taibach at the bottom of Goytre hill, and thus began another interest which has remained throughout my life: the steam engine. On a Sunday morning there would be several tank engines in steam waiting to be coaled ready for Monday's work. Sometimes a 'named' engine would be in the yard for the weekend, perhaps a 'Hall' class, and I began 'collecting' engine numbers. This was the last days of the Great Western Railway before it passed into British Railways ownership. Then we would return, with a huge appetite, to a steam-filled kitchen and vegetables ready to be served. It wasn't long before I had my first Hornby

St David's Day, Central School c.1951. BHL 6th from the left in the back row..

train set for Christmas. When older I would dash to the railway station to watch a 'Castle' class locomotive speed through pulling the up "Red Dragon" express at 0845 before rushing to school.

Primary School

I cannot remember much about my early years in primary school at the Central Boys School, across the road from the infants and girls' departments.

The Headmaster was Mr Pandy Rees, a friend of my father, who was strict but fair, although I was once sent to him for six of the best across the palm of my left hand for something or other. There was also a gentle teacher called 'Gammy' Rees; quite often he came to play chess with my father, and I discovered that his real name was George Rees. My class teacher was an interesting man known throughout the town as 'Daddy' Harris. He looked cadaverous and wore a bow tie. He was interested in the classics and the classroom wall was covered with photographs of the Acropolis of Athens and maps of the Fertile Crescent and the Babylonian Empire. It was Daddy Harris who planted in me the love of the ancient world. When I visited the Babylonian site of Mari on the banks of the Euphrates in Syria in 2005, I told my son, Mark, of Daddy Harris as I wanted his memory evoked in that ancient place.

After a few years I crossed the road again as the boys joined the girls department, where the Head Teacher was a maternal woman, Miss Lewis; the boys department was required for an expansion to the grammar school, and I enjoyed coeducation for the rest of my school life.

School holidays seemed endless. It was my treat to go with my Mum to the cinema on the Friday when school broke up, and I remember the elation, as I ate my sweets in the dark, at the prospect of no school until September. The days of fun stretched away into the distance of my mind. Most years we would take a Paddington train to Badminton where we were met by the publican from the village of Grittleton, a Mr Christie, who drove us in his Austin to the home of my Uncle Fred and Aunt Annie. They lived in a large old house in Grittleton, where the delicious smell of ham, eggs and chips awaited us. Old Fred Lucas was my father's uncle and he worked on the Grittleton House estate. We stayed there during the day, when Barbara and I would play with our cousins in the meadow behind the house. From time to time I would be sent across the road to the farm for a jug of fresh, foaming, creamy milk. Annie's daughter, Edna, had married a George Smith, and they lived with their two children in Castle Combe, about three miles away. As my grandfather Philip Lucas and my Grandmother, together with their other two sons, Harold and Gordon, would be staying with Fred and Annie, we had to walk each evening along dark country roads, with Barbara asleep in her pushchair as owls hooted overhead, to my cousins' home in Castle Combe where we slept each night. But not before the Clan Lucas had beaten the local team in several games of cribbage at the Neeld Arms. One day I walked with my Dad and Uncles past nearby RAF Hullavington; it was 1947, and for half a mile we walked under the wings of Lancaster bombers lined up on the perimeter track awaiting disposal.

I had so many cousins, but the only boy of my age was Malcolm, the son of my mother's sister and my Godmother, Auntie Meg. I cycled to his home in Margam one day and he persuaded me to cycle to Cardiff, thirty miles to the east along the arterial A48 road. It took us nearly four hours. We slept for an hour under a tree in Victoria Park, and then set off on the return journey. It was dark by the time Malcolm turned off in Margam and then I was stopped by a policeman for not having lights on my bike and was instructed to walk the last mile. I arrived at my back gate as my father was coming out to cycle to the police station to report me missing. He was very angry when he saw me, such was his relief. My mother, who must have been sick with worry, could only cuddle me, and tuck me up in bed with a glass of hot milk. The only part of my story I left unsaid was that three miles into the journey my bike skidded on gravel and I fell off into the road as a heavy lorry roared past six inches from my head. I decided that they had worried enough.

My mother's closest friend was Mrs Morfydd Watts, who lived next door. She had a daughter, Vashti, about my age, and with whom I would enjoy picnics on the hillside when we were old enough, and a younger daughter, Margaret, about Barbara's age. Their son was much younger than us. Auntie Morf, as we called her, was exuberant about life, and was, until very recently, given to preaching in the local chapels, and is quite a character. Her late husband, Cliff, was Church in Wales and an altogether quieter man.

For the rest of the holidays we spent as much time as possible on the beach. On a Saturday my father would arrive home at midday to find sandwiches packed and bottles of lemonade ready. We would set off carrying windbreaks, buckets and spades, food, and even a Primus stove for a hot cup of tea. Bus queues were long and so we would walk through the docks, where my Dad was well known, and catch a ferry boat to the far side, which left only a half mile walk to the beach. If the tide was out it meant a long walk to the water, but the sand dunes behind us afforded more than enough fun. The long walk home, with tired limbs, is best forgotten.

A Vocation in Embryo

About the age of eight, I joined St Theodore's Church choir, and after passing the scholarship to cross the road again and enter the Port Talbot Secondary Grammar

St Theodore's Church Choir Outing, c.1951. BHL left in back row behind his sister Barbara.

School, I was confirmed and became an altar server. The Vicar, the Reverend Eric Roberts (later Bishop of St David's) was rather a remote figure living in a huge Vicarage near the church, but the Curate was known to all and sundry as 'Father Bowen', a splendid priest who didn't miss a trick when it came to cajoling young lads to attend church services. It is hard to imagine a 14 year old today getting out of bed at 7.00am to cycle the half-mile to the church to serve at the altar at a 7.30am weekday service of Holy Communion, and being ticked off if he cut it fine. But I did, and endured Father Bowen's gentle, "Come on Brian, mun; you'll be late for school if we don't get on." The discipline was made easier because I was not alone: some of my friends were doing the same thing on the other days of the week.

In that way my vocation to the priesthood became an embryo, which developed as the years went by. Every year for nearly twenty years there were ordinands in that parish, so offering oneself for the priesthood was no big deal. This abundance of ordinands was largely due to Fr Bowen's unsung, energetic work about the parish. Young people flocked to him and to the dances he arranged in the Mission Room; he was short and rotund, and his bald patch made him appear tonsured. When he visited our home he didn't say very much, but holiness and goodness flowed from him, and we were glad he had called. I have ever since considered that to be the essence of a priest. He married my former Head Teacher, the maternal Miss Lewis, and together they quietly but busily served the parish.

Secondary School

The Port Talbot Secondary School was at the end of George Street, so I was always running down the lane at the last moment to arrive in school as the bell was ringing. It was a good grammar school with an enviable record of Oxford scholarships each year. The Headmaster was Mr Gomer Rees, a former chemistry teacher. He was a small man in stature but a giant when it came to running a good school. His word was law with staff and students alike. Always wearing his academic gown, as did all graduate members of staff, he knew the five hundred pupils by name and by their strengths and weaknesses. In my last year I was appointed by him as Deputy Head Boy, and I began to know him better. He was a firm but very fair man, with a nice sense of humour unknown to the student body, which referred to him as 'the Boss'.

One day in October 1953 my grandmother struggled up the hill to Pen-y-Cae Road where I was playing with Dinky Toys at the home of David Singleton, one of my friends. She told me that I had another baby sister. I had guessed something was afoot some weeks earlier when a pram appeared under the stairs. My mother had gone into hospital a few days ago and now all was revealed. Having been assured that Mum was alright, I continued my game until tea-time. I cannot remember the

Dyffryn Grammar School Orchestra 1955.

even tenor of my life being changed unduly by the new member of the family. Joan was as uninteresting as Barbara had been as a baby.

After the first few years in the grammar school, I began to grow and exercise my wings like any fledgling. I had for years enjoyed organizing my friends. I had a gang which met in the lean-to shed at the bottom of my garden where my father kept his bike along with mine. Six of us would squeeze in this tiny space, and in the absence of windows we stuck stubs of candles in bottles and planned schemes borrowed from the action scenes in the comics we read avidly. After half an hour we'd emerge gasping for air and somewhat sooty. Little wonder that about this time I began to wear spectacles. Older, now, I contributed to the school magazine, The Wayfarer, I joined the Christian Endeavour Society, the Forum which was the debating society and the Photographic Society. Instead of the garden shed, I now made a dark-room under the stairs, and emerged after a processing and enlarging evening with eyes streaming from inhaling photographic chemicals. I also took up the violin and joined the school orchestra, but having reached Grade Three in the Associated Board exams, my family could no longer tolerate the dreadful noise which emanated from my bedroom, and, to be frank, neither could I.

An interlude in Germany

On Friday, 9th September 1955, I joined the school party to Frankfurt am Main and Heidelberg. We travelled by train to Dover and crossed to Ostend on the Belgian

State Line ship R.L. Peeters. A train then took us from Ostend to Mainz where we changed at 0500 for a local train to Frankfurt. I was introduced to another 15 year-old boy, Peter Meyer and we took a taxi to his house at Oberlindau 29, where his father and mother, brothers and sister were waiting with coffee and rolls. It was just ten years after the war, and I was astounded at the amount of damage due to allied bombing. Apart from Swansea and an occasional visit to London, I had seen very little bomb damage. Frankfurt was in a mess; near Oberlindau was the US "IG" Building, their military headquarters in Western Europe. It was formerly the head office of an industrial firm. Peter told me that the Americans were always afraid that the Russians would take Frankfurt and that they had built huge ovens at the rear of the building for rapid destruction of documents if their fears were realized. At the other side of a park was the Opera House; an empty shell, the grand porch leaning out at a dangerous angle from the facade. Dr Kurt Meyer was an inventor and was at work all day, but after breakfast one morning Mrs Meyer told me how she had managed to survive the war by feeding her crying children with berries and leaves from the garden; it seemed that food was in much shorter supply than in Port Talbot. One of the reasons for this journey was to take part in a Youth Sports Competition and in a musical evening in a local school. I was impressed by a huge notice at the Stadium which displayed the "World Champions Participating: London, Vienna, Brussels, Berlin, New York, Amsterdam, Port Talbot." I described it in my journal that evening as "peculiar but pleasing."

For the middle weekend of the fortnight holiday we all journeyed by train to Heidelberg to take part in a Rugby match and a concert, and I stayed with the Knauer family in Ziegelhausen above the River Neckar. This was a delightful interlude spent with a jovial, happy family who, unhappily, spoke little English. But they owned two cars, one a luxury Mercedes, which impressed me mightily. And they were most kind and generous to a young Welsh lad abroad for the first time. The second week sped by in Frankfurt, and so, too soon, and to the sound of the school war-cry, "Talbot aye-oh" ringing through the platforms of the Hauptbahnhof, the train carried us home. The great impression recorded in my journal is of early morning crowds of people going to work in the offices and shops, as though, with a common purpose, determined to build a new state from the ashes of war. I am still in touch with Peter Meyer, now a Doctor of Law and assistant to the Finance minister of North Rhine-Westphalia.

· · · · · · · · · ·

The actor Richard Burton was an old boy of the school, indeed, he took his name from the English teacher, P H Burton. The annual school play had continued since his day, and so I joined the cast for several school plays under the direction of the Head of English, Mr Selwyn Davies. I have always found it difficult to retain information, and while I learned my lines, I was never confident and was content

The German Prisoner in Journey's End with the British Legion Players.

to play only small parts. But I enjoyed the buzz of playing to an audience and receiving its appreciation.

This inability to retain information was probably because I didn't apply myself sufficiently to studying the matter in the first place. I was too busy enjoying life. The 'O' Level examinations therefore came as a shock and horror for me. I did not shine as a star, but I scrambled through sufficiently to enter the sixth form. I had always delighted in the English language and chose it for study at 'A' Level, together with Geography and History. At the end of my first year in the sixth I was appointed a School Prefect for the following year along with several of my friends. I was also appointed Captain of my House—Leisan. This responsibility did not prevent me from putting an alarm clock in the desk on the stage in Hall, timed to go off while the Headmaster was conducting Assembly. It rang loud and clear and he was so furious that I lacked the courage to tell anyone that I was responsible for it, so it was rather a pointless exercise.

I obtained a Provisional Driving Licence in February 1957 and my father's younger brother, Gordon, a primary school teacher and an excellent actor, arranged for me to have lessons with a former police driving instructor. I learned to drive in a big Austin Twelve, and passed my driving Test first time. Uncle Gordon had a Ford Popular, and allowed me to borrow it freely. The Forum joined in debates with other schools; there were six form conferences in Dyffryn House, the Education

11

Authority centre near Cardiff, and so several of us would set off in the Ford to conference reunions which I delighted in organizing.

I remember one sunny morning watching a pilot performing aerobatics in a Tiger Moth aircraft over Port Talbot and with the certainty of Toad of Toad Hall, I knew in my heart that I wanted to be up there; I wanted to fly. When a Royal Air Force schools liaison officer visited the school a year later I applied for an interview. I told the large, squadron leader that I wanted to fly. He told me at once that as I wore spectacles, I could not fly, but might apply for a ground commission. I thanked him for his candour, declined, and returned to the Library. I didn't want to mend aircraft, I wanted to fly them. As it appeared that this was not going to happen, I put the idea out of my mind.

Since the summer of 1956 I had been taking casual work in the holidays to earn some pocket money. At first they were jobs like hiring deck chairs on the beach for the local council. The job was short-lived as it rained for two weeks and Hubert, my boss, was despondent. Until one day a wind got up off the sea and peeled back the roof of our shed, exposing two hundred deck chairs to the elements. "Bloody Hell", cried Hubert, as he wound the handle on his ticket machine. When the issued tickets reached his knees, he cried out again, "Bloody Hell, I have to account for all

The Council Road Gang 1957. Dai, Mac, BHL, Danny the Driver.

these tickets." My job came to a rapid end. That Christmas I worked as a Telegram boy at the Post Office. One afternoon I cycled the two miles in heavy rain to deliver a telegram to Richard Burton, who lived just outside the town centre. He opened the door to this dripping young lad, read the telegram and with a curt, "Thank you", closed the door again, and I cycled the two miles back to the warmth of the office. That was the only delivery which did not net me a tip.

The following Summer I worked as a member of a mobile road gang. Every morning I would cycle to the Council Yard and load a ton of tarmac on the back of the lorry, throw the barrow and tools on top, climb into the shed that occupied half of the back of the lorry and Danny the driver would take the five-ton Commer to patch the road outside some Councillor's house before breakfast on the lorry. If it was hot and sunny, we would then hide in a leafy lane outside the town and pick nuts; if it was raining we would play cards in the yard. The Foreman was known to all as Mac; I once espied him saluting himself in a mirror in his office. Another member of the gang would salute every Mitchells & Butler pub we passed. The following year I worked as a dustman, heaving heavy bins of rubbish into a lorry. I got on well with them all, and learned a great deal about life as they related their experiences.

As soon as I was eighteen my father invited me to join him on Saturday mornings for a pint at the Aberavon Workingman's Club, where he would spend a convivial hour with his friends and clients before lunch. It was here, under the critical gaze of the older members, that he taught me to play snooker. "Is that Fred Lucas' boy?" they would mutter as I miscued a shot.

Further horror came too soon in the guise of examinations. It came as no surprise to me that my 'A' Level results were not good enough for university entrance, so I spent a third year in the sixth form. So did Peter Walters, the Head Boy, but he was away much of the year sitting entrance scholarships at various universities, hence, in the following term, I was appointed by 'the Boss' as the acting Head Boy. I passed English, Geography and History at 'A' Level, and was offered a place at St David's College, Lampeter, starting in the Michaelmas Term 1959.

A Romantic Interlude

It was the custom then to hand around an autograph book during the last few days of school before scattering to the next stage in life, and one of the Prefects, Joy Penn, who was also leaving, signed her name in my book adding, "With Love". I had been courting Gillian Humphrey, a distant cousin from Hagley, near Stourbridge, for the previous two years. We corresponded and stayed at each other's home for a week most holidays, but this signature in my autograph book interested me. Nineteen months my junior, Joy Penn had been a year after me throughout secondary school. In the lower school she had a long plait which I would try to tie to the back of her chair during music lessons. She was a slim, attractive girl with dark hair and a wonderful smile, who lived in the village of Cwmavon, two miles up the Avon valley from Port Talbot.

On a sudden whim, when an afternoon attempting to learn Classical Greek from scratch had left me listless, I caught a bus to Cwmavon, found her house, and rang the bell. Joy answered the door and invited me into the front parlour. She had accepted a place to read for an honours degree in History, which she later changed to Geography, at Swansea University. After a short conversation about the future, I asked her to come with me to the nearby seaside town of Porthcawl on the Saturday. She said that she would like that, and I left after arranging to meet in town at her bus terminus. I almost skipped across the road; I knew this was good.

We went to Porthcawl on the bus, because I didn't want to borrow Uncle Gordon's car and thus declare what I was up to. We walked along the promenade and clambered over the rocks before having coffee and cakes in Louis' Cafe on the seafront. I discovered her keen sense of humour, her high innate intelligence, and her thrilling laugh. I was falling in love.

CHAPTER TWO:

Wider Horizons

Collegiate Life in Lampeter

St David's College, in the small market town of Llanbedr-pont-Steffan, or Lampeter in English, was a men-only college in mid-Wales which granted its own degrees of BA and BD under Charters dating from 1822, making it the third oldest degree-awarding institution in England and Wales. It had a student body of just fewer than two hundred men. The Old Building was like a small Oxbridge quad with a tower over the gatehouse, which contained the Porter's Lodge. Facing 'OB', as the quad was known, was Canterbury Building, a later accommodation and lecture block dating from the turn of the century. I applied to read an honours degree in English, and while I had matriculated with a State Scholarship, I was offered a place provided I passed an entrance exam for the Honours School. For some reason, this included a paper on classical Greek grammar. Greek was a subject taught at most public schools, but not at Port Talbot Secondary. I bought the book, '*Teach Yourself Greek*', and set to work during the summer holidays, alas, to no avail. I did not pass the Greek paper and so I could not read for an honours degree, but I was entered for a General Degree in the humanities. With hindsight, I would have chosen this degree above all other as a first degree, for it covered a range of fascinating subjects. Most students entered this course; the honours schools had very few undergraduates.

I drove up to Lampeter for the beginning of term in my uncle Gordon's Ford Popular, with Dad and Gordon (who was to drive back) and my cases, my steel trunk having been sent in advance by rail. I had been allocated a room on the ground floor of Canterbury Building, with its floors of brown linoleum and walls of dark-stained pitch pine, and once my bags were stowed in the room, I said 'cheerio' to my family and began the process of settling in and making new friends. The first task was to join a couple of other chaps in manhandling the college four-wheel trolley up to the railway station to collect trunks. With much hilarity, and a pint of beer in the station buffet, we piled the trunks high and returned to the college more or less in safety.

Born at the beginning of 1940, I was among the first to avoid National Service, so many of my new companions had seen something of the world, and the men in their second or third years were certainly well learned in the school of life. I grew up very quickly in their company. All three daily meals were taken in Hall and the Senior Scholar intoned a Latin grace before Dinner. Motor cars were forbidden, and we could not travel more than five miles outside Lampeter without permission from the Censor. Licensed premises in the town were 'out of bounds' to the college undergraduates, and the Censor, the Senior Lecturer in Philosophy, dressed in academic cap, gown and hood, would patrol the premises in the evening and 'Gate' any student caught imbibing. It is hard to believe that such restrictions were placed on a student body; apart from the strict no-men rule at her women's hall of residence, Beck Hall, Joy had no such limitations at Swansea. However, I discovered that because it was slightly remote from the town centre, the Station Buffet bar kept the station viable through its bar profits.

The railway ran from Carmarthen to Aberystwyth, and I would catch the 0830 train from Port Talbot, my friends from further east hanging out of the carriage windows as it drew into the station. A good connexion at Carmarthen would get us to Lampeter at 11.00am. But with only five trains a day it was only a matter of time before Dr Beeching's axe would kill the line.

The college had been going through a financial crisis in the years before I arrived, and in my first term its future was by no means assured. The Principal, Canon J R Lloyd Thomas, was the right man in the right place at the right time; he was a tall, handsome man; I believed he had served in the Royal Navy during the war. He was known to the body of undergraduates as 'Prinny', and was authoritative, eloquent and fought the college's battles with guile. The University Grants Commission would provide for higher education in Wales only through the federal University of Wales. During my first year he had persuaded University College Cardiff to apply for funds for Lampeter, thus permitting essential refurbishment and modest expansion in the teaching staff. When he addressed the Junior Common Room (JCR) to announce this he would have been lifted high on the senior men's shoulders were it not for his stern demeanour.

In my second year some of the older men in their third year, all of them having completed National Service and led by Bob Price, enlisted my aid in a spoof. The sixth-formers coming for interview seemed so fresh-faced, keen and young that Bob Price and his merry men felt obliged to test their mettle. They were met at the station and led to a lecture hall in Canterbury Building for their initial 'interview'.

Facing them down the hall was the interviewing panel in borrowed graduate gowns and hoods, with me as the clerk pretending to write notes. The youngsters were brought in one by one. '*Do you smoke?*' was the first question. '*No, Sir*.' '*Why not? Do you have a girl?*' '*No, Sir*.' '*Good Lord, not queer are you?*' And so on. It was outrageous. But at the third interview the pendulum swung against us. Half way through the interrogation, for that is what it was, the doorway suddenly framed a familiar large figure, who leaned nonchalantly against the jamb. We all stood up as Bob muttered, '*Sir*'. The gruff voice of authority replied, '*Carry on, Gentlemen*' and Prinny watched us squirm as we attempted to bring the interview to a convincing end. When we had dismissed the unfortunate, we awaited our fate, but the wily old bird just snarled out of the corner of his mouth, '*Five bottles of Port for High Table should set the record straight, Gentlemen*.' I learned my first lesson in leadership from Canon Lloyd Thomas.

Lampeter nestles in the stunningly attractive valley of the River Teifi, a celebrated salmon and trout river. My friends and I would often spend a delightful hour or two walking along the banks of the river. One Saturday afternoon early in my second term, my Cornish friend, Dick Adams, joined me in a stroll upstream. The sun was warm for January and we were developing a thirst when I noticed a small cottage set back from the river in a copse. Unbelievably, a sign hung above the door bearing the words, '*Fisherman's Arms*' which were barely legible due to weathering. We entered and found ourselves in a small, dark front room facing a polished oak counter, behind which were three barrels on trestles. A tiny old lady in a spotless white apron, her grey hair pulled back into a bun, appeared through a curtain to one side of the bar and asked in Welsh what we wanted to drink. I ordered two pints of bitter. She drew them foaming from a cask and set them before us as I paid her. Then she asked if we wanted to go into the back room. As I have always considered that life is an adventure to be enjoyed, I nodded, and propelled Dick through the curtain into a totally black chamber.

As our eyes began to pick out features in the dark we found two chairs by the curtain next to a man in uniform, which I considered risky given that Wales had strict laws about drinking after hours. Then I saw the nine inch black and white television screen in the corner, and remembered that Wales was playing England at Twickenham. Almost at once it was Half-Time and a dim bulb lit up the small parlour as twenty thirsty, sweating men passed their glasses to the old lady to be re-filled for the second half. The uniformed chap next to Dick, with 'Milk Marketing Board' on his cap badge, spoke to him in Welsh. I explained that Dick was English, or rather, Cornish, and had no Welsh. The MMB driver then informed us that his daughter had two spokes. While I turned this information over in my mind he added, '*She speak Welsh <u>and</u> English*.' Wales was defeated convincingly; not even the young Dewi Bebb could overcome Dickie Jeeps' team, but we all trooped out into the wintry sun having enjoyed some good Rugby. It was Dick Adams who taught me the splendid game of 'Fives' and we spent many hours exercising on the two courts in college.

When in my first year the President of the JCR, Eric Flood, announced to the JCR that the Principal had lifted the ban on visiting pubs the cheer was heard in Aberystwyth, as we marched behind him in cap and gown to the Red Lion. There was a tension between St David's College and University College, Aberystwyth. One Rag Week some members of our Rugby XV dressed in warehouse coats and in a hired van drove up to their Students' Union building and removed the front doors under the gaze of the Porter, who had been told that they were being taken to have the College Arms embossed on them. In my third year we captured their Rag Queen, an attractive girl who enjoyed our hospitality under guard in a room in the Red Lion Hotel for a few days. A suitable sum of money deposited in our Rag Fund ensured her release.

My degree course was based loosely on the Literae Humaniores (Lit Hum) course at Oxford: but with the addition of English taught by Professor Stanley Boorman and Mr James Sambrook, and History taught by the Reverend Fred David. The traditional Lit Hum subjects were Ancient History taught by Mr Frank Newte, Philosophy and Logic taught by the Canon Raymond Renowden, and classical Greek taught by Professor Arthur Harris. The latter was a fine elderly scholar, whose MA gown was green with age, and who lived in a house on the campus near an ancient mound known as the 'Ziggurat' out of respect for his knowledge of the ancient world. I can hear him now, speaking in a soft Herefordshire accent as he handed back a piece of translation I had submitted, *'My word, Mr Lucas, your translation is best where it approximates to the original Greek.'* Mr Newte was a timid bachelor who lived in isolation in the gatehouse tower. If he emerged to find a lady guest waiting in the Porter's Lodge, he would scuttle back to the safety of his ivory eyrie. He was a very kind man who had written a definitive work on the Punic Wars, but was too bashful to publish it. Mr David was known to all as 'Dicky Dai', and in my final year was elected Mayor of Lampeter and rejoiced as some of the students hauled him around the town on the Porter's trolley on Mayor-making Day. Mr Renowden was a gentleman, who suffered a slight ill health, possibly caused by taking his Censor's duties too seriously. His delightful wife, Ruth, taught Mathematics.

It was at the end of my first year that I bought a car, and kept it illegally in a lock-up garage in the town. A neighbour in George Street owned a black 1936 Morris Ten, registration CNY 311. Every Saturday he would wash and polish it before putting it back in his garage. He was an Elder in his chapel, and when he heard that I was considering Holy Orders, he offered the car to my father for £50. That was a lot of money then, but as the car was immaculate with a low mileage and one owner, Dad stumped up the cash and bought it for me. It was a beauty and weighed just over a ton. It made it far easier to spend Saturdays with Joy in Swansea.

Once, before I had the car, Dick Adams and I caught the early train from Lampeter to Carmarthen and from there a train to Swansea for the day. Joy and her friend Iris met us and we spent a lovely lazy day by the sea. It was so enjoyable that Dick and I decided to catch a later train back to Carmarthen and take the late bus from there. As we neared Carmarthen the rain began to lash against the carriage window, filling us with dismay and gloom. We then discovered that we had missed the last bus by ten minutes, and so we began to walk along the Lampeter road in the pouring rain with no outer coat to protect us. We tried to hitch a lift, but in the driving rain no one stopped. After half an hour a car stopped and gave us a lift for a couple of miles, and then we were back on the open road again. It stopped raining about four o'clock in the morning and we reached college about an hour later. The Morris Ten put an end to such calamity. I would advertise discreetly on the notice board outside the Dining Hall in Old Building that there were two or three seats available to Swansea on Saturday, and so I never travelled alone. We would set off at 0700 and at 0830 they would alight in the centre of Swansea while I parked near Beck Hall.

I became involved with the Drama Club, and played the part of Aslaksen, the printer, in Ibsen's '*An Enemy of the People*.' The play contains a line which has

St David's College Dramatic Society, Enemy of the People. John Oliver, Richard Theobald, and BHL as Aslaksen the printer.

19

remained in my mind throughout my life, '*For God's sake admit the enormity of the perversion when fools are allowed to govern the wise.*'

The College had a newspaper called '*The Gownsman*', which was quite independent of the College authorities; it was administered by a limited company, Gownsman Publications. A mature student who had been an accountant was Chairman of the Board and in my third year I became one of the two Directors; Stephen Thomas was the other. It wasn't onerous and I learned a lot about advertising revenue, marketing skills and cash flow. The Editor was Bruce Parker, a second year undergraduate with a shock of blond hair and a gregarious spirit. He was a very good editor and went on to become a television presenter for the BBC in Plymouth. His journalistic prowess brought the *Gownsman* a major scoop. After polling closed on the Welsh Referendum on the Sunday Opening licensed premises in 1961, Bruce and Stephen were positioned in the printers in Aberystwyth while I awaited the result in Carmarthen. As soon as it was announced I telephoned Bruce and the *Gownsman* was the first on the streets, beating even the *Western Mail* and the *Cambrian News* in telling the world that Carmarthenshire had 'gone wet'.

At the end of my second year I was elected as the College representative to the National Union of Students. This involved travelling for day conferences at the other Welsh University colleges and to the National Conferences at Margate and Liverpool. I enjoyed representing Lampeter in this way and tried to punch above our weight, for we were numerically very small. I stood for election as President of the JCR but was beaten into second place by the Chairman of the Socialist Society, Steve Wall. At this time I was Chairman of the Lampeter Branch of FUCUA: the Federation of University Conservative and Unionist Associations. On Saturday 3rd February 1962, I attended a Conservative conference in Hereford and ended the evening in the company of the splendid broadcaster of 'Tonight' fame, James Fyffe-Robertson, in the bar of the City Arms Hotel, where many of us were staying the night. In mid-March I was in London for the meeting of the Central Council of FUCUA when the Prime Minister, Ian McLeod and Enoch Powell were the keynote speakers. Earlier that week I had been given the last of my Smallpox vaccinations as the disease was then widespread in Wales, and I was not allowed to visit England without vaccination. I was on the Tube en route to Church House to hear Enoch Powell speak when I became very hot and broke out in a sweat. I left the train at the next station and fainted on the platform. As I came round I was looking up at a circle of anxious faces. '*It's alright*', I said in my slightly Welsh accent, '*It's only my smallpox...*' The word 'jab' was not heard, for I have never seen an Underground station clear so quickly.

Steve Wall and I were good friends, and one Saturday evening I spoke at a meeting of the Socialist Society as I was in agreement with the matter under debate. I cannot recall the subject, but the result was that I was telephoned by

At a Universities Conference in Hereford. Stephen Thomas, BHL, Garth Turner, David Moore.

Conservative Central Office in Cardiff to be told that I had to toe the party line and undertake not take part in such debates without prior clearance. This did not thrill me at all, and I declined to give any such undertaking. I resigned as a member of the Conservative Party and I have never had any political allegiance since. I prefer to be a free spirit.

All the while a conviction had been gaining strength that I would have to test my vocation to the priesthood. I wasn't absolutely sure of it, but sure enough to take it further. My father had always talked of my taking over the administration of his printing business while he ran the workshop. The time had come to advise him about my future, and I wasn't looking forward to it, for I felt that he would be disappointed. When I explained how I felt, there was no hint of disappointment; on the contrary, he expressed delight at my intention and assured me of his total support. However, a year or two later he sold the business and became a Transport Manager in the Steel Company of Wales at the Abbey Works. If he was sad at the way things had turned out, he hid it superbly.

With the help of Joy's hard work in reading my set texts and making copious cramming notes, I eventually passed my Finals examinations and was admitted as a Bachelor of Arts. Meanwhile, Joy had specialized in Geormorphology for her final year and she was awarded a very good honours degree in Geography.

Oxford

I was sent by my bishop to train for the priesthood at St Stephen's House, Oxford, (popularly known as 'Staggers'). I had asked to go there for that was where Fr Bowen was trained. It had an excellent reputation as the Catholic College of the Anglican Church, and is now one of six religious Permanent Private Halls of the university, thus permitting men to begin training for the priesthood while reading for the University degree in Theology. I was interviewed by the Principal, Canon Arthur Couratin, a scholarly Liturgical expert and martinet, described by some wag as *'Noel Coward in a cassock'*, who concluded that *'it will be hell if you come here boy, but you had better come.'* St Stephen's House had a short term in July and August while the University was 'down'. I was to start in that Long-Vac Term in 1962.

I set off from Port Talbot by train in the company of a previous Head Boy at our school and fellow chorister at St Theodore's, Richard Hanford. He had finished a Mediaeval History Degree at Keble College and was half way through a degree in Theology at St Stephen's House. He was kind in showing me the ropes and we have remained good friends to this day.

In my time the college was in Norham Gardens and I arrived at the same time as the new Principal, Father Derek Allen. He was an amazing man. He was 6ft 7ins tall, and of slim build. In his soutane cassock he looked rather like a telegraph pole. His day began at 5.00am, two hours before we struggled down to Matins at 7.00am and found him at his prayers. Matins was followed by private meditation until the Eucharist at 8.00am. The Eucharist was notionally optional, but when men began sloping off to read the papers before breakfast, Arthur Couratin had reminded everyone who it was that left the Last Supper. That became a part of the 'oral tradition' of the House, and it was very rare in my day for anyone to leave after meditation.

Breakfast was a simple meal; boot polish (Marmite) on toast having a regular place on the menu. One morning Archbishop Michael Ramsey came for breakfast. I sat across the table from him and was totally fascinated by his eyebrows and enormous jowl. He spoke to us in the Common Room afterwards and held us spellbound by his sheer goodness and erudition.

Among the new arrivals that term was David Hope who had read his first degree in Theology at Nottingham and was reading for a D.Phil through Linacre Hall. I had hardly settled in when my Bishop, Glyn Simon, paid a visit to the college and tried to persuade me to read for a BA degree in theology through St Catherine's Hall. I resisted; I had discovered that I am no academic but a practitioner and I wanted to get on with my training and so make my way in life. I have long regretted my obstinacy, as a solid course in theology would have focussed my understanding of the Bible and the Church. Bishop Simon knew this, but he never mentioned it again.

In addition to Richard Hanford, my particular friends were Hugh Mead, who had read History at Kings College, Cambridge, and was now reading for an Oxford B.Litt at New College, and the college Chaplain, Fr Neville Tidwell, who taught me Old Testament, and doctrine. Neville was a Hebrew scholar and was always working on ancient Hebrew texts for learned journals. His great passion was teaching; he was a great communicator. He asked me to be his Best Man at his wedding, and he undertook the same duty at my wedding. By an amazing coincidence, when my younger son, Simon, applied to read for a degree at Crewe and Alsager, a campus of Manchester Metropolitan University, Neville was the Admissions Tutor, and telephoned us after years of lost contact following his sojourn as a college principal in Umtata. When he came to stay for a few days in 1999, not long before his untimely death, I asked him about the millennium from the perspective of other faiths and from the comfort of his arm chair he began to deliver a small lecture full of learned comment; I could hardly write it down fast enough. He was known by

St Stephen's House, Oxford, 1963. Clergy, left to right: Fr Michael Sanderson (Tutor), Fr Alan Carefull (Vice-Principal), Fr Derek Allen (Principal), Fr Neville Tidwell (Chaplain).

his close friends as 'The Rev', and he and Mead and I would spend hours together in his room or in the nearest pub, often joined by Nicholas Menon, another good friend, talking about all kinds of subjects ranging from church history to the Welsh coal industry, via Hebrew texts relating to the concept of the Royal Highway in ancient Israel, the Beatles and Beethoven.

A close friend from outside St Stephen's House was David Miller, who was at Magdalen College reading for a B.Litt in the works of the Bolshevik poet Vladimir Mayakovsky. Miller, Mead, Nev and I would happily spend a hilarious evening in 'the Greyhound' pub in North Oxford, on Wednesdays, when we didn't have to be back until Night Prayers at 10.00pm. The landlord and his wife, Frank and Betty, became firm friends, too. David Miller entered the Foreign Office and was sent as a Second Secretary to our embassy in Moscow. He was evidently very good at his job as some years later he was declared PNG by the Soviet, which resulted in his recall and a spirited defence by Sir Alec Douglas-Home, the Foreign Secretary, in the House of Commons. David was the first resident British Ambassador to Armenia when he arrived in Yerevan in July 1995. He asked me to pay a visit, but, sadly, I never made it.

The theological colleges in Oxford had a combined rugby club called the Mongrels; our team transport was an old fire engine. To arrive for an away game with bells clanging was worth three points before we took to the field. The New Zealand All Blacks used to begin any tour of the UK with a match against the university, and the day after the game they would send team members to local rugby clubs for a convivial evening. One such evening I was enjoying a pint of beer with the great All Black lock forward Colin Meads, talking about Welsh rugby, when he asked if I was free the following day. Assuming I was about to be invited to a party, I said I could be available all day. Turning to his brother, Stanley, he called out, 'We've got a prop for tomorrow.' Then he explained that they were short of a forward for a friendly in Cowley. A frozen grin disguised my horror; an image of my body being pulverized swam before my eyes as my legs became unstable. Then I heard faintly the voice of Stan Meads saying that the coach had already found someone, and life returned to my body.

I attended lectures on Hebrew Prophecy offered by Dr Eric Heaton at Wadham College, Early Church History by Professor Greenslade in Christ Church and Genesis by Dr Sparks at Oriel, among others, in addition to lectures and tutorials delivered in St Stephen's House. All lectures were in the morning, with afternoons devoted to reading and preparing essays, although, as my room overlooked the University Parks, there was a great temptation to walk in the Park or take a punt on the River Cherwell which bordered it. We all helped out with chores about the college, and at weekends, when Mr Whipp the odd-job man was off duty, it fell to me to stoke the boiler in the basement each morning and evening. Even when the temperature froze the Cherwell one winter, it was always hot in the boiler room, which accounted for the horrid sight each morning when I switched the light on: there were literally hundreds of cockroaches scuttling for cover.

During my time at college I worked during the holidays for the local civil engineering firm, Andrew Scott. I was sent as the assistant to the Plant Manager in the massive Abbey steel works. He and I shared an office with the pay clerks, under the direction of a wiry, elderly man by the name of Bill Barnet. He was a martinet and even the burly foremen had a measure of respect for him; he was Fagin to their Bill Sykes. The pay clerks had enormous ledgers filling their desks; each man on the payroll had a strip across the entire page with the details of his hours entered each morning as the contracts came in from head office. By Wednesday the ledgers were filled with detailed figures which would result in the calculation of each man's pay.

One Wednesday, one of the foremen asked me if I could balance a bowl of water on the end of a broom, and offered to start me off. Before I could answer he had half-filled a bowl with water, climbed on a chair and rammed a broom under it to keep it firm against the ceiling. Then he handed the broom handle to me. Foolishly I took hold of it, and at once the men removed all the chairs and desks beyond my reach and went for lunch. It was clearly a trick they had employed on all new comers. I tried to slide the bowl across the ceiling, but it nearly fell, and would have destroyed the week's pay sheets for the workforce, and I would have been history. So I stood feeling utterly ridiculous until Bill took pity on me and came to my rescue.

Then the Plant Manager went on two weeks holiday and left me in charge of the plant desk. It was my task to receive the contracts as they came from the pay desk and allocate lorries, vans, diggers, compressors, excavators and the like to the appropriate contracts. Every item on the inventory had to be accounted for each day, and if they were idle in the yard they had to be noted as 'standing'. I had a small Thames van and first thing every morning I would tour the steel works noting where the vehicles were working and which, if any, were in the yard. The second week on my own I lost a Scammell low-loader; for three days. On the Thursday I was about to telephone the head office and confess, when I heard a foreman asking a driver if he'd brought the Scammell back from the paint shop.

Once it became known that I was 'going into the church', they began to apologize for their bad language. I replied that they had no need to apologize to me for I had heard it all before, but I suggested that a 'swear box' might alleviate their guilt. Someone duly produced a box and I imposed a fine of a shilling a word, all money to go to a charity of their choice. The fund grew considerably when a foreman came in one morning in a temper with one of his men, put a five pound note in the box, and left vent his spleen. They decided to support The Children's Society, which was most grateful to them.

The following year, when the Plant Manager was away, a foreman asked me why I hadn't booked any pudlocks to any of the contracts. So I sprinkled a few on each contract. Bill Barnet went mad when he saw what I had done. It appeared that 'pudlocks' were the holes drilled in walls to accommodate the ends of scaffolding poles. *'You can't charge people for boring holes in their property'* he screamed, as I saw the foreman in question grinning outside the door. It was all good fun, and I was growing up all the time in such company.

Glyn Bowen had fostered my vocation; Derek Allen spelled it out for me. Both in his tutorials in spirituality, when we were together in his study, and during periods of quiet meditation in chapel, I began to experience the Christ who had called me. In his quiet and authoritative voice, Fr Derek explained the truth that Christ loved me so much that he had died for me and that now he was calling me to be his hands and his feet and his voice in his church. Without the devotion and the discipline of the two years I spent at St Stephen's House, I doubt if I would have been well enough equipped to see me through my ministry. I left with the utter conviction that Christ was with me in all that I was to do; a conviction I hold to this day.

CHAPTER THREE:

Holy Orders

It was late afternoon on the eve of my ordination in July 1964. I had been in silent Retreat all week in St Teilo's House, Roath, Cardiff. A small group of us had slipped out and were sitting on a bank beside the lake in Roath Park, idly throwing stones into the water. I confessed that I hoped I was doing the right thing in offering myself for Holy Orders. It was a last-minute panic attack which was over by the time we returned to the Retreat House. At the memorable service the following day, in a packed Llandaff Cathedral in a suburb of Cardiff, three of us from the parish of St Theodore, Port Talbot, were made deacons and one ordained priest. The Anglican Church, like the Roman Catholic Church, has three orders of ministers: bishops, priests and deacons, the latter being a kind of probationary order for the first year of one's ministry, though not necessarily so.

It had been just after Easter that year that I had paid a visit to the Bishop's Palace on the Cathedral Green, to discover where I was to start my ministry, or 'serve my title' as it is called. My bishop, Glyn Simon, was of the old school and directed his clergy with an iron will. He had wanted me to read for an Oxford degree in theology at St Stephen's House, but I refused as I wanted to be ordained without delay. He was not best pleased, so I was astounded when he announced that I would serve my title on the staff of the cathedral at Llandaff, Cardiff; hardly a punishment appointment. I was to be an additional member of the staff, the first deacon since the middle ages. As the Cathedral had no accommodation for a fifth cleric on the team, I had to undertake not to marry, and live in lodgings.

The Cathedral Church of St Peter and St Paul is an early 12th century foundation with a history of ruin and restoration. In the sixth century St Dyfrig founded a community here and was succeeded by St Teilo and then Teilo's nephew, St Euddogwy. These three Celtic saints share the patronage of the cathedral with St

Peter and St Paul. A land-mine destroyed the roof and most of the interior during the Second World War, and the present restoration was undertaken by the architect George Pace.

I arranged an interview with the Dean, Eryl Thomas, who returned to Llandaff later as the Bishop. He was assisted at the Cathedral by two Minor Canons, one of whom, David Jones, was a St Theodore's ordinand, and by an assistant curate, for the cathedral was also the parish church. The Dean had been in the headlines of the national press and television as an outspoken opponent of the factory farming of chickens; he kept free range chickens in the Deanery garden. He was an impressive man who spoke Welsh fluently, and had a formidable reputation of getting his own way.

I arrived at the Deanery and Mrs Thomas showed me into the study to await the Dean's arrival from a meeting. I sat in the book-lined room and watched the cat being sick on the rug before the fire. I knew how it felt. Then the Dean came up the path and into his study. For some reason I apologised for the cat as if it were my fault. We talked a bit about St Theodore's Church and my time at Oxford and about cathedral ministry, and then he told me that he would oblige the bishop and take me on as an additional Assistant Curate, but as he was away in July, I should also have a break and start work on Saturday, 1st August. I would receive a stipend of £560 a year, slightly above the parochial rate; have a day off a week and the usual holidays.

The Cathedral Parish of Llandaff

Eryl Stephen Thomas worked hard and played hard. He would not tolerate any slackness and was not slow to admonish any of the staff whom he considered were not pulling their weight. Each weekday morning we began with Matins at 7.00am, followed by the Eucharist and private meditation. Evensong was sung at 6.00pm except for Wednesdays, when it was said. Each of the clergy was given an area of the parish and was expected to visit it and care for it pastorally. Every Monday morning at a staff meeting in the Deanery we had to provide written visiting lists to hand in to the 'old man', as we called him. The Dean would scrutinise them and suddenly ask, '*What about old Mrs Jenkins?*' He knew all his parishioners by name. '*I called on her on Wednesday, Mr Dean*.' '*Odd that; my wife visited her in hospital on Tuesday*.' Years later, when visiting the extremely long Fen Road at RAF Marham in the teeth of driving rain, it was only the sound of Eryl Thomas in my ear, '*This list is written on rice paper, pay attention to your visiting*', that kept me going.

Despite his strict discipline he was careful in training a new curate, not least because St Michael's Theological College was in the parish, and the staff and students often attended the Sunday services in the cathedral. So he shielded me from preaching in the cathedral until mid-October, when he put me down to preach the sermon at Cathedral Evensong. During the week prior to my debut, he asked to see the sermon and he went through it with me, offering excellent advice about content and delivery. The clergy robed in the Minor Canons Vestry in the Processional Way. This is a corridor beneath the Choir Song Room, which leads from the Prebendal House to the north-east of the cathedral, to the Welch Regiment Chapel, and thence through the ancient North Door into the nave. This was all a part of George Pace's design for the rebuilding of the cathedral after extensive war damage. As I processed behind the choir through the nave for Evensong, to the accompaniment of thrilling organ music, I noticed the Dean waiting with Bob White, his verger, in the north aisle ready to follow our procession, and to my horror I saw that behind the Dean was the Bishop's Verger, Hugh Williams, with Glyn Simon bringing up the rear. The bishop had come to hear me preach. As the dean passed my stall he slipped a piece of paper on my reading desk; I looked at it and saw, in Eryl's scrawl, '*Don't let the Episcopal presence put you off, give 'em hell!*' I relaxed and thanked God for a boss who understood.

Two days before my first Christmas as a clergyman the Dean said to me, '*Meet me in the Deanery at 11 o'clock in the morning. We are going to the bank. And wear your cassock.*' I assumed that he would be carrying a large sum of money and required help. On Christmas Eve I turned up at the appointed hour, and, both wearing cassocks, we set off for the National Westminster Bank in the High Street, Llandaff. The Dean greeted the cashier and walked straight ahead into the Manager's office; the Manager, Harold Thomas, was a member of the Cathedral Church Council. There were four or five other parishioners in the office and we all had a glass or two of sherry and passed a convivial thirty minutes. Then the Dean announced that it was time to go to the Butchers. I had a vision of us making a progress along the entire High Street drinking sherry with the shopkeepers. We all drained our glasses and followed the Dean up the street to the Butchers Arms near the cathedral. The bar of the pub was packed with men, some of whom I recognized as members of the cathedral congregations, and a cry went up, "*Make way for the Dean.*" He climbed on a chair as someone handed him a pint of beer, and as carol sheets were passed around he announced the first carol and led the singing in his fine baritone voice. I was captivated with the sheer leadership in Christian ministry. I couldn't imagine many church dignitaries having the charisma to take over a pub bar and lead a hundred men in carol-singing. In this way, and in others, Eryl gave me confidence to be innovative in Christian evangelism at the very beginning of my ministry. On the stroke of one o'clock a cheer went up as Doris, the landlady, put an enormous plate of hot mince pies on the bar and announced, '*On the House*'. It was close to three o'clock before the party broke up and I stumbled back to my digs for a nap.

Each weekday the 7.00am service was attended by a layman who left for his office in Cardiff Docks straight after the Holy Communion. His name was John Davies and he was a senior executive in the Powell Dyffryn Group managing Cory Brothers & Company from Cory's Buildings in Cardiff docks. During the Second World War he had risen to the position of Regimental Sergeant Major, and was miffed when he was suddenly sent for by his colonel to be told to take immediate leave and buy the uniform and kit pertaining to a captain. As the weeks went by, his wife, Gretna, thought her dream had come true and he had finished with war, but it was short-lived. After a month chafing at the bit he was summoned to a house in Mayfair. He was admitted and asked what he knew about cossac. He informed the officer that it was a Russian horseman, and was escorted to a room upstairs where he waited, and waited. At last the officer returned and told him that Major General McLean was ready to see him and he was ushered into a large office. The general gave John a thick document and told him that he was to master it as quickly as possible and within the next three months would have to know it verbatim. He would not be able to contact the outside world directly and would sleep and take all meals within the building; he would be escorted on short exercise walks. As John read the document in the quiet of his own room upstairs, he started with the title, 'Operation Overlord.' It was typical of the man that he knew it inside out in three weeks, was quizzed on it by McLean, who expressed his satisfaction and took John Davies with him thereafter on his journeys to brief Churchill, Roosevelt and Generals Montgomery and Eisenhower.

What a war, but COSSAC (Chief of Staff to the Supreme Allied Commander) had chosen his man well. John became a friend and the source of sound wisdom and counsel. Known by the clergy as 'John Davies the Ships', he acted as Master of Ceremonies to the altar party at the Sung Eucharist services on Sunday mornings, but after the last Mass he used to hold a generous 'open house' for the clergy and altar servers.

The Dean's wife, Mrs Jean Thomas, was a very intelligent, efficient and brisk lady who spoke her mind kindly but firmly. They had three boys, the eldest about my age, and a daughter, Clare. Jean soon invited me to join the family for lunch every Monday after the staff meeting, and I became an 'adopted' son of the Deanery. I discovered a close, loving family, where humour predominated. The conversation was never trivial, and each member of the family felt able to contribute as they felt moved.

During my year as a deacon it was natural that at the High Mass every Sunday, when the Celebrant, the Deacon and the Subdeacon all wore vestments at the altar, I filled the function of the Deacon, and therefore was obliged to walk from the High Altar, down through the Quire, to stand in solemn isolation under the great concrete Pulpitum Arch, which bears the huge statue of Epstein's 'Majestas', and deliver the lines of the Invitation to Confession: '*Ye that do truly and earnestly repent ...*' I knew it backwards. But one Sunday morning I stood there before a full cathedral, and my mind went blank. The space under the arch seemed the size of Cardiff Arms Park. I walked slowly back to the nearest choir boy and took his book from him, only to find that he hadn't been following the service, and I had to find the page. Then, with my cheeks on fire, I walked back to the arch and read the unremembered lines, before returning miserably to the remoteness of the High Altar. We processed back to the Chapter House at the end of the service, and I awaited my fate from the Dean. He said nothing. I divested myself of the robes, but still not a word from the 'Old Man'. As I left the Chapter House his hand fell on my shoulder, '*That will teach you to keep the script in your pocket.*' He never mentioned the matter again and I always keep the script in my pocket to this day.

Llandaff is the only Welsh Anglican cathedral to have its own choir school with twenty choral scholars, and professional men singers. The Director of Music and Cathedral Organist was Robert Joyce, known to his friends as Harry, and we became good friends. He lived with his wife on the Cathedral Green and was an inspirational musician. Evensong was sung daily, except Wednesday, at 6.00pm, with Lay Clerks and Singing Men joining the boys on Tuesday, Thursday and Saturday. For three years I soaked up the classical repertoire of cathedral music week after week, with only a handful of people coming along to share in this rich heritage.

I mentioned that the Dean kept chickens, and this gave rise to an extraordinary scene outside the cathedral one weekday after the morning services. The cathedral is in the shallow valley of the River Taff, so the Deanery and Llys Esgob, the bishop's palace, is reached by a steep alley which ascends beneath the Deanery garden wall to the left and the Palace garden lawns to the right. The Dean and I talked as we walked through the nave of the cathedral on our way home for breakfast, when the Assistant Verger, Ron Roberts, burst through the west door calling, '*Mr Dean, come quick, your chickens have got out, mun.*' Sure enough, chickens were feeding all over the lawns at the west door; they had flown down from the garden high above us. I could only laugh aloud as the three of us, all in cassocks, spread out to drive the chickens up the hill to the deanery.

It must have made a ridiculous sight: three grown men making 'clucking' noises as we tried to gather them in a flock. For a while all went well and the birds went toward the bottom of the incline. Then an errant bird flew over the fence into the bishop's garden and the entire flock followed. '*Damn and blast*' said the Dean, and with a '*Follow me*' he opened the gate into the Palace garden. We were half way across the lawn driving the flock before us, when a casement window flew up on the first floor and the unmistakable voice of Bishop Glyn Simon rang out, '*Mr Dean, get your chickens out of my garden.*' The reply came through gritted teeth,

31

'*I am trying to do just that, my Lord.*' '*Well, get a move on then*' and the window slammed shut. I couldn't catch what the Dean said under his breath, but I do not think it was, '*Have a nice day.*'

The relationship between a bishop and a dean is often difficult. In Wales, the bishop appointed the dean but then had no further authority in the cathedral other than a remote link as 'The Visitor'. In England he doesn't even appoint the dean; that is the prerogative of the Queen. On one occasion I was with Eryl in his study when the telephone rang. He answered it and there followed a brief mono-syllabic conversation ending with the words, '*I'll tell the Bishop*', before he hung up. '*It appears that The Princess Margaret is visiting Cardiff and wishes to pay another ad hoc visit to the cathedral. She will be here in thirty minutes. Now where were we?*' he said. I remarked that he had better let the Bishop know, but was told, '*Oh, there's plenty of time for that*', which explained the photograph on the front page of the Western Mail the following morning of Princess Margaret leaving the cathedral flanked by an immaculate dean on her right and a dishevelled bishop on her left.

After nearly four months in lodgings I felt too restricted to exercise fully my ministry to the young people of the Youth Club, which was one of my responsibilities in the parish. The kind but elderly widow with whom I lodged found it difficult to cope with boisterous eighteen year olds dropping in for coffee in my room, so in November 1964 I found a flat in Pontcanna, the other side of Llandaff Fields. But it was just outside the parish boundary and so I was obliged to seek permission from the bishop. He was sympathetic and gave me his Licence permitting me to live without the parish.

My morning start was now 0630 to allow time for the walk through the fields to the 0700 Service at the cathedral. Returning at 0830 brought me to the attention of the vagrants who slept on the benches in the fields, and to whom we gave a voucher for the Salvation Army hostel in Cardiff. One morning I was approached by one such chap who asked for a clean shirt. This was so off the wall that I invited him back to my flat. It turned out that he was applying for a job that morning and had nothing to wear. I found a shirt for him while my bacon was frying, but I was so moved by his obvious hunger that I offered him breakfast. I have never seen a man devour food so eagerly and rapidly. Swearing him to secrecy, for I didn't want the whole of Cardiff vagrancy to follow in his path, I wished him good luck as he went off clutching my shirt. I saw him a few weeks later pushing a dust cart in the city centre; he hailed me as an old friend, '*I got the job, Father.*'

The flat also gave me independence in another way. I reasoned that I undertook not to marry because of lack of cathedral accommodation. This no longer applied, and as Joy and I had became engaged on Saturday, 5th September, I approached the Dean in his study and explained that Joy and I felt it was high time we wed. He left abruptly and I thought I had blown it, but he returned with a bottle of whisky and two glasses. He raised his glass and we drank to the marriage. He cautioned me that the Bishop would not be happy about the idea during my Diaconate, and urged me to see him before proceeding further. I agreed and the Dean telephoned the Bishop's Secretary there and then. Ten minutes later I was ushered into the Bishop's study.

He greeted me with his customary warm smile and after an impromptu discussion about a book he had been reading on Victorian values, he asked what he could do for me. Taking a deep breath, I came straight to the point and explained that I wished now to marry Joy and live in Pontcanna. His smile changed to tight-lipped and rapid speech. '*The Diaconate is no time to go to bed with a woman, but with the Bride of Christ*', he snapped, and without further comment, he left his study. Ten quiet minutes passed before I peeped out into the corridor. I could hear Betty Horley, his secretary, tapping away at her typewriter, so I went to her office and asked if the Bishop was coming back. She started as she thought I had left. She said that the Bishop had gone into Cardiff in his car. My interview had been terminated.

Returning to the Deanery I saw that Eryl had refilled the whisky glasses, and he laughed aloud when I related what had been said. He told me that if I defied the Bishop, and went ahead with the wedding, the Bishop would postpone my ordination to the priesthood by another year. Later that day Joy and I discussed the matter and agreed to wait a little longer.

The following June I was ordained priest by Bishop Glyn Simon in a service rich in splendid music and liturgy. Afterwards, Eryl and Jean Thomas hosted a reception at the Deanery. The following morning I celebrated Mass for the first time at the 9 o'clock Parish Sung Eucharist in the Cathedral. The Dean acted as the Deacon and David Jones as the Subdeacon. While the choir sang the Sanctus, my eyes focussed on the great Norman arch above the altar, and the sudden realization that I was standing in a long line of priests stretching back to Bishop Urban in the 12th century, who had stood on this very spot and performed much the same action made me feel weak at the knees. I also observed that as I elevated the chalice heavenwards in the act of consecration, I could see reflected in the gilt surface of the chalice the people in the congregation behind me. Then, and now, this represents for me the offering of the life and work of the people, together with the sacrificial offering of Christ himself; the blood of Christ was shed for them and for me. My ministry at Llandaff made real all that I had been taught at Oxford.

It wasn't very long before one of the lay clerks in the cathedral choir, a local doctor, married and gave up his top-floor flat in the house next door to the Bishop's Palace, named Pendinas, with fine views across the Cathedral Green. He tipped me off and I was allocated the apartment. This was much more convenient as I almost lived 'over the shop'.

My Ordination Party at the Deanery, Llandaff, 12 June 1965

Emerging from the Prebendal House one morning I saw the dean talking with some chap by the west door of the cathedral. He beckoned me to join them, and asked, '*Do you know our man at St Marks?*' There had been an interregnum at the neighbouring parish of St Mark, Gabalfa, and as I faintly recognized the man I assumed he was the new incumbent, so I said, '*Yes*', and shook his hand. Later in the day I saw the dean again and he accused me of not recognizing the man he had met at the west door. I protested that I had, until he revealed that it was the actor Donald Sinden, who was appearing in a new play, '*There's a Girl in my Soup*' at the New Theatre; Joy and I had been to see it. The penny dropped; he had recently appeared in the title role in the TV series, '*Our Man at St Mark's*.' I joined Sinden for a hilarious lunch at the Deanery the following day, when he appeared wearing the suit from the play, '*so that I might be recognized*'. It was the beginning of a casual friendship with Donald Sinden which has endured to this day.

Joy and I decided to marry in the cathedral on 23rd July 1966. At the same time, Colin Sykes, the other curate, was removing with his parents into a house which they had bought in the parish, and so Joy and I were offered a cathedral house instead of the flat.

The week before the wedding I moved into the Deanery, and on the Friday Joy moved from Cwmavon to the house in Thistle Way, Llandaff. At Choral Evensong on the Thursday, before the men of the choir and the clergy joined me in my 'Stag Party', the Minor Canon solemnly announced a change from the advertised anthem to one based on Psalm 30. Harry Joyce conducted the choir in a motet which included the words, 'Heaviness endureth for a night, but joy cometh in the morning.' At the conclusion the choir turned to face me and bowed. In turn I rose in my place and bowed to them, before we all knelt down for the prayers. It was a good Stag Do, and the dean and I walked back to the Deanery as dawn broke over the Taff below the cathedral.

The dean married us and Fr Derek Allen, my Oxford principal, celebrated the Nuptual Mass assisted by the two minor canons. The Vicar of Cwmavon, Joy's parish priest, read the Introduction. In addition to the lay clerks, the headmaster of the Cathedral School gave the twenty choristers leave to sing at the service; the head chorister was a lad named Simon Hughes, later to become a Lib Dem MP. The music was glorious, although Harry Joyce had to cry off as he had been invited to give a recital at the refurbished organ at the Royal College of Organists, and felt that not even our close friendship could prevent him accepting it. So my old school and Oxford friend, Richard Hanford, deputized, as the Assistant Organist was in his recording van outside the building making a record of the service. My tutor at St Stephen's House, Fr Neville Tidwell, made a splendid and reliable best man. We had a kind letter from the bishop apologizing that he could not be present to give the blessing as he was away, but wishing us much happiness, and thanking me for heeding what he felt obliged to say to me the previous year.

Music has always been important to me, and I chose carefully for the wedding. As Joy arrived at the great west door on her father's arm, the choir of twenty boys and twelve men stood just inside with the dean, crucifer, acolytes and vergers and sang Martin Shaw's 'Fanfare for Christmas Day' in greeting. The choir sang, 'Haec Dies' by Byrd before the Mass, which was set to Jackson in G. Finally, after the Mass, as we all stood before the High Altar, the choir sang Jackson's setting of the 'Te Deum.' As we processed to the great west door Richard Hanford played, 'Marche Triomphale' by Karg-Elert.

It was a splendid affair, but Joy said afterwards that she would not have gone along with it had she known it would last one and a half hours. Later that day I drove to Howtown for a honeymoon in the Lake District. Driving back the following Saturday, we listened to the final of the World Cup from Wembley, and I nearly hit the central reservation of the M5 when England won, beating Germany 4-2.

Our married life settled quickly into a busy routine; I would set off for the cathedral at 0640 and Joy left for a brisk fifteen minute walk at 0715 to catch the 0735 Express coach to Port Talbot, where she was a Geography teacher at our old grammar school. She returned just in time for us to have a cup of tea before I left

Our Wedding Day at Llandaff Cathedral

for Evensong at 1740, followed by Youth Club or meetings of one kind or another. It was a busy priestly life, undergirded by the sound and spiritual foundation I had established at St Stephen's House, which gave me the confidence and ability to tackle difficult and sensitive situations with authority.

As I crossed the Green on my way to the cathedral after breakfast one wet morning, I met the bishop emerging from the Deanery, his cloak about his shoulders. He hurried over to me in a state of agitation. That morning, Friday 21 October 1966, at 9.15 am, after several days of heavy rain, over 40,000 cubic metres of coal waste on the side of Merthyr Mountain slid down the hillside and smashed into the village of Aberfan in a slurry 12 metres deep. The pupils of Pantglas Junior School had arrived not long earlier for the last day before the half-term holiday. They had just left the assembly hall, where they had been singing 'All Things Bright and Beautiful, 'when they were buried alive. In total, 116 children died with five of their teachers. The bishop was about to leave for the stricken site and had advised the dean, but he knew that I was to address the Men's Society in Barry that evening and he gave me the substance of an alternative address there and then, in the rain, in three minutes. Glyn Simon was quite brilliant at thinking on his feet.

I took Holy Communion to the homes of many sick people in my area of the parish. One was Lady Reardon Smith, whose family owned the shipping line of that name. On one occasion, when I had arranged to visit her, the maid asked me to wait while she went to see if madam was at home. Her Ladyship was rather deaf so the maid had to speak up, '*The Curate is here to see you, ma'am.*' The old lady shouted in return, '*Snails?* (she never did get my name right) *Tell him I am not at home. Doesn't he know Wimbledon is on?*' Another person was a splendid and very sick man Arthur Cosker, who was confined to a wheelchair. It was always a joy to visit him, and after some months I discovered that he wrote poetry. He trusted me enough to let me read some of it. I considered it excellent and his insights quite moving. I took it to the poet Vernon Watkins in Swansea, and he, too, admired it. I learned so much about life and how to live it from the elderly and infirm.

My three years at Llandaff went very quickly and was a rapid learning curve at the top of which I felt I was well prepared to move on to new challenges. The bishop stopped me on the Green one morning and said that it was time I did some real work. I protested that I hadn't stopped working since the day he put me in Llandaff, but he said that '*anyone can work in a cathedral*' and now it was time for me to move on. '*I want you to go to Neath to build a new church in the Cimla*', he said, '*The people are looking forward to a new priest who will move things along.*'

The end of my ministry in Llandaff was shrouded in tragedy. On 1st September, my dear friend David Jones, the Minor Canon who had been a mentor in my early days at the cathedral, and who with his lovely wife Joan had invited me to join them for Sunday lunch up to the time of my marriage, had been admitted to hospital with carbon monoxide poisoning. I went with Eryl to see David in hospital; he seemed lifeless and with little chance of survival. Eryl considered he had let his colleague down because David had not felt able to confide in him, and he retired to the Deanery in misery. I felt equally miserable as I had known David longer than anyone in Llandaff. A retired Canon who lived on the Green, Fr Harold Rew, agreed to preach in Eryl's place at the Parish Eucharist on the Sunday, and I believe the bishop preached the sermon at Cathedral Evensong. It was judged unlikely that David would ever return to work, even if he survived, so in order to give the dean and my colleagues time to rearrange David's duties, the bishop agreed to extend my time at Llandaff by two weeks until 23rd September 1967. My successor was moving into my house in Thistle Way, so we removed our furniture into the flat in Cimla, Joy went to her parents' home in Cwmavon, and I lodged with my good friend 'John Davies the Ships' in Llandaff.

Cimla, in the Parish of Neath with Llantwit

Three years of this busy routine, during which I learned my '*craft and noble art*', as Dylan Thomas might have described vocation, those three years prepared me in full measure for what was to come: a sprawling housing estate without a church of any kind on the hillside above the town of Neath. The Church in Wales had bought a parcel of land for a church building between the fire station and a filling station, and my job was to build it. The Borough Council had allocated a small council flat for the priest, and after organizing a dynamic Ordination Service in the cathedral in the morning, Joy and I were reunited, not in the comfortable house in Llandaff, but in the Spartan one-bedroom upstairs flat on the hillside. At least it would make life easier for Joy. She was now the Head of Department of Geography at her school, and Steel Thomas, the German teacher, lived across the road from the estate on a small private development, so she could travel with him each day. His wife, Charmian, had been a senior hospital midwife, and when our son was born she looked after him while Joy was at school. It was a perfect arrangement.

The contrast with Llandaff was invigorating. The prayerful discipline I had learned stood me in good stead. The Rector was Canon J F Williams, known to all as 'JF', and he was assisted by three assistant curates. The Reverend Albert Way had been with him a while and looked after St Thomas' church, but the Reverend Bob Blackmore, to work at St Catherine's, arrived with me. I was also accompanied by a deacon who had been ordained in the cathedral service that morning, the Reverend Dennis Morris, who was to assist in St David's church.

The Reverend Philip Berrow, who had been a curate in the parish of Neath before leaving to join the Army Chaplains' Department, had established a worshipping community in a surplus site office donated by the National Oil Refinery, Llandarcy. My task was to increase this to the point where a permanent building could be erected on the site. I wore my cassock everywhere to establish my presence in the community. After a morning 'on the knocker' I would call in at the pub, the Cimla Hotel, for a pint of beer before lunch. At the beginning of the second week one of the regular drinking men who assembled there sidled over to me and asked, '*What are you up to, Vicar? You come here every day but you won't convert us.*' I answered gently, '*I come here for a pint before lunch, does that cause you a problem?*' '*No offence meant, Vicar.*' '*And none taken*', I told him. The following day I was invited to join them, and we became friends. And I did convert them, for they were good people and they became ready labourers when required on site, and some became members of the regular congregation.

Meanwhile I had been taking stock of the Parish of Neath. In the town was the old Parish Church of St Thomas, which had been vandalized inside by the Victorian restorers. Literally a stone's throw away was the 19th century church of St David, which had fracture plates recording cracks in the tower, and the south porch moving away from the south wall of the church. It was a very large building and cost a small fortune to maintain and heat. Alongside it was the big Parish Hall. Nearby were a lovely Georgian Rectory and a terraced house for Fr Albert Way. In the Melyn area to the south was the church of St Catherine, with a hall alongside it and the house where the Revd Bob Blackmore lived. To the northwest was a tiny gem, the 12th century church of St Illtyd. I was tasked with building a fifth church in the parish; it seemed excessive. I collected data regarding the number of worshippers in the various churches, and the cost of heating, lighting and maintaining them. With the help of a local architect, who was already involved in the temporary church of St Paul, Cimla, I devised a plan for the future.

My plan involved selling St Thomas' church at a commercial price to the Roman Catholic congregation, which had no church building in Neath but worshipped in their club; demolishing St David's church and the adjacent hall, selling the building stone, and clearing this large site right in the centre of the town; selling St Catherine's church and its hall to local industry once a 'change of use' had been agreed; selling the Rectory and all the clergy houses; finally, decline to build the new church in Cimla. St Illtyd's church would survive unscathed. Then the building would begin on the central cleared site with a hall to accommodate 300 people seated in comfort, with committee rooms along one side. Above it a church to seat 300 would be built. The vertical build would leave room to build a new Rectory and a Parish Office, together with three clergy houses, the whole forming three sides of a quadrangle, and all linked to one central heating system. Two buses were to be bought, with 'The Parish of Neath' emblazoned along the sides, which would tour the town on Sundays driven by part-time taxi drivers, picking up worshippers.

My research had revealed about 200 folk worshipped more or less regularly on a Sunday morning, but they were dispersed in small numbers. How much better it would be for their soul if they were to join in worship as a single, large congregation. I had learned the truth of that in Llandaff where the cathedral is the only place of worship in the entire parish. The income from the sale of premises and stone, together with savings made in operating and maintaining the three churches and clergy houses, would not match the new building works, but with St Thomas' church alone costing £18.00 every time a service was held there, I calculated that the parish would be making a profit after five years of operating under my scheme, and that week by week thereafter the profit would increase to form a sizeable investment for the future.

It was not to become a reality. The Rector refused even to take the scheme to the Parochial Church Council. 'Sell the Parish Church to the Roman Catholics? Are you mad?' And that was that. I was prepared for opposition, for sometimes you have to do unpopular things if you believe it is right, but I had hoped to have an opportunity to explain my proposal in some detail.

I was disappointed, but not downcast. I had a job to do, so I got down to it and determined to make it a success. It was decided to build the permanent building joined to the temporary Church, which would then function as a Church Hall but would also have sliding and folding doors to enable the Hall to provide extra capacity at Festivals. The diocese offered a grant of money and an interest free loan to assist the building of the church. We added to this gifts from local industrial firms and asked parishioners to let us have any sum of money they considered 'spare' as a five or ten year interest free loan. 'JF' refused to start building until the money was in the bank, and I supported this tough stance, despite frustration expressed by many that nothing seemed to be happening. The Rector and Parochial Church Council had the responsibility for the budget, but they left the day to day management of the work to the architect and me. Ken Davies was appointed the architect; he lived in Cimla and had helped with the erection of the temporary church of St Paul some years earlier. He confided that he had never designed a church, his work being largely engaged with private dwellings and pubs. He had, however, been to see the Roman Catholic Metropolitan Cathedral in Liverpool, which had excited him. I took him to see the new church of The Holy Family in Blackbird Leys in Oxford which was also built 'in the round' and was built and consecrated in 1965. It came as no surprise to me to see his drawings reflected what we had seen; our new church was to be octagonal with a roof which sloped almost to the ground. Ken affirmed that roof is cheaper to build than wall, and it reminded him of the Old Testament tent pitched where the Ark of the Covenant rested. I was impressed with his scholarship.

But the work of building up the Body of Christ had to be tackled first, for it is people who constitute a church and not building materials. So I pressed on with my visiting programme, strengthening the Ladies' Guild, founding a Guild

Palm Sunday Procession crossing Cimla Common, 1969

St Trinian's. The After-Eight Club take part in the Cimla Carnival, 1969

of Servers to add dignity to the worship, building up the Sunday School, and gathering candidates for Confirmation. As far as I was allowed, I went where the people gathered; so I visited the Fire Station, the school and of course the Cimla Hotel. I discovered quite a number of adults who wanted to learn more about Christianity and were willing to join an Adult Confirmation Class. Members of the choir and the ten year old children in the Sunday School made a sizeable Junior Confirmation Class. But the teenage youngsters tended to go down the hill into town for their leisure time and it was difficult to meet them.

I decided to try a Senior Youth Club for young people over seventeen years of age called 'The After-Eight Club', which would meet in St Paul's Church/Hall at 8.00pm and adjourn to the Cimla Hotel next door for a nightcap. Given the ambivalent attitude to alcohol in Welsh religious life, this was a risky enterprise, and I expected opposition from parents. It was a success from the start. The young people were quite willing to meet in St Paul's for a lively no-holds barred discussion; the church became known by them as the 'Holy Hut', and I was known by my Christian name and Joy by hers. In a very short period of time we had a regular membership of two dozen young men and women aged between eighteen and twenty. Nearly all of them attended the Sung Eucharist on Sunday morning, even though they were not obliged to do so. Parents told me they were delighted to know that when they went for a drink in the pub, as they would do anyway, they were in safe company. The club put on a Revue for the good people of Neath in the St David's Hall, which was so well received that the following year it was fully booked almost as soon as tickets went on sale. We filled a coach for a club outing to Oxford, which was hilarious; especially the afternoon spent punting on the River Cherwell, which demanded all my skills to maintain some vestige of control.

One evening one of the lads, a popular fellow called Fred, asked to have a quiet word with me. I assumed it was girl friend trouble, but he revealed that while he enjoyed his place in the pack of the grammar School Rugby XV, he really wanted to referee. One of the men in the Llandaff Parish Choir, Vivian Phelps, was secretary of the Welsh Rugby Football Referees Committee. He had once told me that he was looking for young men who wanted to referee rather than players who were too old to continue and who changed to refereeing. I related this to Fred and offered to put him in touch with Viv Phelps. He was delighted as was Viv. We called him Fred, but his name is Clive, and Clive Norling later became a most successful international Rugby Football referee. He refereed a then record thirty-five Test matches and officiated at all the major rugby stadia in the world during the 1980s and 90s, and became the director of referees for the Welsh Rugby Union.

In the meantime, the bishop had given me an additional diocesan job, that of forming a Guild of St Teilo for young lads considering ordination. I set about it and soon had about a dozen youngsters on my books from all over South Wales. I would arrange to meet as a group in Cardiff twice a year and correspond with them when necessary.

One of the many fund-raising ventures we employed was the Bring and Buy Sale. For such events in the hut a folding wooden door was drawn across the width of the building to screen the sanctuary. At one such sale the building was full of stalls containing books, knitwear, antiques and nearly-new items; it was a dark evening at the beginning of November, but a large number of folk had turned up and it was hectic. A Neath churchwarden, who was also the Borough Treasurer, had come along to spend some money in a good cause, and had put his hat down near the door. When he came to collect it as he was leaving, it was missing. My wife confessed that she had sold it by mistake to some lads. At once she drove him around the streets of the estate in search of his best hat, and shared his horror when she saw it on the head of a Guy Fawkes which was being hawked around the houses in a wheelbarrow.

On 14th February 1968 the Electoral College of the Church in Wales met to choose a successor to Archbishop Edwin Morris, who had been Bishop of Monmouth since 1945. The College elected Eryl Stephen Thomas, Dean of Llandaff. Eryl asked me to be one of his chaplains at his consecration with Canon (later The Very Reverend) Frank Jenkins, Vicar of Risca, as the other; we were his first and last curates. The next step was for the Holy Synod to approve the election. The Holy Synod of the Church in Wales comprises only the Diocesan Bishops, and after Evening Prayer, on an overcast Thursday afternoon on 28th May 1968, Frank and I led Eryl, dressed in cassock with academic gown and hood, into the nave of St Asaph Cathedral, the home of the senior bishop. Sitting in a semi-circle behind a table were the five bishops in Convocation robes; this was the Church in Holy Synod, and I was moved by the almost Celtic simplicity of the proceedings. At 10.30 the following morning I followed Eryl

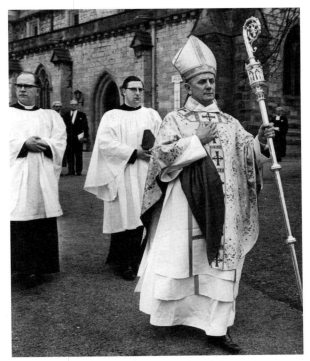

Eryl Thomas' Consecration as Bishop of Monmouth
His Chaplains: Canon Frank Jenkins and BHL

into the cathedral for his consecration, when he took the Episcopal name 'Stephen Monmouth' in order for his friends to continue calling him Eryl. Wearing the dalmatic of a deacon under the chasuble, he looked every inch a leader and a prelate.

Soon afterwards he asked me to move to his diocese of Monmouth as he had work for me to do, but already my fellow clergy were saying to me that I would have an assured future as a friend of a bishop who was clearly destined to go far. I concluded that whatever mark I might make in the church it would be attributed not to my endeavour but to my mentor. I declined to join Eryl.

I had been fascinated by the aerobatics of a Tiger Moth over Port Talbot when I was a lad, and from that day I had a desire to know more about flight and wanted very much to become airborne. The Biggles stories and wartime exploits outlined in books such as '*Enemy Coast Ahead*', written by Ralph Barker, later to become a friend in the Savage Club, served only to deepen this desire. Knowing of my interest in aviation, 'JF' mentioned to me that he had been asked to become the Honorary Chaplain to the Neath Squadron of the Air Training Corps but felt that I was closer to their age group. I went to the Drill Hall to meet the Officer Commanding, Flight Lieutenant Eric Witts, and warmed to him at once. It was another ready-made youth club. The duties of a chaplain were not onerous, and involved getting to know the lads and the staff. The boys were courteous and clearly enjoying the evening's tasks. The ATC was meeting a need in the town. I became the Honorary Chaplain and my life changed because of it, but I didn't know that then.

My life was to change in a more fundamental manner at 01.30 on the morning of Wednesday 19th March 1969, when Joy gave birth to a baby boy in Neath Hospital. We had agreed to name a son Mark Stephen, and once I had recovered my composure, I set off in the car to inform our parents in Port Talbot. Half way down Cimla Hill I saw Felix Crossland, one of the Church Council members, taking his dog for a late walk. '*Felix!*' I called out, '*Joy has a baby boy.*' To my utter astonishment he replied, '*Oh, you've had it now until they screw you down.*' I told a policeman on his beat in Briton Ferry who was more joyful about the news. Joy's parents were in bed so I dropped a note through the door and continued to George Street where my parents were rousable, and toasts were drunk.

On Sunday, 20th July, the Bishop of Monmouth came to Cimla to baptize Mark during Evensong in a packed church. Eryl and Jean were his Godparents, as were John Davies 'the ships' and his wife Gretna. We all hurried back to our flat following refreshments after the service to watch the first Lunar Landing on television.

I continued to pop in once a week for an hour with No.334 (Neath) Squadron, ATC, but on Saturday, 26th August 1969, I went with the squadron on Summer Camp to RAF Lyneham in Wiltshire. I met Padre John Thomas, the Station Chaplain, in the church on Sunday morning, and he invited me to join him for the day on the Tuesday. In the morning he took me to nearby RAF Colerne and after lunch at Lyneham we went to the RAF Hospital at Wroughton, where I visited one of the wards while he did another. Here was a man doing priestly work, but in uniform and ministering to aviators. The seed of an idea fell on fertile soil.

That evening I had my first flight; it was in a Lockheed Hercules transport aircraft, registration XV210, and we took off at 2200hrs to carry out a two-hour sortie of 'circuits and bumps'. During the flight I spent half an hour on the flight deck, including some time with my head in the astrodome, gazing at the clear moonlit Wiltshire countryside below, and the RAF roundels shining on the wings, as the four propellers reflected the flashes of the anti-collision beacon. The following day we had a two and a half hour flight in a Bristol Britannia up to Prestwick and back. I was in my element. I was thrilled by the power of the aircraft at take-off; by the teamwork evident on the flight deck, but chiefly at the different perspective of the earth's topography below. That seed of an idea was well watered.

In September Padre Thomas wrote to me telling me that he had spoken to the Chaplain-in-Chief about my time at Lyneham, and, if I was interested in joining the RAF, the Chaplain-in-Chief would like to see me. I replied in the affirmative and a rail warrant arrived in the post for me to travel to the Ministry of Defence for an interview. The seed of an idea had germinated.

Meanwhile, on a fine morning in 1969, work commenced on the permanent church building. It was an exciting time; each morning, returning home from Matins in St David's Church, I would call at the excavation and greet the tradesmen. Before long the steel arrived for the structure, and, once the roof was on, the floor and internal fittings began to arrive on site. One morning an instant decision would be made regarding the route of the embedded microphone

St Peter & St Paul, Cimla, begins to take shape, 1969

The new church building at Cimla, 1969
Left to right: Bill Powell & Isaac Richards (Churchwardens), Ken Davies (Architect), Mrs Gravell, BHL

points; another day the site of an under floor safe would be agreed. Day by day the arrangement of organ, font, choir stalls and altar were discussed and agreed.

Less than three years after the project began, the new building was ready for consecration by Glyn Simon, now Archbishop of Wales. The Church in Wales had recently added the name of St Paul to that of St Peter in the church's Calendar, and as I had come from the Cathedral Church of St Peter and St Paul, I asked the Archbishop to add St Peter to the existing St Paul's Church in Cimla. Thus, the building was consecrated in the title of St Peter and St Paul, and opened for worship on 18th May 1970. The archbishop asked who was to celebrate the first Eucharist in the new church. When I said that I would be doing it at 7.30am the following morning, he explained that it was the prerogative of the bishop, but as he was unable to be present the following day, he would delegate the privilege to me. A few days later I received a sealed Licence giving me his authority to celebrate the first Eucharist in the new church.

The building itself had cost £17,000 with an extra £3,000 for the organ. The foundations and drains for the original building plus materials we had to buy-in for use by volunteers added up to £2,000, so that the whole project had cost £22,000. Twenty years later I was honoured to return as the guest preacher at the dedication of an extension to accommodate the growing congregation, and in 2010 I was invited once again to preach in celebration of the fortieth anniversary. They were splendid people, and I loved them dearly.

The new church of St Peter & St Paul, Cimla 1970

The following month I was commissioned into the Chaplains' Branch of the Royal Air Force, much to the displeasure of the Archbishop of Wales, who told me that I would be wasting my gifts. I replied that he could well be right, but they were my gifts, and I wanted to test my vocation in another field and free of any taint of patronage. Glyn Simon was a good man who wanted only the best for his diocese. I found no fault in him despite the rebukes I endured.

CHAPTER FOUR:

A Chaplain in the RAF

When I joined the Professionally Qualified and Re-Entrant Course at RAF Henlow in June 1970, there were eight Commands in the Royal Air Force: four overseas commands, and four in the UK. The Venerable Len Ashton was the Chaplain-in-Chief, always affectionately referred to by chaplains as 'the Chief', and he led a team of ten Assistant Chaplains-in-Chief. During my interview with him I must have mentioned the large congregations I had experienced at the cathedral and in the housing estate, for I remember him saying, 'If large congregations are important to you, then don't join the RAF. But if you want a daily ministry which will stretch you to your limit, then we will make you welcome.' I was confident that if I worked hard then large congregations would follow, so I applied for a commission: the arrogance of youth.

One week after I had signed the final acceptance papers for my commission, and received confirmation of a place at Henlow, Joy was invited to apply for the post of Tutor in the Geography Department at Swansea University. It was a post she had dreamed about, but as I was committed to the RAF, she saw her place at my side and declined the invitation. I shall never be able to repay in full her loyalty and sacrifice.

Back to the Classroom

I celebrated the first Holy Eucharist in St Peter & St Paul's church at 7.30am on Monday, 22 June 1970, and then drove to RAF Henlow in Bedfordshire and reported to the Officers' Mess. Flight Lieutenant Ken White, Officer Commanding Professionally Qualified and Re-Entrant (PQRE) Flight, met me in the foyer with a big smile of welcome; the comforting aroma of toast wafted from an anteroom; members of No.71 Course were assembling for afternoon tea. They had come from far and wide. There were doctors, dentists, nurses, Royal Canadian Air Force pilots transferring to the RAF, and three chaplains, one of whom was a priest from the Exeter diocese by the name of Robin Turner, and the other a Free Church minister. We were already commissioned and ready to be trained in the mysteries of service life. The nurses and pilots were Flying Officers; the professional men were Flight Lieutenants. After one year of satisfactory service, chaplains were then advanced to the relative rank of Squadron Leader and to Wing Commander after fourteen years. A chaplain's rank was 'relative' to their position in a military society; like the medical and legal branches, we had completed a degree course and several years post-graduate training, followed by at least two years in full-time ministry, so we were older than a newly trained officer in other branches of the RAF.

The first task was to be kitted out and to order our tailored uniforms. Until they were ready we were issued with 'hairy blues', a tunic and trousers in a coarse material, which was uncomfortable and inelegant. The course was a part of the RAF Henlow Officer Cadet Training Unit. It meant that there were large squads of men and women marching everywhere as part of their training to be commissioned as officers. They saluted every officer who came near them. As I was now wearing the rank of Flight Lieutenant on my shoulder slides, I left the safety of the Mess with caution and huge anxiety, for I was still uncertain how to salute correctly. My time with the Air Training Corps had taught me a lot, but I was not confident. If I saw a party of marching men approaching, I would dodge around the back of a building to avoid it. On day three I dodged right into the path of a solitary man with gold braid all over the peak of his cap. Rooted to the spot I gave him the best salute I could muster. To my dismay he burst into hoots of laughter. He saw the

No.71 PQRE Course, RAF Henlow, 1970. BHL is 5th from the left in the back row

misery on my face and controlled himself. 'It's all right, Padre', he said, 'You don't have to salute me, I'm a Corporal Bandsman.' I readily joined in the laughter and I learned that day the difference between 'scrambled egg' and gold braid; you salute 'scrambled egg' on a cap.

It was unfortunate, but I upset the Drill Warrant Officer on my first day. I had parked my car beside other cars near the church. I was aware that it was technically the edge of the parade ground, but assumed it was permitted. An enormous shout of 'You, sir' from the other side of the world caught my attention. It was followed by a bellow, 'Stand still! Stand still!' A warrant officer was marching towards me across the parade ground at a rapid pace. I could see two bulging eyes separated by the peak of his cap. He crashed to attention before me, saluted, and pointing to the church with his pace stick cried, 'That, sir, is a church into which I do not go.' Then swivelling on his heels, he pointed at the Square and bawled, 'And that is my parade square on which you will not park your ruddy car. MOVE IT. NOW!' Quietly and with dignity, I moved my car.

He remembered me when, a few days later, No.71 PQRE Course pitched up for our first lesson in drill. He walked along the two ranks we had formed, looking at us as if we disgusted him, which we probably did. One of the doctors, Philip Hoesli, was a tall, languid man with a shock of blond hair. The warrant officer stood behind him and for the first time I heard uttered the immortal words: 'Am I causing you pain, sir?' The doc drawled, 'Not in the least, Warrant Officer.' 'Well I should be 'cos I'm standing on your hair. Get it cut.' He was almost emaciated and, with a bald head on his shoulders, he was known to all officer cadets at Henlow as 'The Screaming Skull', but was addressed as Mr Jordan. He stopped in front of me as I stood at attention. Recognition dawned on his thin face. 'We have met, sir. We shall get on well you and me.' There was a chill in his tone which did nothing to encourage me.

Two weeks later, while we were enjoying a period of drill on the square, I was right marker and on the command I turned right and marched off in the lead. There is little more daunting than to hear the sound of marching boots receding in the distance when you are supposed to be in the lead. I looked nervously over my shoulder and sort of stopped or halted. The command had been to turn left, and they were all at the other end of the square and marching well. I glanced over at Mr Jordan, and he smiled an evil smile and beckoned to me with a bony finger. I marched up to him and he pointed to the ground beside him. I stood at attention beside him surveying the rest of the Flight marching back across the square under the direction of the Drill Flight Sergeant. 'When I tap my Pace Stick on the ground, I want you to halt them, and fall them into two ranks in open order, sir', he whispered. Before I could marshal my thoughts he tapped his stick loudly on the ground. I have no recollection what I actually barked out at the top of my voice. I

No.71 PQRE Course Visit Old Warden Aerodrome, 1970. Padre Robin Turner, BHL, Dr Philip Hoesli

know I began with, 'Number 71 PQ and RE Flight ... HALT', but what followed is a blank. However, though it might not have been in the Drill Manual, my colleagues caught the drift and did what I wanted. They ended in two ranks in open order and standing at ease. The Screaming Skull looked at the Flight and then at me with an old-fashioned look and whispered, 'Very well. You are going to buy them a lot off beer in the Mess tonight.' It was the closest he came to smiling. And he was right about the beer.

There was a great deal to learn in the four weeks of the course; the Manual of Air Force Law (MAFL) and Queen's Regulations for the Royal Air Force (QRs) became additions to the Bible for reading and inward digestion. At the end we had an examination and I was delighted to gain an A grade.

At the beginning of the third week we received our Posting Notice, advising me that I was going to RAF Halton, about an hour's drive to the west of Henlow, so I paid a visit to the Families Office to obtain a married quarter there for the following week. The Families Officer was a nice chap, but, having telephoned Halton, told me that there was a long waiting list for quarters. I explained that was rather difficult for my wife and baby who would be homeless a week

Friday when my parish flat was required for my successor. He took pity on us and arranged for us to occupy a 'Transit Quarter' at RAF Henlow; it was fully furnished, so our own belongings would have to go into storage for the time being, at my expense.

Having completed my course, I drove to Neath, packed up the flat into a local removal company's van, and returned with Joy and Mark to 14 Western Avenue, RAF Henlow. The following day, after introducing my family to the Chaplain, John Boatwright, I left for Halton to start work.

Learning the Ropes

I was posted to RAF Halton, the No 1 School of Technical Training, as the assistant Anglican chaplain. Padre Alan Vickers, who had processed my commission as Staff Chaplain, was the new senior chaplain. There was also a Roman Catholic chaplain, and a Presbyterian, Methodist and United Board chaplain, the Reverend Graham Corderoy, a Baptist Minister who became a good friend and a source of kindness. The Commandant was Air Commodore Bob Weighill, who, not long after I had arrived at Halton, gave me a lift in his staff car to watch the station Rugby team play against RAF Lyneham, where his friend the international rugby referee Larry Lamb was station commander. I lived in the Officers' Mess awaiting a married quarter. The Mess was Halton House, formerly a Rothschild mansion, and was known to the living-in officers as 'The Gilded Cage' so sumptuous were the furnishings. At my first Dining-In night I had to endure an initiation ceremony. Another officer was appointed as my assistant and helped me to carry an enormous brass gong up the wide and elegant staircase, and on reaching the top assist me to sit in the gong, which he then propelled down the stairs. It was a terrifying prospect as the array of officers in their Mess Kit below me zoomed closer until they parted to allow me to spin across the floor of the Grand Salon, coming to rest against the far columns. When the Commandant of the RAF Hospital at Halton came down with three nursing officers on his lap, overturned the gong halfway down, and nearly broke several limbs, the President of the Mess stopped the game.

The PMC, as the President of a Mess Committee is known, was a very able Group Captain, Brian Davis, who invariably came into the Mess for a drink in the bar before lunch on Sundays. This was also my habit after church, together with a handful of regulars. The Mess at Halton also catered for Chequers, the Prime Minister's country house nearby, and shortly after a Mess Meeting had voted in favour of inviting the PM of the day to become an Honorary Member of the Mess, the PMC rang me up to make sure I was coming for my usual on Sunday morning. He explained that the new Hon Member was coming in for a libation, but it was important that the news didn't get out for then the bar would be packed with members who never came in at the weekend. The usual gang was assembled around the bar counter on the Sunday at noon as the PMC came in with Edward Heath. He was bronze from his recent return from an ocean racing trip. He was introduced to us in turn and I quizzed him about his sailing. The sport clearly exhilarated him, and for an hour there was lively and relaxed conversation with much humour and heaving shoulders.

I hated the separation from Joy and Mark, and drove the thirty-five miles to Henlow on Friday evenings to spend Saturday together. It was worse for Joy for she did not drive and was stuck in the married quarter in Henlow, knowing no-one, and occasionally getting a bus to the shops in Hitchin. She never complained about her situation. At the very end of July I was walking up the hill at Halton to the Mess for lunch when an RAF ambulance stopped alongside me. I was appalled to see Joy inside and climbed aboard. Mark had been diagnosed with a hernia and was on his way to the RAF Hospital when Joy had spotted me. He spent two nights there before returning to Henlow after a successful operation. At last we were allocated a Type V, Flight Lieutenant's house, at 22 Mansion Hill, near Halton House and on the rise of the Chiltern Hills. I arranged for our furniture to come from South Wales, and we moved in on 27th August; we were together again as a family. That autumn we enjoyed many lovely walks along the paths of the Chilterns, and explored Aylesbury and Wendover. And my next door neighbour, Flight Lieutenant Toby Taplin, took me flying in a Chipmunk trainer over the Downs.

However, after five months I decided that I might have made a mistake in joining the RAF. Halton had two thousand young men, known as 'Brats', who were mostly three-year apprentices in aeronautical trades; the remainder were pursuing a one year course for mechanics. They marched between the barrack blocks and the workshops, a band at their head, each morning, lunch-time and at the end of the afternoon. They marched to church on Sundays by wing, an experience which set me firmly against Church Parades, for most of the young men were attending worship under duress. Day after day the chaplains taught these lads, in groups of eighty, from a skeletal and tedious syllabus. With that number of youngsters in a Nissen hut, with only a smoky oil stove for warmth, there was little meeting of minds. Worse, Alan Vickers would not let me visit the married quarters in my free periods, on the basis that there was no time for that, so I spent hours sitting in the office wasting my time.

In December I wondered whether to resign my commission, but at Joy's behest I went first, one dark, wet evening, to see Padre Dennis Clark, the chaplain to Halton RAF Hospital. He is an astute priest and listened to my anger with great patience. He persuaded me to give it more time, and he would see what could be done. Two months later I was posted to RAF St Mawgan in Cornwall as the station chaplain.

My First Station

In February 1971, I arrived in Penzance on the over-night motorail train and drove to RAF St Mawgan in snow. Again, there was a problem over accommodation. I had become a member of the so-called 'Kipper Fleet', the close-knit family of what had been Coastal Command but was now No.18 group, Strike Command. RAF Ballykelly, in Northern Ireland, had closed in December, which meant that many of the Shackleton crews had been posted to St Mawgan to convert to the Nimrod aircraft, then coming into service. Thus all the married quarters were full and there was a waiting list. A quarter became available in March in nearby Padstow, but the Chaplain-in-Chief had decreed that the chaplain must live in the main 'married patch' in St Eval, so I lost my place in the queue. I also lost my rag and decided to put a bit of stick about. I asked for and received an interview with Wing Commander John Trevains, the Officer Commanding Administration Wing, usually abbreviated to OC Admin. I made it clear that I was not a happy chap and was, in fact, the most disadvantaged officer in the whole of the RAF. The good Wing Commander understood the drift of my argument and agreed with me. He telephoned the Chaplain-in-Chief and having received no change of heart, he said he would do what he could.

In the meantime I lived in the Officers' Mess, in a hut alongside the main building which contained the dining hall and the public rooms. The initiation ceremony for new members on their first Mess Night was less dangerous than that at Halton. In the foyer of the Mess was a gold fish pond backed by a tall plinth. The new member had to climb on top of the plinth without falling in the pond. It looked easy and it was, but once seated securely on the top, smiling with success and much beer, one became aware of a damp sensation in

Outside St Eval Church, 1971

the nether region as someone switched on the fountain which dribbled out off the top of the plinth. The trick then was to get off quickly without losing one's grip or one's dignity.

The bulk of the married quarters, and indeed my office, were about eight miles away from the station on the disused airfield of St Eval, so I arranged an 8.0am said Eucharist at St Mawgan and a 10.30am Sung Eucharist at the old village church of St Eval. An RAF bus came from St Mawgan picking up the congregation en route. The local Methodist minister held a service once a fortnight in a little chapel in the Families Centre by the NAAFI, and the Roman Catholic priest invited his people to attend the Mass in a convent in St Mawgan village.

Now, at last, I was exercising my ministry in the environment I had hoped for. In 1971 there were three squadrons at St Mawgan: No.22 Squadron HQ, operating Whirlwind helicopters from detached flights, No. 42 Squadron operating the Shackleton Mk 3 aircraft, and No.7 Squadron operating Canberra TT18s, the latter I called my 'Youth Club', for the squadron was reforming, largely with first-tour aircrew. There was also an Operational Conversion Unit, training aircrew to operate the Nimrod MR 1, then coming into service. It was a busy station with a long history of maritime aviation.

In April, OC Admin did his stuff at last, and Joy and Mark came down from Halton as we moved into 30 Lerwick Road, St Eval. As the weather became warmer we explored the bays and headlands of the north Cornish coastline, and introduced Mark to the delights of sand and sea. As I had moved out of the Mess, I was entitled to the services of a batman. 'Batting' had ceased for squadron leaders by this time, but as the men were on a contract, they were still available. Mr Morgan was assigned to me; nearing retirement he said to Joy, 'I don't move furniture and I don't clean windows. But I like ironing.' She warmed to him at once.

One sunny Friday afternoon in the Officers' Mess, excitement was in the air. The station was hosting an Open Day for the general public on the morrow. Display and static aircraft had been arriving for some hours and their aircrews were now enjoying a convivial party in the bar. The Red Arrows were there in their smart red flying suits; the Patrouille de France in their distinctive blue flying suits, and the Diable Rouge team from Belgium in orange. Everywhere you could see pilots using their hands to explain their display routines. From my perch at the corner of the bar I saw a resident Shackleton crew from No.42 Squadron enter from the terrace in their drab, olive-green flying suits. They had returned from a long and tiring sortie over the Atlantic and were ready for a beer.

From the door they looked in disbelief at the cabaret in full swing in their Mess. After a moment's pause, their Captain led them into the middle of the crowd, where they extended their forearms, and began to make a low growling sound, as they slow-marched in a circular movement, their hands absolutely level, mimicking the relentless monotony of a Shackleton sortie, when compared with the short, dazzling sprint of a display team's routine. It didn't take long for the chaps in the pretty flying suits to get the message that the maritime air force was a world away from tight formations and breath-taking cross-overs.

I have related this episode in detail because it indicates that to serve in Coastal Command and its successor formations requires a certain type of personality. At the very least, one has to possess an inner conviction that you are doing a worthwhile job, even if it goes largely unremarked; from the beginning it was known as the Cinderella Command. One also has to operate in extreme conditions, and often at an uncomfortably low level. And then there is the loneliness and endurance; a twelve-hour sortie was common, and would take you far out over the ocean. It is all down to you, your crew and your aircraft. The interdependence is absolute.

My vocation hadn't changed since my time in Llandaff. I was there to bring people into the presence of Christ, but how was I to live it out in this environment? I decided to 'loiter with intent'. More theological clergy call it a ministry of presence. It is essential that any priest working in a secular environment is accepted first as a human being. If the people do not get to know you as you are, they are not likely to trust you when they are in need of help. You have to get alongside people where they are and engage with their concerns. I discovered at once that the advantage for the priest in uniform is that you can be with them in their workplace.

So, overcoming my reticence, I went into the crew rooms and drank coffee while leaning on the bar. This is not easy and not for the prude, but a Shackleton crew of ten is used to welcoming newcomers and I was accepted warmly. I learned to play Uckers and Polar Bears, but never got the hang of liar dice. But the door really opened when I asked if I could fly with them. They considered that I was mad, but they agreed readily and I was kitted out with a flying suit and a flying helmet or 'bone-dome'. After that, I went aviating as often as I could: in the Shackleton, a flight was often an eight hour sortie over the Western Approaches; the Canberra a couple of hours towing targets; and the OCU Nimrod mostly circuits and bumps. I loved it and at the same time the chaplain became a part of squadron life.

On Tuesday 6th July 1971 three Welshmen took to the air. Flight Lieutenant Dave Humphries-Evans, a Canberra pilot on No.7 Squadron, with his Welsh navigator, had agreed to fly a training sortie over Port Talbot for me to take some photographs of the town. On the approach to the coastline in Swansea Bay I unstrapped and stood beside Dave and navigated him up the River Avon towards Cwmavon, banked to the right over Velindre, and I could see my parents in the garden of their home waving at the Canberra aircraft with its unmistakeable yellow and black striped underside. I had been granted a wish, as I was flying in the exact airspace in which the Tiger Moth had inspired me as a young boy. We completed one more turn over the town as the force of gravity in the turn had pulled my camera arm down. Then we climbed away to beat up David's uncle's farm near Llandeilo before crossing the Brecon beacons to fly over the Navigator's home in Abergavenny.

In June, after twelve months of 'undetected crime', I had been promoted to the relative rank of squadron leader. It meant that I had to work harder at being addressed as 'Padre' rather than 'Sir'. I felt that I had been successful in this respect when, in the first week of August, Flight Lieutenant Colin Hughes, known throughout the maritime air force as 'Huggiss', telephoned me in my office in the Families Centre in St Eval to say that I had no option but to join his crew in a remarkable flight the following week—the last flight of a Shackleton Mark 3 out of Home Waters. In short, a training flight to Gibraltar. I lost no time in 'persuading' the Vicar of St Eval to cover my Sunday services, and the game was on.

I should have checked the date, Friday 13th, for it was a tedious flight outbound. We flew to 10 degrees west, turned left and then played for ages with a submarine in the Bay of Biscay, tracking it when submerged with the aid of sonobuoys. But tedium heightened to terror when I heard Huggiss confessing to his co-pilot on the crew intercom that he hadn't been to Gib since the frontier with Spain had closed, and therefore hadn't done a descending turn onto the runway, which jutted out into the bay. My relief on landing was changed to alarm as the pilots and navigators abandoned the aircraft as soon as the engines had been shut down. Clearly something was seriously wrong, so I raced across the grass after them, over the road and a low wall, to find them ordering beer from the Officers' Mess beach bar before it closed. That weekend I was led, willingly, into all kinds of trouble culminating in the Station Commander ordering us 'off the Rock', but I managed a day trip by ferry across the Straits to Tangier on the Sunday.

Take-off on the Monday was as tense as the landing had been. At midday in August in Gibraltar the heat can be oppressive and does not produce much lift under the wings of an aircraft attempting to defeat gravity on take-off. We taxied to the very end of the runway before turning to face east into what little wind there was, and Huggiss ran the engines up to full throttle, holding the aircraft on the brakes as he said over the crew intercom something like, 'In the event of malfunction below 90 knots the engineer will call, "Abort! Abort!" and we shall brake hard and turn off into the parking area; in the event of malfunction above 120 knots I shall call, "Abort! Abort!", and we will continue the climb-out, dump fuel and return to land. In the event of malfunction between 90 and 120 knots the Padre will say, "Our Father..."' And with that he released the brakes and we roared down the runway and, eventually, staggered into the air.

I discovered that weekend that observing, and helping out with the men at work, and joining with them at leisure, offered immense pastoral opportunities to a priest. A word of advice here, one of consolation there, and an occasional rebuke along the way, all made for solid friendship and trust. I also discovered, leaving Gibraltar that day, that the Mediterranean would have a life-long fascination for me. The warm sunlight, the clear air and the smell of the sea combine to make the ambience irresistible.

It was refreshing to work as a part of a large team of highly professional men and women. Every Friday at 1700hrs there was a Happy Hour in the Officers' Mess bar. I attended this every week, for it was an essential meeting of colleagues from all departments on the

Passing the time during a long Shackleton flight

Station. Pilots would have a beef with Ops about take-off slots; engineers would have a go at pilots for breaking their aircraft; the chaplain could make an informal case to the Motor Transport Officer for a staff car; and the Senior Medical Officer, for some reason known only to himself, took to banging all and sundry on the head with a tin tray. One of my good friends at Happy Hour was the Officer i/c RAF Police, Flight Lieutenant Martin Mortimer, and it wasn't long before my sessions at Happy Hour paid off.

Late one evening when I was at home in St Eval a lady telephoned me in some distress from her home in Bodmin. Her husband, a corporal, had beaten her and left the house with her young son. She was very frightened. I noted the address, told her to lock the doors and windows, and await my arrival. I changed into uniform and telephoned Martin Mortimer to ask for the loan of a Policeman for a few hours, the way you do. He said at once that he would come with me, and asked me to pick him up on the way. As we set off for Bodmin, I asked if he had a plan of action. His broad Scottish accent was reassuring as he said simply, 'We'll see the lady and then go straight to the 'Nick'; I've telephoned ahead.' We calmed the woman as she told her story, then making sure she was safely locked in, we went to the Police Station. They already had a patrol car looking for the man and in minutes they had tracked him to a pub and were bringing him in. I didn't see him, but they gave me the boy to reunite him with his mother. She was unwilling to remain alone in the house, so I had arranged with the St Mawgan Duty Officer to allocate a room in the WRAF Block for her and her son. We returned to the Police Station for a cup of tea and discovered that arrangements had been made for a police car to take the two of them to St Mawgan. Martin and I spent a convivial hour in the 'Nick' before I drove us back to our homes. I reflected that in a parish I would have had to sort something out on my own. The following morning I was able to talk to the corporal and his wife in a calmer atmosphere.

Another big difference, which I discovered very early in my RAF ministry, was that I had to learn again how to communicate the Gospel of Christ. In the parish everyone in the congregation is more or less 'on message'; they have some understanding of the service and the context of the Gospel. That cannot be assumed in the Armed Forces. There will usually be a small nucleus of committed Christian folk in church on a Sunday, but there will also be casual visitors; men and women whom you might have seen at work during the week, and have come to see how you operate. It might be the only chance you will have to persuade them of Christ's love of them. It is a huge responsibility for a priest, and he has to grasp the opportunity.

I also understood what the Chaplain-in-Chief had said at my interview about large congregations: at the 0800 Communion on base, there was usually one corporal and me. Once an airman strolled in, greeted the corporal with, 'Hiya, mate, what's your name?' Only to be told, 'My name is John, but you can call me Corporal.' The situation at St Eval was little better. I used the parish church which was about a mile towards the sea from the quarters, across the disused airfield, and the MT bus stopped briefly at the quarters to pick up any families, but hardly anyone used it. Mr Morgan, my batman, who had lived locally all his life, described St Eval in his charming Cornish accent as 'Hell's back yard, m'dear.' Despite its distance from the operational side of life, my office was alongside the Families Office, so I knew at once when families were arriving or departing from married quarters.

The coast of North Cornwall had more than its fair share of wintry Atlantic weather. There were days when force eight fog would roll in from the sea at cliff top height and all flying would cease for the day. Many of the aircrew, both officers, and Senior NCOs, would adjourn to 'Auntie Pearl's', so called after the owner of the Riviera Lodge Hotel, an establishment at Mawgan Porth. Pearl would dispense beer while Flight Lieutenant Johnny Johnston would accompany our raucous singing on the piano. I felt totally at home and among friends in situations like this.

The last Mk2 Shackleton to return from Singapore when British Forces pulled out of the Far East in 1971 brought with it a memorial cross to be installed in St Eval Church. It was originally found on Sin Cowe island, with 'B 205' laid out in stones on the coral. It marked the grave of a single body, Flight Sergeant Dancy, who was killed when the 205 Squadron Shackleton, 'B' for Baker, crashed in the South China Sea while on an anti-piracy patrol in December 1958. His was the only body recovered as it had been fished out of the sea and buried by fishermen who had seen the aircraft dive into the ocean, and who made the rough cross to stand over the grave. The cross was taken to RAF Changi, where it remained until 205 Squadron disbanded and the memorial was flown home to St Mawgan.

The Labuan Cross. The last Shackleton Mark 2 from Singapore brings the Cross to RAF St Mawgan. It is received by Padre Lucas for a permanent home in St Eval Church in 1971

In December 2008, on the 50th anniversary of the fateful crash, I preached at a memorial service in St Eval Church when the widows of Sgt Dancy and Flight Lieutenant Boutell, the pilot, were present; it was the first time they had met each other.

I forged a very good relationship with the Senior Medical Officer, Wing Commander Douglas McLeod. We worked well together and trusted each other. He was a brilliant doctor who certainly knew how to enjoy life. After one Mess Night some young officers took to leaping across the pond in the foyer. Douglas tried it but didn't quite make it, banged his shin on the far side and ended up sitting in the pond, which was getting redder by the minute. The Junior MO was called and cross at being called out in the early hours he stitched his boss' leg without the benefit of anaesthetic, as we all crowded around offering advice and solace.

I had been in Cornwall for eight months when the Assistant Chaplain-in-Chief, Strike Command, Padre Hewitt Wilson, came to pay a formal visit. During the debrief before he left, he suggested that a weekly Sung Eucharist was rather excessive and that once a month would do, with Morning Prayer on the other Sundays. I replied that I took a different view and had concluded that weekly Eucharist was better nourishment for a committed congregation, but I acknowledged that he was more experienced and, if he wasn't happy with what I was doing, he could post me. Wise man that he was, he just sucked on his pipe and smiled.

As we were preparing for Christmas, the time came for Joy to give birth to our second child. Tucking Mark in the back of our car, I drove as quickly as I dare to the Treliske Hospital in Truro, where Simon was born some hours later, in fact not long after I had arrived home and put Mark to bed. Two days later Mark and I brought Joy and the little one home to St Eval. He was the best of Christmas gifts.

I always experienced an excitement climbing aboard a Shackleton for a flight. There was a sense of history in having to climb over the wing spars inside the aircraft, and the fragrance of old leather mingled with aviation fuel. The noisy growl of the four Rolls Royce Griffon engines driving the contra-rotating propellers, combined

*Flight Lieutenant Colin Hughes (Huggiss), right, with his crew before flying Mark 3 Shackleton
'J' for Juliett to a Museum*

with the vibration of the airframe to give a sense of adventure as the pilot opened the throttles for takeoff. The journey to the primitive Elsan lavatory in the tail required much perseverance. My first flight of 1972 was in a very different aircraft.

It was a return trip to RAF Kinloss, in Scotland, in Nimrod XV257 captained by Squadron Leader Brian Burton. After takeoff I went forward to the flight deck, and when the co-pilot went aft for his lunch I took his right hand seat and strapped in. We were to the west of Edinburgh. Brian asked if I would like to fly the aircraft, and took my huge grin for assent. He explained again the instruments and emphasised that as we flying along an airway it was essential that we maintained our height of 32,000ft and kept on the compass heading. He switched off the autopilot, and with that he said, 'My throttles, your stick.' I repeated what he had said and took control of the aircraft as he let go.

The Nimrod had "feel" built into the controls to stop the pilot pulling the wings of the aircraft, or so they told me. That means that you have to pull the aircraft about a bit, and it took me some minutes to keep the artificial horizon level and at altitude. I looked out of the windscreen as the real horizon tilted, and I had to bank the aircraft rather sharply to starboard, resulting in some blasphemy on the intercom over spilt coffee. Eventually I was comfortable with my flying, and the instruments told me that I could breathe out. I smiled to myself in sheer contentment as I realized that my flying suit was damp with sweat. I looked across at Brian; he grinned at me and said you'll have to hand over soon; we're over Bristol and close to descent. I had been flying the aircraft for fifty minutes, but it had been sheer joy to be able to move this big four-engine beast about the sky.

I was on leave in Port Talbot after Easter 1972 when I had a message to telephone OC Admin Wing as soon as possible. Fearing an accident or worse, I rang St Mawgan and John Trevains told me that I was to be posted in four weeks time. I groaned until he added, 'To RAF Luqa in Malta, but report to St Clement Danes for further details as the Chaplain-in-Chief is away.' I completed the week's leave with our parents, and returned to pack my kit. I went up to the Central Church of the Royal Air Force in London and saw Padre Thomas, who I had met in Lyneham when I was with the Air Training Corps, and who was now the Resident Chaplain at St Clement Danes. He gave me the bad news that there could be a six-month wait for quarters in Malta. Joy was to be alone again, this time with two young children.

In December 1971, Dom Mintoff, the Prime Minister of Malta, had told the British Forces to leave the island forthwith. In Operation Withdrawal, the RAF squadrons departed: Nimrod aircraft of No.203 Squadron to Sigonella in Sicily, and the Canberra aircraft of No.13 Squadron to RAF Akrotiri in Cyprus. The families were repatriated to available quarters all over the United Kingdom. A skeleton force was

Preparing to read the Committal Service over the intercom on board No.42 Sqn Shackleton 'H' for Hotel prior to scattering the cremated remains of a former squadron officer on the sea in the Bristol Channel, 1971.

retained at Luqa to run down the headquarters and outlying sites and equipment before the final withdrawal date of 31st March 1972.

In the final week, Prime Minister Edward Heath signed a Military Facilities Agreement with Mintoff, enabling the British Forces to remain while renting the bases for a further seven years. That signalled Operation Reactivation. My posting was a part of that operation. The Chaplain, Padre John Daimond, was actually on his way home when the Agreement was signed, and offered to return, but the Chaplain-in-Chief decided that he had done his bit.

Consequently, there was little time for a hand-over, so I arranged for a Canberra of No.7 Squadron to fly me to RAF Benson. John Daimond met me and we drove to a nearby pub for the hand-over. He had brought the church silver with him in the aircraft home and it was placed on the table between us in a cardboard box. As we drank our ale he produced a silver chalice, I checked it in the Inventory and signed for it. Another quaff of ale and a pair of silver candlesticks was produced and signed for. So it went on until the table was full of silver. Then I noticed curious glances from elderly men sat at the bar. We drank up and left, before we had to explain to the local constabulary. Two hours later I was back in Cornwall.

CHAPTER FIVE:

The Maker's Rep

I wondered whether Hewitt Wilson had taken me at my word when I was posted in 1972 to RAF Luqa, Malta. As the crews of No.42 Squadron converted to the Nimrod MR1 they were posted to No.203 Squadron in Malta, so I knew the majority of the families from the outset; I had baptized some of their children.

I returned to the Mediterranean on a hot Saturday morning in May 1972 and was met at the aircraft and taken straight to the Officers' Mess to 'freshen up'. As I checked in at the reception desk I was aware of three Wing Commanders looking keenly at me. One of them came forward with his hand held out and introduced himself as Don Biltcliffe, OC Engineering Wing. He then walked out to the reception desk to make a telephone call. He returned in two minutes to let me know that a car would be brought around for me in ten minutes, and that meanwhile I was in need of a drink. It was a splendid welcome to a new station. Don explained that all RAF cars had been returned to UK following the withdrawal, but a local hire car would be mine until the Service Mini arrived back. Ten minutes later the keys to a Triumph Herald convertible were left for me at reception. What a refreshing change to my unsuccessful fight for transport at St Mawgan.

Royal Air Force Station Luqa was under the control of the Commander-in-Chief, Near East Air Force, from his headquarters at RAF Episkopi in Cyprus, and my immediate ecclesiastical superior was the Assistant Chaplain-in-Chief at that headquarters, Padre Ray Bowen, another Welshman. My office was a Nissen hut between Admin Wing Headquarters and the Transit Mess on the airfield site. My clerk, Joe, was a locally enlisted airman who spoke very good English and was a most willing clerk.

I discovered that there was, indeed, a long waiting list for married quarters and so about a hundred and twenty officers were living in the Mess. I had a room on the ground floor in a shady courtyard known as the Bullring. Nevertheless, once the sun had gone down there was a boisterous evening of revelry in the bar and terrace. For the sake of sanity and liver it was urgent that I resumed normal service. After a fortnight of riotous night life, I sat Joe in the Triumph, and toured Malta visiting 'Hirings': locally owned properties which were approved by the RAF Families' Officer.

By far the nicest I looked at was a house in Marsascala, a fishing village located at the end of a long inlet in the east of the island, about a twenty-minute drive from RAF Luqa. The furniture was standard RAF issue, but there was no cooker or fridge. When the occupants had removed in a hurry to England the previous December they were allowed to wrap the cooker and the fridge in carpets, and take them home with them. Worse, the remains of their final cooked meal were still in the pans on the window sill covered in cockroaches. Nevertheless, I told the Families Officer that I would take it, and he issued a 'Call-Fam' notice to enable Joy and the children to travel to Malta.

Meanwhile, in St Eval, Joy arranged a 'March-out'. This was an incredible ceremony when the Families Officer met the occupant in the married quarter and checked the inventory from beds to teaspoons. At the same time his warrant officer would dismantle the cooker looking for evidence of grease, and rub his white glove over the top of doors looking for dust. The officer's wife was usually manic at the time of march-out due to the weeks spent in preparing the house for the inspection. Joy had to handle all this by herself, for I was in Malta. Moreover, she had two children, one just three and the other six months, and packed suitcases by the front door for a car journey to Bodmin Road railway station en route to Malta via RAF Brize Norton in Oxfordshire.

It is almost unbelievable, therefore, that during the march-out she received a signal—a military telegram—which she thrust into her pocket to be read when the formalities had been completed. At last, she was complimented on a most satisfactory preparation and all was well. Gathering the children and suitcases, Joy crossed the road to the house of a friend for a welcome cup of tea while waiting for the RAF car to arrive for the journey to the station. Then she remembered the signal, and tearing it open read it. It was a brief message: 'Your flight to Malta delayed twenty-four hours. Do not, repeat, not report to RAF Brize Norton today.'

She telephoned Brize Norton and asked if she could stay there the extra night as she had vacated her house and had nowhere to sleep, only to be told by a young female officer, 'That's your problem, Madam.' And the line went dead. But Joy was made of sterner stuff, and remembered that I had stayed at the transit 'Route Hotel' when at the ATC camp in RAF Lyneham. So her friend found the telephone number for RAF Lyneham and Joy spoke with the officer in charge of the Route

Hotel; he was all kindness, and advised her to catch the train as arranged and take the Lyneham bus at Swindon station, for accommodation was now booked for her.

The car arrived a few minutes later and she made her way with children, cases and pushchair to Bodmin Road railway station to join the train to Paddington and thence to Swindon. On the platform she saw several wives with young children and noticed the RAF Luqa flight labels on their suitcases. When she spoke to one of them about the nuisance caused by the delay, she discovered that they were airmen's wives and had not been informed, so she told them to stick close to her. Thus it was that Joy arrived at Lyneham with four extra families all of whom were readily accommodated. It was an appalling incident, which I referred to Brize Norton for comment, but received none.

I hired a Ford Escort for a week and met my little family as they emerged off the aircraft into the warm sunshine on 21st May, and then drove east across the island to Marsascala. The chief clerk in the family's office had loaned a camping stove for the few weeks until a cooker was available, and I had hired a fridge from a store in nearby Zabbar. Joy set to work cleaning the house from top to bottom, for it had been empty for five months in a dusty atmosphere. It wasn't long before a Maltese lady asked if we required a maid. We liked Doris Mercieca at once, and she was employed on the spot. She was an enormous help for Joy and became almost a member of the family. She adored the boys, and they loved her.

The Station Church of St Christopher was situated off the roundabout at the entrance to No.2 Site at RAF Luqa and was therefore outside the airfield security

St Christopher's Church, RAF Luqa, 1972

Church Council, RAF Luqa. Left to right: WO 'Chalky' White, Miss Liz Manhire, BHL, Mrs Silk, Sqn Ldr Chris Burton. Back Row: Sqn Ldr John Cartwright, Sqn Ldr Norman Walter, Ch Tech David Nye

zone. I arranged for the church building to be cleaned and started holding Sunday services there. I kept the former pattern of a said Holy Communion at 08.00 and a sung service at 10.00. When Joy arrived, she agreed to play the piano I had obtained on loan from the Officers' Mess at the 10.00 Sung Eucharist on Sunday. For weeks we had to clear away crown corks from discarded beer bottles as they dropped out of the piano and rolled about the floor during the service. Mark sat on the organ stool with her and quietly read his books while Joy played the piano, but we left baby Simon behind in Marsascala. Doris' father kept the newspaper stall on the promenade, and Simon spent his Sunday mornings in a baby-relaxer on the counter, being spoiled with hugs and sweets from the Maltese ladies who came to buy at the stall. Some service wives had been jostled in the streets of Valletta by young activists, and our friends thought we were taking a risk by leaving Simon so prominently, but he was never safer.

The Nimrod crews of No.203 Squadron had returned to RAF Luqa on 23rd April, from their withdrawal to the United States Naval Air Station at Sigonella, in Sicily, and, when their families returned, the majority of them occupied hirings in a large apartment block built around a swimming pool at Bugibba, in the north west of Malta. Slowly, the other families began to return to the island and as I received the weekly report of arrivals I would visit and welcome people to their new home.

Over the months the congregation built up and I soon had a choir to enhance the music, and a small Sunday School. I appointed two 'Churchwardens'; one was Squadron Leader Chris Burton, the CO of the Police and Security Services, and the other was Warrant Officer 'Chalky' White, the SWO. On Sunday mornings at 1000 they would frame the doorway and welcome people as they arrived, although I once had to rebuke Chalky for greeting an airman with the word, 'Haircut.'

Overseas, the church becomes a little piece of home life, and even folk who have drifted from regular worship return to it in a foreign land. It offers continuity and a feeling of comfort, and there's nothing wrong with that as long as it leads to a closer walk with God. For many in St Christopher's church it did mean that, without any false piety or pretence. The church was full most Sundays for the Sung Eucharist. I gave one of the regulars a lift to the Sergeants Mess after the service one Sunday, when a voice I knew well called out, 'Good Morning, Padre. I knew you when you were poor.' Rising out of a chair behind the hedge was the unmistakably gaunt figure of Warrant Officer Jordan, 'the screaming skull' from Henlow. I parked the car and went over to greet him and he insisted that I joined him for a beer in his mess. I was glad to accept, and found him to be excellent company.

One of the first to greet me when I settled in was the minister at the Church of Scotland Kirk in Valletta, the Reverend John Milne, a bachelor who was also the Officiating Chaplain to the C of S and Free Church personnel. After a long career as a chaplain, he had retired in 1964, and knew many of the older former Shackleton chaps. He lived in the Manse in Straight Street, Valletta, known infamously as the 'Gut', and came to the Mess each working day at lunchtime for his gin and tonic.

The role of the squadrons at RAF Luqa was largely one of reconnaissance. The Nimrod aircraft of No.203 Sqn were superbly equipped for searching for surface and submarine vessels of our allies as well as the Soviet fleet, and then tracking their transit through the Mediterranean. To find submarines the crew dropped sonoboys, which deploy one or more hydrophone sensors below the surface while sending information to the aircraft through a radio transmitter. The aircraft had Autolycus, a short-range instrument for the detection of diesel fumes from submarines either on the surface, or while snorkelling, and projecting from the tail was the Magnetic Anomaly Detection boom, which contained apparatus for detecting a distortion in the Earth's magnetic field caused by a submerged steel vessel. No.13 Sqn operated the Canberra in a photo-reconnaissance role, often flying at a very high altitude.

Two days before No.13 Squadron returned to Malta in October, from a sojourn in Cyprus following the withdrawal, the squadron families arrived from UK and occupied hirings all over the island, chosen by their husbands *in absentia*. The next day one of the aircraft crashed into Akrotiri Bay in Cyprus killing both crew members. As there was no officer from 13 Squadron in Malta, I was asked to break the news to the wife of the navigator; the pilot was unmarried. I have undertaken this task many times since, though I am firmly of the view that it is the work of the Squadron Commander. In this case, it took a while to determine where she was living, but as dusk was falling I tracked her down to a remote village.

She was so pleased to see me until I asked her to sit down and the gravity of my tone gave her a clear signal of pain, even before I told her of her husband's death. Such news is so devastating that it is vital that you make sure you are talking to the right woman before giving her the message; nothing is gained by informing the wrong wife that her husband has died, and I have heard of that happening. I always took an airwoman or a neighbour with me to take the children into another room, make a cup of tea, or to fetch a close friend. In this case she had a sister who was a squadron leader in the Ministry of Defence, so I arranged for her to fly to Malta overnight. A few weeks later I accompanied them to the aircraft as she returned with her sister to the UK.

It was a tragic episode, but it meant that I was readily accepted by squadron members on their return, one of whom, Flying Officer John Armitage, joined the church choir. Tall and with a shock of blond hair, John had a lovely tenor voice, and threw himself into church life with gusto. I was not in the least surprised when, the following year, the Commander-in-Chief, Near East Air Force, chose John as his ADC, and he left for Cyprus.

Another wife who returned to Malta was the wife of the Prime Minister, Mrs Moyra Mintoff, for she had been living in England. As she was a devout Anglican she began to attend the 0800 Communion service. Wishing to keep a low profile she would arrive just as the service was about to begin and left as soon as I had pronounced the final blessing. The second week I beat her to the exit and greeted this new arrival. She introduced herself and explained that she could not avoid the social whirl in the cathedral in Valletta so she preferred the quiet devotion of St Christopher's church, if that was alright with me. I advised the Air Commander Malta of her attendance, for it was, after all, a military establishment, but made him promise to keep it to himself and not to intrude on her privacy, to which he agreed.

After a few weeks, she asked why she hadn't met my wife. I explained that Joy was my organist at the 1000 service, but that she would be welcome at our home in Marsascala at any time. A month passed by before the door bell rang one evening as Joy was bathing Mark before bedtime. I answered the door, carrying Simon wrapped in a towel, to find Mrs Mintoff. 'Oh, I've called at a bad time' she said. I welcomed her and explained that Joy was bathing the older lad but would not be long. 'Give him to me' she said, and taking Simon she went up the stairs towards the bathroom. I called out, 'Joy, Mrs Mintoff is coming up to say hello.' Within minutes there was the sound of laughter and squeals emanating from upstairs, so I poured a large Gin and Tonic and hoped for the best. They put the children to bed and came downstairs. With a glance at my glass, Mrs M said, 'Yes please.'

After that Moyra, for she soon insisted on Christian name terms, would visit us in the evening when Dom was in Parliament, for she knew she was safe and that we would never repeat anything she told us. We liked her very much; she was clever, witty, with a keen sense of humour and always enjoyed good, challenging conversation. She had an attractive low voice similar to that of the actress Fenella Fielding. She was a slightly built lady, but drove a big, battered Mercedes. Moyra Mintoff was always a welcome visitor. We kept in touch until she died. On a visit to Malta following my retirement in 1995, I invited her to afternoon tea in my hotel. When she arrived, the manager diverted us to a small private room, whispering 'You should have told me, sir.' She smiled at the silver service which followed. She had hardly changed over the years, and was alert and shrewd and humorous. And she still drove the same big Mercedes, though, on that occasion, she asked me to park it for her.

Life in Malta became more regular and less like a holiday as new equipment and personnel retuned. A brand new organ arrived for the church, we had a new cooker and fridge at home, and I was issued with an RAF Mini. Remote as we were from the church and the NAAFI shops it became imperative that Joy learned to drive. Maltese law only permitted learners to drive in the company of a licensed local instructor, and then only on their allocated section of road. So Joy passed her test at the former RAF Ta'Qali airfield even though she had never before encountered a hill-start.

One evening Joy and I arrived home from a Ball in the Mess in the early hours of the morning and having taken Doris home, we were preparing to go to bed when a distressed wife arrived at the door, her dress covered in blood. Her husband, a Flight Lieutenant, had beaten her. Joy took her upstairs, cleaned her and put her to bed. The following morning, I called at her house before the neighbours were about and asked her husband to bring clean clothes for her. He was indifferent until I threatened to make life difficult. He came half an hour later to take her home. I reminded him that I would be taking a close interest in them from now on. I didn't report the incident as I should have done, but he knew that I knew, and that was enough. A chaplain is never off duty in the RAF.

On another occasion, when we arrived home from a Ladies Night in the Mess, we encountered a stranger looking after the children. Doris had been required at home as her mother was gravely ill, but such was her dedication to us that, instead of asking someone to telephone us, she had found this young woman to take over before going to her mother's side. I took the girl home and then, still in my Mess Dress, I went to Doris' house and joined the family around the old lady's bed. She was close to death, and they asked me to pray with them, which I did. The next day Doris told me her mother had died shortly after I had left.

Perched on a bar stool in the Mess one evening a new officer came and stood alongside me. He introduced himself as Mike and I bought him a drink. We had an interesting conversation about Malta, and then, when I asked him what he had come out to do, he revealed that he was the new Station Commander. Group Captain (later Air Chief Marshal Sir) Michael Armitage was a tall, distinguished looking man of great ability. He did not take kindly to the fact that I was not on the telephone in Marsascala, because if I was required on base after working hours a car had to be sent to inform me. I explained the background to the quartering problem, so he decreed that as it was too expensive to lay a landline to my house, the first married quarter to become available with a telephone was mine. In September 1973 the Families Officer offered me a wing commander's house with a telephone at Kalafrana. I explained to the Station Commander that there was a quarter available with a 'phone, but it was inappropriate to my rank. His reply was immediate, 'If you and Joy like the house, Brian, it's yours.

It was a lovely house, and one of the earliest RAF houses to be built, for the RAF crest with the date '1922' was carved in stone above the pediment. The two larger bedrooms and the lounge were on the first floor, and French windows led from our bedroom and the lounge to a deep balcony which ran the entire length of the house, and looked over the garden to the sweep of Birzebbuga Bay, and beyond to the Mediterranean Sea.

It was on the big balcony that we held monthly drinks parties after the 10.00am service on Sundays. I would put out a box of spirits and crates of beer and Francis, a bar steward from the Officers' Mess, dressed in white shirt and black tie, would arrive with all the glasses, mixers and soft drinks while we were in church, and when we arrived home the bar would already be set up in the lounge and Francis would be waiting at the top of the stairs with a tray of drinks in his hand. All I had to do was to hoist the Welsh flag from the flagpole at the end of the balcony. The glorious thing was that you could arrange a party months in advance and be assured of brilliant sunshine.

The downside to our move to Kalafrana was that we had to part company with Doris, for she would not leave her father, and although it was only a few miles away there was no transport link. We employed a local maid named Rita, who would sleep in the guest room when we were going to be late back from functions at the Mess. The house was, however, convenient when Mark was old enough to start school at Luqa, for a school bus stopped outside the house to pick up children from next door, and Mark would set off happily clutching his packed lunch.

BHL with Group Captain Mike Armitage, Station Commander, RAF Luqa

The Station Commander instituted a practice that I had not experienced before or since. Early one evening he telephoned me and invited us to go with the children to Luqa House for a drink; he asked if I would give the Station Warrant Officer a ring and bring him with his wife. While Joy and the children with Marjorie White joined Gretl Armitage in the lounge, Chalky and I sat with Mike Armitage on the terrace enjoying single malt whisky as the evening sun went down. He said that he saw the SWO and the chaplain as men with no axe to grind, who were secure and confident in their position, and yet with their finger on the pulse of the station, and he wanted any candid advice we thought he required. Chalky needed no further encouragement: 'That Routine Order that went out last week went down like a bag of nails in the Sergeants Mess, sir. It doesn't stack up. It's daft.' For my part, I was able to deflect a suggestion for the new President of the Officers' Mess Committee which, if implemented, would have been most unfortunate. This informal meeting was repeated about three times a year after that, and proved most useful to all three of us, to the detriment of the Boss' whisky stock.

An Interlude in Singapore

Flight Lieutenant Colin 'Huggiss' Hughes and his crew, which had taken me from Cornwall to Gibraltar a year or two earlier, were now on 203 Squadron operating the Nimrod, and were to represent the RAF in the international maritime competition for the Fincastle Trophy in Australia, and again it was suggested that I should go with them. Huggiss' crew were the competitors, but following behind them on their transit as far as Singapore, and only taking-off each day after they were safely airborne and reported as serviceable, was the reserve aircraft, captained by Flight Lieutenant John Bird, but barred by competition rules from actually flying into Australia. I joined the crew of this aircraft.

On 19th November 1973 the four Spey engines lifted Nimrod MR1 XV 240 from the runway. The first leg consisted of a transit to the RAF base on the island of Masirah, off the Indian Ocean coast of Oman. We climbed to about five miles high and flew to Cyprus where we turned left over the high mountains of central Turkey with mount Ararat in the distance, and on along the old CENTO route over Iran and then letting down over the vast Omani Empty Quarter to RAF Masirah, just over seven hours after leaving Luqa. I was met at the foot of the aircraft steps by the chaplain, Peter Levingston, who took me to his quarters where, over glasses of whisky, he pumped me for all the information and gossip on the Chaplains' Branch, for his was a thirteen month unaccompanied posting.

The following morning saw a departure for RAF Gan, the staging post on Adu Atoll in the Maldive Islands just south of the Equator. I had been foolish enough to mention to Dave Murphy, the Air Electronics Officer (AEO), that this was to be my first time in the southern hemisphere. For much of the tedious transit across the Indian Ocean I sat in the port beam lookout position, for the window was concave offering almost 180 degree vision. Then the Captain advised us on the

DESTINATION	TR	DIST.	LEG TIME	ETA	REV. ETA	TIME	OBSERVATIONS	W/V	VAR.	HDG	DR	G/S	TMN
							This is to certify that Rev Brian Lucas crossed the equator						
				at Position O/O N/S 7332E (NW of Gan) AT 201008 ʒ									
				at 33000 ft en route Luqa to Tengah.									
				He underwent with vigour and fortitude the aircrews									
				initiation ceremony									
									J.S. Bird	CAPT			
								D	Buchanan	Co Pilot			
								T	Raffles	NAVS			
								P	Curry				
								D	Murphy	AEO			
									J.S. Bird. Captain.				

Crossing the Line 1973

intercom to fasten seat harnesses due to clear air turbulence ahead. The AEO came behind me and yanked my harness so tight that I could hardly move as I heard over the intercom, 'Nav to crew, one mile to run to the Equator', the Captain replied that he had the line of oil drums in sight. I was still laughing as he pulled the aircraft up and over an imaginary barrier, when I went totally blind. Crew members were busy squirting shaving foam in my eyes, ears, down my neck and down the front of my flying suit. There had been no turbulence: I had crossed the line in style.

I stood behind the pilots to observe our descent to RAF Gan. At first I saw a tiny smudge of lighter green than the dark ocean; then it became evident that it was a coral reef, and then the lighter green of grass with white specks on it could be seen. As we touched down the white specks were playing cricket. It could only be a British base. The tour of duty at Gan was six months unaccompanied and even that short length of time was too long for some men, for it is a very small island. Transit aircraft carrying families kept their passengers out of sight of resident personnel, for the sight and sounds of wives and children was too much for some to bear.

After parking the aircraft, we went to the Mess and sat under a steel canopy outside and drank cold beer while a sudden monsoon storm broke overhead. As the water rose around us we hoisted our feet higher on the stools as a Mess waiter came with rolled up trousers and trays of more beer. The rain stopped after thirty minutes and five minutes later the water had all drained away and normality was restored. I went swimming in the waters of the clear coral lagoon, and enjoyed the sight of innumerable brightly coloured fish. Walking back to my room I was fascinated to watch the fruit bats flying so low that they grazed your hair as they came in at dusk to roost upside down in the palm trees.

It was hot and hazy as we lined up to depart for Singapore the next morning, for a five hour flight to RAF Tengah, Singapore. I was back in the port beam lookout as we flew over mile after mile of tropical forest on the Indonesian island of Sumatra. The Officers' Mess at Tengah was being redecorated, so we were accommodated in Singapore in the luxury Equatorial Hotel.

The following day, both crews enjoyed wandering through the bustling streets of old Singapore City, and the tourist trail—Raffles Hotel and Bugis Street. Before we left the hotel, Dave Murphy, the AEO who had initiated my 'crossing the line' ceremony, advised me to put my RAF Identity Card and my money in my socks. Feeling foolish, and suspecting another spoof, I stuffed my ID card in my sock, but left the money safely buttoned in my hip pocket. Near Bugis Street a 'lady of the night' approached us and slipped between us. We said firmly 'No thanks' and she returned to her rickshaw and was gone. So had my money, which gave my so-called 'friends' much hilarity when the tale was told.

It was dusk by the time we settled down at some tables in the infamous Bugis Street to watch the night scene. It was just after midnight that the transvestites emerged. One sat at a nearby table and I announced to my colleagues that I was going to do some research, and I joined her/him at his/her table. I shall refer to 'her', for she looked every inch a beautiful young woman. I told her at once that I was a priest interested only in trying to understand her way of life. She told me her name was Nancy, and we talked for nearly half an hour about her hopes and aspirations. She was from Bangkok, had a boyfriend in Stoke on Trent and hoped to marry him. She thought and behaved as a woman. I could not begin to understand her life or her attitude to it, but neither could I judge her. Nancy was a lonely person living a dangerously vulnerable life, and I said a silent prayer for the Almighty to protect her, as I bought a ridiculously over-priced orange juice for her and bade her farewell. When my friends asked for 'the gen', I told them to buy their own programme.

The next day, Huggiss and his crew flew the last leg to Edinburgh Field air station in Adelaide, Australia, to enter the Fincastle Competition, and on landing sent a signal to say that the aircraft was perfectly serviceable, which meant that our job was done as he didn't need us for spares, and so we could return to Malta. On the Monday morning, the flight engineer discovered that the pitot head heater was not working, so we could not fly until a replacement heater unit arrived from UK. I hired a car and drove across the Causeway into Malaysia. I thrilled at the sounds of the jungle, and later the scenery of the mangrove swamps bordering the Malacca Strait. On Sunday 2nd December I had assumed that I would have been in the pulpit of St Christopher's Church, Luqa. Instead I was preaching in the pulpit of the Station Church at RAF Tengah.

We took off at last on 4th December and landed at Gan after a seven and a half hour flight. I went for a swim in a tropical storm and nearly stepped on a deadly stonefish but was alerted by the co-pilot as my foot hovered over its spiny back. It was in Gan that I noticed that the chaplain had the sign, 'Maker's Rep', on the front of his bicycle. Reflecting on it I thought it was an accurate description of the priest's role in an aeronautical environment. We had a day's delay at Gan due to technical trouble, but later that morning we received a signal informing us that Huggiss and his crew had won the Fincastle Trophy; the Nimrod had beaten all other NATO and allied air forces' nationally selected crews in submarine detection. Flight Lieutenant Hughes was awarded the Air Force Cross the following June.

We left Gan after lunch the following day for the four-hour flight to Masirah, and on 7th December departed Masirah for Malta. We landed at RAF Akrotiri to refuel, and forty minutes later we were airborne again for RAF Luqa, where we landed at 1705 local time, eight days late.

While I had been on detachment to the Far East I had relied on the Anglican clergy at the Royal Navy and Royal Marine establishments to cover my church services for me, and they had not failed me. Shortly after I had arrived at Luqa I had called a meeting of Padre Milne and the other local civilian clergy who acted as Officiating Roman Catholic chaplains, to discuss ecumenical matters, and once the Royal Navy chaplains arrived at HMS St Angelo and No.41 Commando, Royal Marines chaplain at St Andrews Barracks, the eight of us formed the Joint Services Chaplaincy. We met regularly at various units.

Apart from the daily 'Pause for Thought', we organized a weekly radio broadcast on BFBS, the British Forces Broadcasting Service. It was a fifteen minute programme which went out live on a Sunday night called 'Viewpoint', the material being prepared as a group some weeks in advance. Padre Ian Thompson, the RN Free Church chaplain, was a good broadcaster and acted as chairman; we invited a guest to join us each week, a wife or a serviceman with attitude; a retired army major acted as a 'Colonel Blimp' to wind everyone up, and I made often controversial statements to get things going. It attracted a good audience and ran for months. I discovered a flair for broadcasting and did a lot of it from then on.

On a Friday evening I led a team of six young pilots from Luqa as guests of No.41 Royal Marine Commando at a Dinner Night in their barracks. It was an excellent,

RAF 'divers' with tridents welcome No.619 Squadron, Royal Navy, to RAF Luqa. BHL is on the extreme right

quite riotous evening, and their chaplain and I were already good friends, but it was very late when the transport returned us to Luqa. The following Monday morning I received a telephone call. 'Good morning Padre, the Adjutant from 41 here; it's all fixed for your parachute course in Cyprus, the papers are in the post to you.' I sat bolt upright in my chair. 'Sorry, Adj. wrong chaplain. This is Padre Lucas from Luqa.' 'Yes, Padre, you told the Colonel on Friday evening that you would like to join the 'ab initio course' in Cyprus and it's all arranged. Cheerio.'

I could remember nothing of this; clearly the man was delirious. Two days later when I opened the mail it was I who had delirium. There was the application form, to be signed by the Station Commander. That was a way out, for my boss would look after me; I urged Group Captain Armitage not to bother himself with reading the form, just to sign the bottom not approved. 'Brian, what good PR for the RAF, a chaplain parachuting with the Commando. Approved.' As the date of the course drew closer I prayed more fervently, and to good effect. My guardian angel arranged for HMS Hermes to carry off the entire Commando to patrol the Lebanese coast in case of an emergency there.

When HMS Ark Royal paid a visit we were delighted to accept an invitation to a Cocktail Party on board. The 'Ark' was moored in Kalkara Creek. Access to the ship was by a walk-ashore, a series of pontoons lashed together, followed by a long gangway up the side of the carrier now looming above, and in through an entrance in the side of the hull; all very tricky for ladies in cocktail dresses, but fine entertainment for the chaps.

Once on board, we found the party in full swing on the hangar deck, where the longest bar in Christendom had been erected along one side of the aircraft maintenance area. In such a gathering married couples move quite independently of each other greeting and laughing with friends and hosting officers. Joy and I were no exception. We met up again eventually as we went up to the carrier deck for Beating Retreat by the Band of the Royal Marines. There wasn't a dry eye as they performed the Sunset Ceremony, and the great White Ensign was lowered as the lights of Valletta shone across Grand Harbour. Then it was time to go home. Joy and I had become separated again, but we would meet up at the car parked beside the wharf.

I was with a group of No.203 Squadron Nimrod officers and their wives, talking animatedly as we went below and out onto a pontoon and into a motor launch, which chugged off across the water. How fine Ark Royal looked, all lit up across the shimmering harbour. Then we rounded the point and came alongside Sliema seafront. The Nimrod guys wished me goodnight as they climbed into their cars to take them back to Bugibba in the northwest of the island. Then the horrible truth struck—I hadn't arrived at Ark Royal by motor launch. Here I was, standing alone in a Dinner Suit in Sliema, with no money but only my car keys in my pocket. Somewhere in the blackness across the water, a good twelve miles by road, was Joy standing on the dockside, in a cocktail dress, by our locked car, on an increasingly chilly evening.

But I was in Malta, and wearing a clerical collar. Around the corner came a taxi. I hailed it. The conversation was something like this: 'Yes Father?' 'I want to go to Kalkara Creek.' 'Jump in, Father.' 'But I haven't any money.' 'Don't insult me, Father. Jump in.' We set off in a cloud of exhaust fumes and he talked all the way around Msida, Floriana and into the dockyard area of Birgu. As we drew near to the car park I told him he could drop me here, and thanked him profusely for the free ride. He would hear none of it other than to seek my prayers for him, a wish I readily granted. As I closed the door my solitary car was illuminated in the taxi's headlamps, and standing alongside it was my shivering wife in an attractive cocktail dress. Everyone else had long since left. I cannot imagine what the taxi-driver thought of this priest going to a deserted quayside where an attractive young lady awaited him late at a night. All I can tell you is this: the priest was more alarmed at the thought of the sermon the young lady was to preach to him.

This kind of social interaction lingers in the mind with fond memories. Joy and I will never forget the Royal Navy summer ball at HMS St Angelo, the great fortress which juts into Grand Harbour; the remembrance of us dressed in Tropical Mess Dress, dancing in the warm evening air to the Royal Marine Band on the ramparts of the fort, with the lights of Valletta gleaming across the water, is still enchanting. Again, at the RAF Luqa Battle of Britain Cocktail Party in September 1993, Joy and I were hosting the Deputy Prime Minister and Minister of Justice (later the first President) of Malta, Dr Anton Buttigieg. He was a cultured man, and a published poet. We enjoyed his company for his conversation was wide-ranging and well-informed.

It all seemed light years away from the 'Cold War', until the day I took Padre Ian Thompson on a Nimrod sortie off the North African coast. As we approached the Soviet anchorage in Hammamet Bay my RN colleague could only gasp in amazement at the rows of warships. As we flew up and down the lines of destroyers, cruisers, frigates, minesweepers, Ian said aloud, 'In my entire career in the Navy, I have never seen such a fleet. If only the British public could see this.'

The following July I arranged to take two Royal Navy chaplains to Cyprus on board a Nimrod taking part in a NATO exercise based at RAF Akrotiri. We hired a car and I drove them to Kyrenia, where we stayed in a hotel for a few days and enjoyed Greek and Turkish cuisine. A British European Airways Trident crew were also stopping-over in the hotel for the weekend, and we had a good party in the bar. We flew back to Luqa on the Friday, bringing with us Padre Howard John, a

Baptist minister who was the RAF Free Church chaplain at Akrotiri, for a short holiday in Malta.

The following Monday, 15th July, I was leaving Luqa Primary School after assembly when the Headteacher came running out after me shouting that President Makarios had been assassinated in Nicosia. I was shocked, not least because I had been driving through Nicosia on the Thursday morning without any sign of trouble, and this had happened on Sunday. The BBC World News was full of the killing of Makarios and the implications for Cyprus of the coup led by Greek officers of the Cyprus National Guard at the direction of the ruling junta in Greece. They installed Nikos Sampson as President. The New York Times described him as, 'the Al Capone of Cyprus'. He was also described as a 'thug and vicious killer' and a 'playboy gunman'.

On Tuesday, rumour began to circulate that Makarios had escaped. He had been airlifted from the coast at Paphos by an RAF helicopter, and taken to Akrotiri where he transferred to the Argosy for a flight to Malta, and at 2100 that evening, a Royal Air Force Argosy aircraft arrived from Cyprus with President Makarios on board. Early on Wednesday I was on my way to Ops, and as the locally-employed RAF Malta policeman opened the security barrier for me to pass, I saw that standing alone inside the barrier in a tee-shirt and slacks was Dr Buttigieg. He should never have been allowed to pass the barrier, but the Maltese policeman had recognized him. 'Good morning, Minister,' I said; 'Can I help you?' He remembered me at once and asked how Joy was, but I was curious about his presence. He explained that he was waiting for the Archbishop to arrive. I said that I was unaware that Monsignor Gonzi was visiting the station, but he said, 'No, Archbishop Makarios, President of Cyprus.'

I asked if the Archbishop was alright, and he replied that Makarios was calm, very calm. At my prompting he explained what had happened, 'The President was entertaining some Egyptian dancing girls in his palace in Nicosia', then added as I smirked, 'Schoolchildren, Father Brian. There was a sound of gunfire, and his aides rushed in and escorted him out to the rear yard. They were driving him away when an armoured car blocked the front gate and fired at his car, but he escaped through a small entrance and drove up into the Troodos Mountains, where he spent Monday night in the place he knew well: Kykkos Monastery. Yesterday he was rescued from near Paphos by a Royal Air Force helicopter, and flown here. He spent last night with the Governor-General, Sir Anthony Malmo. He is now worried about his colleagues.'

I asked him if he would prefer to wait inside with a cup of coffee, but he was content to wait by the barrier. I found a telephone and informed the Station Commander that the Deputy Prime Minister of Malta was outside Ops and related

Archbishop Makarios boards an RAF Comet at RAF Luqa, 17 July 1974

what I had been told. Within five minutes the Station Commander arrived and the Air Commander was right behind him. I slipped into another office and watched through the window as a motorcade drove up to the RAF Comet aircraft, where the great and the good were assembled. Makarios spoke briefly with Dr Buttigieg and the others in the group before walking up the steps and turning to wave defiantly, before entering the aircraft for his flight to London and New York, where on the Thursday he addressed a meeting of the United Nations, as the Turkish armed forces halted the coup in Cyprus by occupying nearly half the island. Nikos Sampson was de facto president for only eight days.

The Trident aircraft, which once belonged to BEA, is parked at the now-derelict Nicosia International Airport to this day, its airframe riddled with shell holes. I often wonder what happened to the crew members who were such good company in the bar. Life at Luqa became very busy as the Nimrod aircraft flew ops over Cyprus. It was Huggiss and his crew in their Nimrod five miles high, who reported the Turkish armada sailing towards the north coast of the island, thus heralding an invasion. At the same time, No.IX Squadron flew their Vulcan bombers to Malta for safety.

On another Monday morning when I was leaving Luqa School, the Headteacher called me to say that little Johnnie, a sergeant's son, had just told him that his Dad had been in jail all weekend. I knew that the boy's mother was in the hospital maternity ward, so who was looking after Johnnie and his little sister? At once I checked with his squadron ('He's on a few days leave, Padre; his wife is expecting, you know.') and then the Police Flight ('No-one in the Nick this weekend, Padre'), and so I had to call at his flat.

To my surprise the Sergeant opened the door himself, 'Hello Padre, come in.' He made me a coffee while I wondered how to answer his question about my reason for calling. I told him that I was just passing, but he saw through that, so I related what Johnnie had said in school. His face darkened like thunder, and I feared for the boy, when suddenly the Sergeant began to laugh until the tears flowed down his face. 'Follow me, Padre,' and he led me along the corridor to the little boy's bedroom, 'I am still in jail, I haven't thrown a double-six since Friday night', he said, indicating the game of Monopoly on the bed.

In late summer we discovered that Joy was expecting another baby. It was due in April, just about the time we should be coming to the end of my tour of duty in Malta. So I wrote to the Staff Chaplain seeking an extension of my tour to include Joy's post-natal care, until, say, August. It was decided instead to bring us home early, in February. We decided to keep the baby secret from our families until we arrived back in UK.

When I arrived in Malta, one of the first things I did was to pay an official call on the Archbishop of Malta, Monsignor Sir Michael Gonzi, at his palace in Valletta.

BHL with Mgr Michael Gonzi in the Archbishop's Palace, Valletta

I was accompanied by the Roman Catholic officiating chaplain to the RAF, Fr Ivo Tonna. It was like speaking to an historical figure, for he had been Archbishop of Malta since 1943. Mgr Gonzi told me of the difficulties between Mr Mintoff's Labour Party and the church, but that he was ready to fight his corner all the way. In 1961 he had placed the Labour Party under interdiction, and I believe he had excommunicated Mintoff at some point. He told me that now that Dom Mintoff was Prime Minister he was having to do battle for the Church all over again. As the time drew near for me to return to the UK I paid him a farewell visit. Three years had passed, and he looked aged and drawn, and I was not surprised when he retired in 1976.

Then came sad news. On 27th January, a friendly officer broke the rules by phoning me with the contents of a Ministry of Defence signal. My mother, who had just passed her 60th birthday, had been admitted to hospital in South Wales, and my father had asked for me to be present. A flight home in the morning was soon booked for me. I phoned Neath Hospital, but the nurse would only say my mother was comfortable, and, stupidly, did not pass the phone to my father who was sitting nearby. I was anxious for my mother to know that Joy was again pregnant, for the prospect of another grandchild would have been a tonic for her.

Next morning I had a call saying that my mother had died. In an act of kindness the duty officer did not release the signal until I was airborne, for once my mother had died my presence at home was no longer urgent and I would have dropped to the bottom of the passenger list and might have missed the flight. Arriving at Brize Norton, I found a car had been very generously organized to take me straight home to my father.

A Requiem Mass was said for Mum on 31st January at St Theodore's Church prior to her funeral service. Afterwards, my sisters, Barbara and Joan, and I walked with Dad at Porthcawl in the cold air above the rocky coastline. That loving, gentle, forgiving woman, with not one ounce of malice in her soul; who had nurtured me in my youth and taken great pride in my successes; was gone from my life and the world was now a more uncertain place. For all my emptiness, I could hardly comprehend Dad's desolation, as we walked together, quietly remembering her whom we loved so much, oh, so very much.

There was just over a week before I was to return to the UK on posting to RAF Honington in Suffolk, so I flew to Malta on the Sunday night BEA flight from Heathrow, arriving at Luqa at 0115. During the past year I had been invited to convert my four-year Short Service Commission to a Permanent Commission, adding another twelve years to the four. Bearing in mind the varied and busy life I was leading, compared with the fairly routine ministry of a priest in South Wales, I applied successfully for the extra term.

An Interlude on P&O Cruising

In the late 1970s and early 1980s I used to take two weeks leave and join P&O as a cruise chaplain. "Nice life if you can get it," I hear you cry. I make no apology for it was hard work (I pause for you to wipe the tears from your eyes). It involved long days and nights, for the ship I joined was the SS Uganda, a school ship. A thousand schoolchildren would fly from the UK to the Mediterranean to join the vessel for a two-week experience of life afloat in the warm sunshine. There were also about three hundred cabin passengers and teachers for whom I had pastoral care. In addition to the ship's company, there was a Headteacher and a Deputy Head as well as a Surgeon, a Matron and a fully equipped operating theatre. There was even a branch of Barclays International Bank on board.

It all began in 1975, when I was based at RAF Luqa, and joined the British Forces schoolchildren from Tal Handaq Secondary School on the school cruise departing on 2nd January from Limassol New Port. The other six hundred children would be from Maltese schools. The cruise was from Malta direct to Alexandria (for Cairo and Giza), then to Beirut (for Baalbek), on to Haifa (for Nazareth), and finally to the Aegean. When countersigning my application, my Station Commander, Group Captain Mike Armitage, was rather keen to join me. However, when my leave application reached Headquarters Strike Command there was a horrified reaction, for Alexandria offered port facilities to the Soviet Mediterranean Fleet in 1975, and as for going direct from Lebanon, on the brink of civil war, to Israel, heaven forfend. A signal came to RAF Luqa forbidding me to go ashore in Alexandria and Beirut, but as it was not copied to me, I enjoyed the cruise enormously. The day trip to Galilee was a highlight, as I was asked to read the Gospel narrative of the stilling of the storm while in a small boat crossing the Sea of Galilee. The experience of encouraging Maltese children to play in the snow high on the Lebanese Mountains was hilarious, as they had never encountered snow before, but with my expert tuition, they soon learned to make snowballs. The Roman Catholic chaplain on board, Fr Patrick Cachia, was a kindred spirit, and we became firm friends. He was the Prior of the Dominican Convent in Sliema, and later in the year he invited me to preach there at the Solemn Mass on St Dominic's Day.

In September the following year I was off again, this time sailing from Liverpool to Madeira with a Music Cruise. All 900 children embarked had either to sing or play a musical instrument to a high standard, for they would be giving concerts in Madeira, Gibraltar, and the Gulbenkian Concert Hall in Lisbon, with a final concert for parents and the public on return to Liverpool. Charles Western was the guest conductor for the concerts, the Lindsey Quartet was on board to give Master classes, and Fritz Spiegl was the guest lecturer and the most amusing company.

As we sailed from Liverpool in the Saturday afternoon sunshine, the children were given streamers to throw down to their parents on the quay; it was a joyous sight. In the bar later that evening, the musician in charge of the wind section of the young person's orchestra, asked if I would like a wind band to accompany the Sunday morning service. I accepted and gave him the hymns I had chosen. The following morning, the Captain turned the ship into wind, so that the after sport deck would be sheltered by the superstructure, and as I followed the Captain and the Headteacher to the stern the band had not only practised the hymns, but it was playing a lively processional march.

As we steamed into Funchal harbour on the Wednesday morning, the band was gathered at the stern, beneath the Red Ensign, playing tunes such as 'Good old Sussex by the Sea', to applause from the owners of private British yachts at anchor. That evening the choir and orchestra gave a fine concert in Funchal Cathedral. After the concert, and once the children had retired to their dormitories, I arranged to lead a party of teachers on a run ashore. As we filed down the gangway to the quay the policeman guarding the ship agreed to find taxis for us and gave me his rifle to hold while he telephoned. It was that sort of evening. The two taxis took us to a bar somewhere in the downtown area, and as we entered in our Dinner Suits, Charles Western sporting a carnation in his button-hole, and the ladies in their long dresses, the clientele went silent. All was well until one of the young teachers began discussing politics with the men at the bar. Then a table was overturned as the man shouted, 'Spinola no good.' I advised the ladies in our group to walk slowly and quietly to the door, leaving their drinks behind. We did so and managed to find two taxis passing by, into which we piled quickly. As we drove off we heard the police sirens coming to quell the full-blown fight, which was escalating nicely. I counselled the young man never again to discuss politics in a foreign country unless he knew the company very well indeed.

However, the lasting experience for all the children, and the cabin passengers, must have been the concert in St Michael's Cave deep in the Rock of Gibraltar the following Sunday, 26th September. The setting is magical; coloured lights illuminate the stalactites hanging from the lofty roof of the cave, and the acoustics are perfect. The border with Spain was closed at that time, and relations were strained over the Spanish claim to sovereignty over Gibraltar. The last item on the programme was Handel's, 'Zadok the Priest', with the resounding words, 'Long live the King, May the King live for ever'. The Gibraltarians went wild with excitement, and I was convinced that the applause could be heard even in Madrid. It was quite wicked of Charles Western, but as an encore he led the children in a resounding 'Rule Britannia.' There wasn't a dry eye in the house.

It was two years before I joined the ship again. In November 1978 I flew to Naples to join a cruise chartered entirely by Cumbria Education Authority. I got to know the PE master from Keswick School, Martin Bellarby, with his school party, at Gatwick, and as we arrived at the SS Uganda to hear a Tannoy message to the effect that sailing was delayed five hours due to fog at Gatwick, Martin and I took a stroll into the city, tasting the wine in a few bars.

Arriving back at the ship, we saw that two Italian Navy vessels had berthed stern-on alongside the Uganda, which towered above them. As we had a few hours to spare I proposed that we said hello to our NATO allies. There were too many senior officers in view on the destroyer, so I led the way up the gangway to the frigate, and asked the sailor on duty for the Officer of the Watch. We waited a few minutes before an officer appeared in a brilliant white uniform with a blue sash, and with a dazzling smile and perfect English, which made me feel inadequate. He asked if he could help us. I explained that I was a priest in the RAF wondering if we could visit the wardroom. He apologised that he was busy for the next two hours, but we would be welcome as his guests at dinner in the wardroom.

I explained that we would have sailed by then, but thanked him for his generosity. I should have left it at that, but he had been so kind that I asked which was his home port. 'Taranto', he replied. My brain dredged up what I knew about Taranto, and I heard myself saying, 'Ah! The Royal Navy still celebrates the Battle of Taranto.' As the words left my lips, I pushed Martin towards the gangway and said our farewell to the Italian Officer. 'What's up?' asked my friend as we reached the quay. The Officer was still smiling down on us, but it was a much thinner smile. I answered Martin, 'In November 1940 we torpedoed half of the Italian Fleet in Taranto harbour. The anniversary is tomorrow.' The ancient Greeks had a saying, 'three things can never be recovered: the spent arrow, the missed opportunity and the spoken word.' How true. We sailed from Naples later that evening for Bodrum —ancient Halicarnassus—in Turkey, and two days later I held a Remembrance Sunday service on the Sports Deck, during which the Captain, John Terry, cast a wreath on the calm waters of the Mediterranean as the Red Ensign fluttered over our heads.

That evening, I officiated at a burial at sea. An elderly passenger had died of a persistent illness, and his next of kin asked for him to be buried in the Mediterranean. It took place from a large doorway in B Deck, close to the water, after the children had settled down for the night. It was reverently done: as I said the words, 'we commit his body to the deep', the Master at Arms raised one end of the bier and the shroud slipped quietly into the water and the Captain threw a wreath onto the surface of the waves. Then we retreated to the First Officer's cabin for a restorative brandy.

After Bodrum we passed through the Dardanelles, and I joined Captain Terry on the Bridge Wing as we passed the huge war memorials on the northern shore.

The largest is the Turkish memorial in the shape of two massive columns with a capstone across the top. Suddenly the Uganda's deep-throated siren sounded a long blast, and a sailor lowered the ensign at the mast head in salute. John Terry told me that every ship which passes through the Dardanelles carries out this act of homage to the dead. At 0800 the following morning we berthed near the Galata Bridge in Istanbul, a city I loved at once, and to which I have returned several times by road from Lincolnshire.

That cruise ended in another city I have loved ever since—Venice. As soon as we berthed in the early morning I was the first to go ashore, and made my way at once through the awakening streets to St Mark's Cathedral. I found it empty of tourists and breathtaking in its intimate yet astonishing beauty. I was moved to write the following short poem:

On First Entering St Mark's, Venice

Humbled by San Marco's intimate piety
I choked upon the tears of simple ecstasy.
My love, I wish that you had been with me
to share th'eternal truth, of life the key;
for as the mighty organ played I kneeled,
Around me God in Christ to man was plain revealed.

Yet another two years passed before I applied for another cruise, and in November 1980 I flew to Trogir, in Yugoslavia (now Croatia), to join Uganda at Split for another Cumbria Education Authority cruise. This cruise took us to Delphi in Greece, to Alexandria and Cairo, Antalya in southern Turkey, before we disembarked at Piraeus for a tour of Athens before returning home. It was while we were at the pyramids of Giza in Egypt that I heard a group of schoolgirls call out to their teacher, 'Miss, Samantha has gone off on a horse with an Egyptian man.' To which the teacher replied, with a sigh, 'Thank God. Perhaps now I'll have some peace.'

In October 1982, by which time I was stationed in Cyprus, I joined the ship for the last time. Two months earlier she had completed her service as the hospital ship in the Falklands War, where her call-sign had been, 'Mother Hen.' We sailed from Piraeus in the afternoon, and as we rounded Cape Sounion I was having a drink with the Captain in his Day Cabin. He suddenly stood up, and invited me to bring my drink out onto the Bridge Wing, which was contrary to his usual practice. We gazed up at the splendid sight of the ruined Greek Temple on the top of the cliff, and then he flung the contents of his glass into the sea. I looked at him as if he was mad. He saw my astonishment and said, 'I always placate Poseidon;

Walking out to the aircraft at RAF Akrotiri to escort SS Uganda to Limassol (BHL second from left, Gp Capt Willis third from left)

I am a mariner.' With that he returned to his cabin. I followed him, uncertain of his solemnity, for Poseidon was the Greek god of the sea and storms. I call that hedging your bets.

The next port of call was Rhodes. I had arranged for the Royal Navy chaplain to fly to RAF Akrotiri, where I was based in Cyprus, to cover my absence for me, but at the last moment, he could not get away. As we prepared to depart from our berth at Rhodes, the Officer of the Watch played the RAF March over the loudspeakers as our sailing music when he saw me leaning on the rail on A Deck. I waved at him on the Bridge Wing, and then I heard my name called from the quay. Looking down, there was my RN chaplain waving up at me. 'Sorry,' he yelled, 'I got away only yesterday and booked this little holiday instead." My reply was happily drowned by the deep sound of the ship's whistle as we were tugged away from the quay. We sailed to Haifa, and this time I made my only visit to Jerusalem and Jericho, before we returned to Venice via Delphi and Split. We didn't know it then, but Uganda had only two months left as a school ship before returning to the South Atlantic as a troop ship for the remaining two years of her active life.

During her last cruise she spent Christmas Eve 1982 in Cyprus, and I arranged for a three-ship of Wessex helicopters from No.84 Squadron to escort Uganda into Limassol Bay. At 1010 we lifted off the main runway, the Station Commander,

Group Captain John Willis, in the lead helicopter. As we gained height, I saw Uganda steaming through a calm sea on passage from Naples, a Greek tanker astern of her and a Cypriot car ferry, the Sol Phryne, about half a mile on her starboard quarter. I had briefed the pilots that students were not allowed forward of the funnel, so we positioned ourselves accordingly around the stern. I could see familiar faces and there was much waving from the top of the steps up from the School Office on the starboard side of 'A' Deck.

Uganda had berthed in Limassol by the time I had driven with my wife and children to the port. She had also visited Cyprus on her previous cruise, and I had taken a group of the ship's company up the mountain to RAF Troodos for the day. Now the officers of RAF Troodos had beaten me to it; one of them had gone on board in a white DJ, bow tie, a napkin over his arm and a flask of iced 'Olympus Surprise' as soon as the gangway was down, for a party in Ron Furlong's cabin. Ron was the ship's Staff Officer, and was known to thousands of young people as 'Action Man', for among other duties, he organized the sports on the after deck. Joy and I had a farewell drink with him, and he gave my daughter Helen a cuddly toy dog and there were also gifts for Mark and Simon.

Soon it was time to go ashore and we stood on the quay looking up at the Old Lady, all lit up. One of the Troodos officers produced carol sheets and we began to sing. Ron rushed down the gangway and began to conduct us. We sang one carol, then another, suddenly applause broke out, and as I looked up I saw around eight hundred students and passengers lining the decks, their voices joining ours. The whole of Limassol seemed to be Harking to the Herald-Angels. Then I heard the crackle through Ron's two-way out-thrust radio; it came on his down beat, "Bridge to Staff Officer, get that **** gangway stowed, the Pilot's anxious. Happy Christmas. Out." And Ron left us to it.

Thus Uganda sailed from Cyprus on Christmas Eve. As she moved away from the quay, Ron still framed in the hull door on 'B' Deck, conducting the carols, I heard for the very last time the sensual note of the ship's whistle as she saluted us, or the tug—it did not matter which. As we lapsed into silence on the suddenly chilly quay, we could hear the sound of the carolling coming to us over the water of the harbour, until she turned the mole and out into the night bound for the Holy Land. And I noticed the coloured lights of a Christmas tree at her mast-head. Half an hour later, having taken my family home, I made some excuse and drove to the southern tip of Cyprus and watched her, a tiny speck of light in a black emptiness, and I mouthed, 'Godspeed you and all who sail in you, Uganda.' Mine was a very private parting.

After her time as a troop ship in the South Atlantic, she was laid up in the River Fal, and began to rust until she was eventually sold for scrap and renamed SS

SS Uganda steams towards Cyprus with RAF Escort. (BHL in the left hand seat of the aircraft). Christmas Eve 1992

Triton. But the fine old lady did not 'go gently into that good night', for on her final voyage to a breaker's yard in Taiwan she was driven ashore on 22 August 1986 by Typhoon Wayne, and there she lay with her back broken. She was still there in 1994 waiting for the breaker's men to come out to her, instead of her being meekly delivered into their hands.

It was a sad end for a fine vessel. Hundreds of thousands of children had their horizons widened immeasurably by the experience of cruising the Mediterranean world with their school teachers. On shore excursions I often took responsibility for a group of children and benefitted from seeing familiar places through the eyes of a child. It was a bad day when Educational Cruising passed from the Cargo Division of P & O to its Passenger Division, where profit was everything.

Our House at Kalafrana, Malta (the Welsh Flag flying above the balcony)

President's XV v. Captain's XV Akrotiri Rugby Club, Cyprus 1984 (President's Squad in blue)

'The Rectory', Bristol House Road, Cranwell

BHL and Helen with Greg and his wife at Sylvanas Restaurant, Cyprus, 2009

With Archbishop George Carey in Lambeth Palace 1991

Archdeacon Brian Lucas in St Clement Danes
A portrait in oil on canvas by Stanley Baldock, 1993

HM The Queen Mother arriving for the Sir Arthur Harris Memorial unveiling service.

Preaching the Sermon in Clement Danes at the Service to mark the Unveiling of the Harris Statue

Padre Ray Brown, BHL and Mgr Tony Harris on a roundabout at RAF Lossiemouth

Lunch with HRH The Princess of Wales

'This should be the other way around' Anna presents BHL with a bouquet at Colditz

The Leadership Team 1992. Left to right: Dermot McKavanagh, Peter Bishop, Robin Turner, Brian McAvoy, Tom Goode and Phil Mortimer. Front Row: Diane, BHL, Barbara

Farewell to Adastral House Party: March 1994 Former Personal Secretaries gather around The Chief.
Left to right: Yvonne, Julie, Paula, Joy and Barbara

Meeting President Lech Walesa in Warsaw, 1995

CHAPTER SIX:

An East Anglian Sojourn

It was good to recover our breath after the hectic departure from Malta at the beginning of 1975. I had several weeks of disembarkation leave before starting work, so while Joy and the children stayed with her parents, Roy and Nan Penn in Cwmavon, I went to collect our Fiat from Brize Norton on Friday 14th February, and then drove to Suffolk to take over a married quarter at 36 St Edmund's Gate, RAF Honington, returning to Port Talbot quite late in the evening. I spent a lot of time with my father and decided that he needed to get away for a break. I had arranged to remove our furniture from storage to Honington on Thursday, 12th March, so I persuaded my father that I really could not manage this on my own, and I would appreciate some help if he was able to join me. We drove to Thetford on the Wednesday, and stayed at the Bell Hotel, enjoying a session in the bar after dinner. We were both a little jaded the following morning as we helped to hump and dump furniture into the house before returning to Port Talbot. The following Saturday, Wales defeated Ireland at Rugby by 32 points to 4, and after the final whistle, we climbed into the Fiat and travelled to our new home in Suffolk.

RAF Honington

RAF Honington is near Bury St Edmunds, and was commanded by Group Captain Martin Chandler, a witty and astute man who closely resembled David Niven. The station was then home to three squadrons operating the Buccaneer aircraft, No.12 and No.208 Squadrons were RAF and there was also No.809 Squadron Royal Naval Air Service, which was based on HMS Ark Royal, but deployed to Honington when the Ark was in home waters. In addition, the Operational Conversion Unit (OCU) operated some Hunter aircraft for pilots converting to the Buccaneer.

On the corner of St Edmund's Gate, where it joined from the main road, was St Edmund's Church. The building had been the station gymnasium, which had been transferred to church use when a new gym was built on base. It had been tastefully decorated and furnished, and the large hall had been divided in two by a folding screen, thus offering a hall for functions as well as a reasonably sized church. However, whereas the church life in Malta had been rich and vibrant, packed with worship, social activities and fun, here the average Sunday congregation was about ten. I believe that many families took advantage of weekends to visit their parents. My predecessor, Padre Roger Huddleston, had been a close friend of The Reverend Ernie Griffin, the elderly Methodist minister who was the Officiating Church of Scotland and Free Churches (CSFC) Chaplain, and had introduced the novel idea of having a joint Sunday morning service every week, taken in turns at 11.00. There was a C of E said service of Holy Communion each week at 0930 which attracted one or two worshippers.

I found this arrangement very difficult to work with and I was not prepared to continue with it. Every other week I would attend the 1100 service as an observer in my own church, and I'm afraid that I regarded the worship as tedious in the extreme. I decided it had to stop. I saw Ernie at his home and explained that I wanted an Anglican Sung Eucharist every week, when I could preach to the gospel reading of the day in order to develop the people's understanding of Christ and attempt to discern his will for them. However, not wishing to deprive him of his opportunity to build up his own flock, I would hold the service at 1000 so that he could continue with his service every Sunday at 1100.

He complained to the Station Commander that I was 'easing him out', and contacted his friend the Archdeacon about me, who in turn contacted the Bishop of St Edmundsbury and Ipswich, who was informing the Bishop to the Forces. I concluded that there was nothing more to be said, and carried on regardless.

In the meantime, I had formed a good relationship with the church organist, Fred Wilson, who lived a few miles away, and we were developing a children's choir, from which grew interest in confirmation classes. In stark contrast with my experience of my Free Church colleague, my membership of the local Anglican Deanery Chapter was a delight, and a source of spirituality and scholarship, and I used to look forward to our monthly meeting, something I have not done anywhere else.

Just after 0015 in the morning of Wednesday, 30th April 1975, I tucked up Mark and Simon in their dressing gowns in the back of the car, and drove to the RAF Hospital at Ely where Joy was admitted to the labour ward. I returned home with the boys, and at 1020 that morning Helen was born. We were delighted to have a little daughter. I drove again to Ely that evening to see them, and two days later Mark and Simon were introduced to their baby sister when Joy brought her home from Ely.

I was invited by Colin Francis, the Headteacher at the village school, where Mark was a pupil and where Joy was doing supply teaching, to lead a monthly assembly in the school hall, and as the Reverend Glyn Owen, the Welsh Vicar of Honington, was a sick man I would take his Sunday services from time to time. Thus we became acquainted with the local people in the village in the gentle valley below the RAF station. Honington Hall was, and is still, the home of David Croft, the Producer and Director of the BBC TV comedy programme 'Dad's Army'. Many scenes in the series of programmes were filmed locally in the Stanford Training Area, a Ministry of Defence swathe of rural Norfolk seven miles north of Thetford. He also used the village church and school as locations for filming. The Church Hall in the series is, in fact, the school hall where I led the assemblies, and the piano the very one which Joy used to play when she did supply teaching there.

One Sunday lunchtime we watched as David filmed the scene where the members of the 'Warmington-on-Sea platoon' are dressed as German soldiers. During a break in the filming, Frank Williams, who plays the Vicar in the series, came over and asked if I was the local vicar. I explained my position and we talked for quite a while. We later became good friends when I met him again as a fellow-member of the Catholic Group in the General Synod of the Church of England. He was my guest of honour when I first took the Chair at a Savage Club House Dinner. In 2007 the actor Bill Pertwee, the Chief ARP Warden in the series, was appointed an MBE and I arranged his celebration party in the Savage Club after the investiture. It was rather like returning to Honington, as David Croft and his wife, Frank Williams and others joined in the fun.

The summer of 1975 was very hot, and we explored the delights of East Anglia whenever we could. Helen was a delightful baby and her brothers adored her. As the time approached to arrange a Harvest Festival, I went to the Catering Squadron for help with producing a harvest loaf. The Officer Commanding was a short, balding man with a military moustache, who was known to his airmen by the nickname 'Captain Mainwaring' after the character in 'Dad's Army' created by Arthur Lowe. When we knew each other well enough, I called him not 'OC Cat Squadron', but 'Magnificat'. His name was Tom Cottew and I liked him at once; we were kindred spirits. Together with his wife Dulcie, Joy and I joined them at the Officers' Mess Summer Ball, and as we approached the buffet table, where his flight sergeant had prepared a fine traditional Boar's Head as a centrepiece, Tom said in a loud voice, 'I see they have found OC Admin Wing.'

Tom Cottew had served in the war as a Wireless Operator/Air Gunner (WopAG) in Liberator aircraft. He had retained his flying category until the Medics discovered he was covering the same eye in his annual visual test and he was grounded. He was later seconded in the rank of 'Lieutenant Colonel' to the British-led Saudifinanced guerrillas in South Yemen where he was responsible for a very mobile intelligence gathering team. He was so mobile that when the British left Aden in November 1967, they forgot to inform Tom Cottew. He eventually found a ship bound for Djibouti in French Somaliland, and remained there for a while before making his way to the Ministry of Defence in London to enquire about his back pay. He was rather coy about how he became a caterer, but he was very good at it, and the Air Force Board later appointed him to direct the catering for Air Board lunches and dinners in London and elsewhere.

He was one of the funniest men I have known, and had a penchant for big cars; his criteria were, 'Grace, Space and Pace' when buying a vehicle. At Honington he drove a Daimler Majestic, and once a week he would arrive outside my office at the church and we would depart very discreetly for the Ingham Arms, about fifteen minutes away, for a pint of ale and a pie. It was while returning from this hostelry one day, that I said suddenly, 'I have come to the conclusion, Tom, that I shall have no great part to play in life; I shall be forever a player of minor roles.' I have no idea what led me to say that, but we both laughed at it, and I felt somehow liberated and at ease with the world.

When I thought later about that sudden revelation, I became aware that I had fallen into the trap of trying to do the right thing in order to get on; there is an element of ambition engendered by Service life which sits uneasily on a priest. The awareness of my part in the great scheme of things came to me as we drove alongside the airfield, comfortable in the silence of a good friend, and at peace with myself as a human being with a sure vocation. It was the certainty of my vocation which gave rise to the equanimity; I did not have to prove myself as a priest, I just had to get on with the work I was doing in the way I was doing it.

When the time came for me to move on to another station, John Neville said at my farewell interview, 'You will miss the lunchtime trips to the pub with Tom Cottew'; which just goes to show that Station Commanders don't miss much. And he was right.

Martin Chandler was succeeded by John Neville as the Station Commander, and in February 1976 he asked me if I would consider moving house to 7 St Edmunds Square, which was next to his residence, as he was fed up with sweeping up leaves by himself. No.7 was the house allocated to the Wing Commander in charge of the OCU, but the new incumbent lived off base and the house was empty. It was an attractive house, with a rear view across the open countryside of the airfield. For some reason we could not identify, Joy and I had never felt really comfortable in 36 St Edmunds Gate, and, as the house now on offer had four large bedrooms and a large garden, we agreed to move the hundred yards or so. Only after we had moved did people mention to us that someone had in the past committed suicide in No.36.

I had always started the working day with Matins and Eucharist in the station church. I continued this practice at Honington, and opened the church at 0730 and said Matins; then, if there was no one for Eucharist at 0800, I would meditate until 0815 when I would return home for breakfast. More often than not, as I walked back with my cassock and cloak flowing in the wind, John Neville would pass me in his staff car on his way to his office. One day he asked me where I had been at that hour of the morning, and seemed somewhat nonplussed when I replied, 'Church, sir.'

As church families moved away on posting to other units, they were not replaced by new families arriving, so the congregation grew smaller week by week. Visiting the married quarters did not result in many new regular adherents either. The situation was not helped by the airman's quarters being dispersed over a wide area of the locality with a small 'patch' at Barnham, another at Stanton and yet another at Watton. When, one Sunday there was only my family and the organist 'reflected in the chalice', I became very despondent. But I remembered again the words of the Chaplain-in-Chief when I was interviewed by him, 'If large congregations are important to you, then don't join the RAF. But if you want a daily ministry which will stretch you to your limit, then we will make you welcome.' During the week I was fully absorbed by squadron life in the hangars and in the crewrooms, but as the Buccaneer was a two-seat aircraft, I missed the opportunity to go flying, and said as much to a Flight Lieutenant Nick Berryman, a Buccaneer pilot whose son was friendly with Mark.

Ash Wednesday dawned as the sort of morning when you wanted to leap for joy. The sky was blue, the air was crisp and the sun promised another astonishing day. It was a day for aviating. As I finished saying Matins in the empty church, the telephone rang on my desk; it was Nick Berryman, "Meet me in Ops in half an hour. There's a slot in the programme for you to fly in the Hunter T7", he said. The Hawker Hunter had thrilled me when I was a teenager and it was flown by 111 Squadron as "The Black Arrows". So I cleared my diary for the morning and was at Operations in good time. I was fitted with an anti-G suit over my flying overalls, and carrying my 'bone dome' we walked out to the aircraft. It stood on the pan, shining in the sunlight, surrounded by ground equipment. It was the two-seat variant and we sat side by side so cosily that we had to bend our heads together in order for the cockpit hatch to close.

I connected my anti-G suit to the aircraft oxygen system, plugged in to the intercom, and Nick ran through the controls with me, including what to do in an emergency, and then, with a 'thumbs up' to the ground crew chief, he started the engine and the aircraft vibrated with power. We taxied out to the end of the runway and, with take-off checks complete, Nick opened the throttle allowing the Rolls Royce Avon turbojet to push the Hunter against the brakes like a greyhound on the leash. I heard in the little speakers in my helmet the Tower give take-off clearance, and at once I was rammed back in my seat as the aircraft sped down the main runway. Then, at 0930 on Wednesday, 3 March 1976, we launched ourselves into the blue sky over Suffolk.

Nick levelled out at a very low height and streaked across the countryside avoiding farms and livestock. We climbed to 2000 feet to cross the coast, and I asked, "Is that Cromer?" Nick dipped the starboard wing towards the town below, "Yes", and flipping the aircraft through 180 degrees onto its port wing, said, "And that's Sheringham." I unclipped my oxygen mask, and pulled a blue bag from the leg pocket of my flying suit and parked my breakfast in it. By this time we were over the North Sea, and we flew along the coast for a while before turning out to sea. "Now it's your turn to do some work", said Nick. "I want you to do a vertical climb and level off at 10,000 feet exactly. I'll operate the throttle." This was not a discussion; he was the captain, and I was crew. This was his office and I was seated at his desk. The control column was similar to that on an old Renault 5—it was an L-shaped lever sticking out of the 'dash board'. I pulled it into my stomach as Nick opened the throttle to maximum. The Hunter stood on its tail and reached for the sky. It was a strange sensation lying on my back watching the altimeter winding up a hundred feet a second as the sea receded to my rear.

A Hunter T4 in flight.

When we reached 9,500 feet I eased the stick back gently, turning it slightly to the right at the same time. As the Hunter turned into level flight I discovered another proof of the existence of God—we were flying at precisely 10,000 feet. I heard Nick say, 'I don't believe it.' Neither did I, but I wasn't going to let on. 'Is that OK?' I asked him nonchalantly. I can't relate his reply; it was unbecoming of an officer and a friend.

He was about to make me do it again when we heard on the radio, 'Aircraft crashed in the Honington undershoot, recover at once or divert.' We had a quick chat about it; our diversion airfield was in Scotland, and I had a service in church at 1900. There was no option; we had to get down quickly. So we called the Tower and requested immediate recovery, and down we went into the approach pattern. We could see the smoke rising from the wreckage in the forest near the airfield, but we learned that both crew members had ejected safely from the RAF Germany Buccaneer. So my flight was cut short, but we had been airborne for an hour, during which I had flown the aircraft for twenty minutes and discovered that fast jet aviation is a class 'A' drug in its own right. While airborne you are on 'a high', and the moment you land you want more.

While I mowed the lawn one evening a lone Hunter took off and climbed to about four thousand feet before it darted and dived, then climbed again before rolling over and swooping higher; in short, it was stooging about in the evening sun. I turned off the mower to enjoy the spectacle. When it landed I telephoned Air Traffic who told me that the Station Commander had been flying the aircraft. When I spoke to him about the lovely little flight the following morning he admitted that after a really bad day he had unwound by putting the Hunter through its paces. I understood that perfectly.

We were about to sit down to lunch one day when a telephone call summoned me to one of the dispersed sites. An airman's wife told me that her neighbour was in a bad way, and, as she knew that I had seen the lady the previous week, she asked if I could help. Three ladies stood in a group outside the house as I arrived in the street about fifteen minutes later. The woman who had telephoned said that the children were with another neighbour.

The poor woman was, indeed, in a state; she sat staring ahead, and when I said softly, 'It's alright, it's me, Padre Lucas,' she gave no indication that she had heard or seen me. The neighbour was showing me an empty packet of pills by the chair when, suddenly, she jumped up and without a word raced upstairs. Shouting to the neighbour to follow me, I chased after her. She had slammed the bedroom door and locked it behind her, and, when I heard breaking noises inside, I did something I had always wanted to do, I raised my right leg, and aiming my foot just above the handle, I kicked the door open. She was standing on the window ledge about to jump into the garden so I ran across the debris on the floor and putting my arms about her ample waist, I pulled as hard as I could until her fingers lost their grip on the window frame, and we collapsed in a heap on the floor. Rolling her onto her back, I lay on top of her, calling for the neighbour to sit on her thrashing legs. Her eyes were rolling in their sockets, and wrenching one hand free of my grasp, she pulled a sleeve of my RAF uniform shirt clean away from my shoulder. Then the poor woman went limp as she passed out. After a minute I decided it was safe to let go and I called for an RAF ambulance which took her to hospital.

All this was because her husband was having an affair with another woman. Some weeks earlier I had asked him to talk it through with me, but he had refused. She spent a week or two in the RAF hospital at Wroughton, near Swindon, and soon after she returned home, they both turned up at my office to tell me that they were posted away from Honington and were going to make a new start together. The high drama of her actions had brought her husband to his senses.

Too often I have spent long hours with couples attempting to salvage a marriage which was fractured. If there is the slightest weakness in a marriage the rigours of Service life will find it and open it up like frost in stone. The isolation of RAF bases (so that the noise generated by aircraft disturbs as few people as possible), the absence of an extended family, the long working hours and frequent deployment away from home, the wives who are tied to school times when casual work is, in any case, thin on the ground: all these factors serve to strain even the strongest of marriages. The RAF does the best it can to reduce tension in family life, but in the privacy of the married quarter it is down to the husband and wife to work things out as best they can. I loved my flock and I shared their pain when they were struggling.

There were some parents it was difficult to love. I was called out one evening by a couple because two young children next door to them were hanging out of the bedroom window. I hurried to the house and discovered that the father was away on deployment and the mother had gone into Bury St Edmunds to play darts, leaving her three year old with her five year old child. I brought the children downstairs where a neighbour began to clean them. This situation had to be resolved at once, so searching in my diary, I found the telephone number of the NSPCC inspector I had met at happy hour in the Mess, and asked him to come over. He arrived in less than half an hour and was angry at what he saw. The neighbour told him which pub the darts match was in and off he went, leaving me with a neighbour and the children. When he returned, having dragged the mother out of the pub, she was far from penitent, and claimed that her friend had promised to come and stay with the kids. I left the situation in the capable hands of the large Inspector.

It was an innovative idea that Joy and Marcia Spackman, the wife of OC Admin Wing, developed later at RAF Marham when they asked the Station Commander to pay for them to be trained to operate a Citizens' Advice Bureau at the base on a voluntary basis. They spent many hours in training and working in an established office at Thetford, but the time came when they were approved by the national headquarters of the CAB, and were allocated an empty married quarter, discreetly located at the end of a terrace, where they set up the first RAF CAB office. They engaged a solicitor from Swaffham to attend and offer Legal Aid consultations, while they offered informed advice on a large range of social problems, and it proved such a boon to families that they soon engaged extra volunteers.

At the beginning of May 1977 there was news of a tragedy near Huntingdon. The Secretary of State for Defence, Fred Mulley, made the following statement: 'A Canberra aircraft of No.39 Squadron was returning to its base at RAF Wyton, near Huntingdon, after a routine training flight. About two miles from the end of the runway it crashed by some houses in the estate of Oxmoor in the village of Hartford, north-east of Huntingdon. Three young children were killed and five people were injured, of whom two are detained in hospital. The two RAF members of the crew were also killed. The crew members did not use their ejector seats.' The next day the pilot was named as Flight Lieutenant John Armitage, the fine young tenor in my church choir at RAF Luqa in 1972.

I learned that the stricken aircraft was heading in a shallow dive directly towards a crowded school playground, so, instead of ejecting, John stayed with the aircraft to turn it towards open countryside. He almost made it, but the undercarriage clipped a chimney of a house and the aircraft crashed in the street. I attended the funeral at which the entire Town Council turned out in their robes to show their respect for his courage and sacrifice. There was a reception in the Officers' Mess at RAF Wyton after the service, and, in accordance with RAF tradition, the cost was charged to the mess bills of the dead officers, and then written off by the Mess. But there were tears mingled in the wine.

Her Majesty the Queen celebrated her Silver Jubilee at the beginning of June 1977, and I was appointed by the Station Commander to form a committee to arrange appropriate celebrations. Remembering how good the Royal Navy is at organizing social events, I asked the Senior Naval Officer, Commander Fred de Labiliere, (brother of General Sir Peter) who was also the President of the Officers' Mess, to join the committee together with his wife, Sue. Fred was a very popular officer who thought laterally. My committee organized an all-ranks tea party for children held in the afternoon of the Jubilee Bank Holiday, Tuesday 7th June, on a large grassed space. That evening, Fred closed the Officers' Mess Bar and set up an open-air bar under a stand of trees outside my house in St Edmunds Square. It was run by the Mess Steward and all drinks were signed for on chits.

My father was staying with us for the week and, when I gave him my Bar number, he thought this was a marvellous arrangement. While he was with us we all went to the river Little Ouse at Santon Downham for a day, and he thoroughly enjoyed messing about in a dinghy with Mark and Simon, especially when I fell overboard. Another day we hired a rowing boat and played pirates on the river near Flatford Mill in Constable country. One of his tricks was to balance a broom handle upright on his index finger, which kept the children entertained.

He died four weeks after this holiday, as I was preparing to move to RAF Marham. My father had been registered partially-sighted for a few years, but refused to carry a white stick. Not far from his home in Port Talbot, he stepped out in front of a car and was admitted to hospital with internal injuries. He was discharged for a few days, but had to return to the hospital and I arrived with my sisters in time to administer the last rites. I met the driver of the car and absolved him from any responsibility; how could he have known that my father couldn't see him? So, for the second time in succession, my posting to a new station was clouded in sorrow. I still miss this honourable man, who, in my teens, taught me to develop a firm handshake, to play snooker, to drink wisely and to behave justly to all men. Dad always gave me his total support, even when my vocation meant that we were not going to work together. But above all, he was such good company.

RAF Marham

The notional length of a tour of duty in the UK was two and a half years, so my posting to Marham, in North West Norfolk, came as no surprise. We moved into 119 Norfolk Road, RAF Marham, on 19th August 1977. The station operated the Handley Page Victor K2, and there were two squadrons of these former V-bombers, now flying in the Air-to-Air Refuelling (AAR) role. The flying component was completed by No.100 Squadron, operating Canberra aircraft. The Station Commander was a delightful gentleman in every sense of that word, Group Captain (later Air Chief Marshal Sir) Benny Jackson.

The church was located in a half of the former Sergeants' Mess, the other half being used by the Church of Scotland and Free Churches (CSFC), with a shared hall in the centre. I also had a colleague, Pat Billington, a Church Army sister. Sister Pat is a warm-hearted lady with a gentle northern accent, who was excellent with the wives and children. It was my real pleasure to marry her with an equally gentle officer who was an Air Traffic Controller, Flight Lieutenant Bill Holland.

My CSFC colleague was Charles McNeil, a minister who joined the RAF from a Kirk in Glasgow and brought his accent with him. As soon as he arrived at

Marham he destroyed all hope of having a good working relationship with the Station Warrant Officer (SWO). It happened on the day before the Air Officer Commanding was coming to inspect the station, and the SWO was drilling a guard of honour outside the Officers' Mess. 'Right, lads, have a break for ten minutes, but if you're going for a smoke move out of sight behind the trees. And watch the white webbing on the Strike Command ceremonial rifles; lay your rifles on the kerb-stone to keep the webbing off the ground.' Meanwhile, Padre McNeil had arrived at the main gate, asked directions to the Officers' Mess, and drove on, his car piled inside with personal effects. He swung around the corner in front of the mess and feeling a thump, thump, thump, decided he had a flat tyre. Getting out of his car to check he saw two horrific images: one was a neat row of bent rifles, the other was the SWO having a fit. They never got on after that.

Between us, Sister Pat and I maintained a healthy congregation, with a good choir and Sunday School. We shared the visiting around married quarters between us, and I had in my area the seemingly endless Fen Road, which on a wet day in the bleak landscape was a trial of duty versus sense. Although I visited all the flying units, Charles and I were each elected as Honorary Members of a Victor squadron: he was with 57 and I was elected to 55 Squadron, where I was welcomed by Flight Lieutenant Dave Cherry, who had been on No.7 Squadron at St Mawgan. He accorded me the honour of becoming his son Christopher's Godfather.

I took my membership of the squadron seriously, as I had done with No.13 Squadron in Malta; I made a monthly contribution to the squadron fund, and Joy and I attended squadron dinners and parties. By dropping in to the hangar and workshops, I became known about the place as 'the squadron Padre', and while I was careful not to get in the way of highly technical tasks being carried out on the aircraft, I was always made to feel very welcome by the airmen and NCOs. They also knew Joy, for at every station since Halton she had taught both airmen and NCOs Geography and English to 'O' and 'A' level at evening classes in the Station Education Centre, as well as for the RAF Education Test which was required for their promotion.

It didn't take me long to undergo the escape test which was necessary before I could fly in a Victor. Only the pilot and co-pilot had ejection seats, so in an emergency the rear crew had to bail out through the door on the port side in a rolling technique which required practice. My first flight was at high level over the sea to the west of Blackpool. The Captain was the Squadron Commander, Wing Commander Peter Beer, who had been Equerry to HM The Queen. The Victor was an airborne filling station for aircraft on patrol to drop by and fill their tanks in a close encounter of the white-knuckle kind. The Victor trailed from under its wings, or from its underside, a hose with a drogue at the end, rather like a shuttlecock. The customer aircraft had a probe jutting out above its canopy or from the side

A Victor aircraft of No,55 Squadron

of the nose, and the pilot had to ram the probe into the end of the drogue; once locked in position, fuel would flow down the hose and into the fuel tanks.

We were at the height of the Cold War, and RAF fighter aircraft were constantly on patrol to escort Russian aircraft out of UK airspace, so the Victor was essential to the Phantom and Lightning aircraft if they were to remain on task for any reasonable length of time. Towards the end of my first flight we had a visit from a Tornado test aircraft. As I hadn't seen one before, the pilot was asked to fly ahead of us so that I could have a glimpse of the future. It was impressive at close quarters, and as it rolled away and climbed into the heavens, I was filled with envy. Soon after this we had a problem with cabin pressure, and Peter asked if I was OK for rapid descent. I said that I was, and he put the Victor into a very steep dive to about fifteen thousand feet and we headed for home.

Standing outside No.100 Squadron hangar one day, talking to a squadron pilot, I saw a Canberra coming in to land. 'It's returning from the wedding of one of our pilots at RAF Lossiemouth,' said my friend. With that there was a loud bang, and the Canberra dipped the port wing which caught the grass, and the aircraft cart-wheeled before my eyes. It seemed to hang in the air; its underbelly starkly outlined against the dark trees beyond it, until it landed with a crump on the runway and skidded along in a great cloud of dust and smoke. 'Please don't catch fire,' I cried out loud. We were both frozen to the spot. Then I came to, and as the crash tenders and field ambulances raced across the grass I ran to my RAF Mini; still no flames at the crash site as I drove to the Medical Centre where I might be of some use.

Ten minutes later the navigator limped in supported by two medics. He told me that when he saw the airfield he bent down to put his maps away when there was a bang and they lost the port engine. When the aircraft came to rest there was grass at his feet, so he unstrapped and got our fast. The nose had broken off, trapping the pilot, who was suffering only a broken leg, and was being cut out of the Canberra. The navigator seemed equally worried about the ceremonial swords on loan from Headquarters Strike Command in the bomb bay. Thank God it didn't burst into flames.

Once or twice a year RAF operational flying stations were obliged to undergo a Tactical Evaluation (Taceval) to prove to NATO that it was safely defended and 'fit for purpose'. An evaluation team would arrive unannounced at any hour of the day or night, usually the latter, and 'capture' the guards on duty as they informed the Station Commander of their presence on base. At once sirens would be sounded throughout the married quarters, calling personnel to report to their usual place of duty. Much cursing could be heard in the middle of the night as officers and men cycled furiously through the streets, and babies began to cry at the noise. At Honington, when the sirens went off I had only to walk to the church a hundred yards away and 'phone in to the Orderly Room. At Marham I had to be checked in at the main gate in order to get to my office, before visiting the Medical Centre for a coffee. Soon the night would be shattered by the sound of Conway aero engines starting up, followed by the roar of aircraft taking to the sky.

More and more people were beginning to buy their own homes and live in the local area. This eventually had an impact on lively nights in the Mess, but at Marham there was still a good social life to be enjoyed. At a Dining In night I was introduced to the game of Jousting. Two SWO's bicycles were 'borrowed' and I was chosen by 55 Squadron as their 'Knight' to challenge OC Admin Wing. Armed with a mop held under the arm, we were propelled toward each other by our 'seconds'. Just as I was gathering up steam along the corridor I was arrested by OC Police Flight for not having any lights on my bike. I was fined a pint of beer and allowed to proceed. I caught OC Admin Wing a fair poke in his ribs and he crashed in a tangle of bar stools, and I was declared the winner. It was that sort of evening.

Padre Charles McNeil had been making wine in one of the many empty rooms in the former sergeants' mess which we used as our churches and offices. He eventually persuaded me to join him in the venture, so I invested in some jars and raw materials, and we doubled the production. One Wednesday morning, we were both on our knees in the little room sampling some of the wine which needed to be racked. I was remarking on the good quality when a large gleaming black shoe entered my field of vision. My gaze rose up the trouser leg to a hat bearing gold braid. There stood the Station Commander and the SWO. I had forgotten the CO's Inspection was due at 1030. Charles didn't even stand up, but in his severe accent said, 'We're saving on the communion wine, sir. We should make the Station a healthy profit.' Gentleman that he was, Benny Jackson just smiled and said, 'I shall hold you to that, Padres; we'll come back in half an hour.' I never again missed a CO's Inspection.

I used to attend the Station Commander's meetings with the Station Executives once a month. At one meeting 'The Station Open Day' appeared on the agenda, and when we came to that item all the wing commanders seemed to be picking up their pencils off the floor or bending down to put papers in their case, and I was the only one sitting upright, so the CO said, 'Brian, you are just the man to organize the Open Day.' 'Sorry, sir, I cannot control aircraft,' I said quickly. 'Not a problem, Squadron Leader Ops will do the flying display.' And so, with huge grins from the others around the table, I became the Officer i/c Open Day 1978.

I arranged for the first meeting of representatives from every section on the station to meet me in the church hall on a Friday afternoon. I could hear them arriving as I gathered my papers in my office, when the telephone rang. It was the Chaplain-in-Chief's Personal Secretary saying that the 'Chief' wished to speak to me. I was obliged to ask if it would be alright if I rang him back in a few hours. Throughout the meeting I wondered about it because it was very rare for the 'Chief' to telephone a station chaplain; he usually worked through the chain of command. It was gone 1600 before I could ring back and speak to Hewitt Wilson. When he told me he usually had chaplains up to MOD for interview on this subject, but as he was going on holiday the next day he thought he'd telephone, my concern grew. Interview? This was worse than I feared. Then he astounded me by inviting me to become his Staff Chaplain. He told me to talk it over with Joy first, but I accepted the offer at once, and he arranged for me to visit him at the Ministry of Defence in September.

The Open Day was most successful and two weeks later, on 10th July, 'Operation Bolthole' began. The runway at Marham was to be resurfaced, which meant that the aircraft were based at RAF Sculthorpe for the duration. Sculthorpe is near Fakenham, about forty minutes' drive away, and was used by the US Air Force. The food was hugely popular, with enormous beef steaks cooked to order. Throughout the winter, however, the ground crews who maintained the aircraft left Marham in the dark and returned home in the dark. They found it very tedious, particularly when Russian aircraft probed our airspace in large numbers and RAF fighter aircraft had to intercept them for hours at a time supported by the Victor tankers.

This support committed several crews to standby on base. The Soviet Air Force seemed to increase the incursions at times of public holiday, when families had to cancel planned visits to their parents. When sustained for weeks on end, it eroded morale, and the Soviets knew it.

During our time at Marham we developed an interest in Speedway, and we would travel as a family to the Saddlebow Stadium in Kings Lynn on a Saturday evening, and take up a position on the 'fourth bend' just before the home straight. The boys would wear the club green and gold striped scarves, while Helen wore cycling overalls in Club colours, complete with clipboard holding the programme. The team captain then was an inspired young rider, Mike Lee, and his number two was Dave Jessup. A few years later, when we were living in Northwood, we were watching on television the World Speedway Championship in Sweden, and saw Mike Lee win the world crown, with Jessup as runner-up. When the commentator announced that both men would be riding for their club later that evening, we packed some sandwiches and drove from London to Kings Lynn in rapid time for a truly celebratory evening. Love of sport engenders that kind of madness.

In late January 1979 I spent a week at St Deiniol's Library, Hawarden, reading and praying about the next phase of my ministry. It was going to be quite different from any work I had experienced; it meant working as a part of a team and keeping office hours, but, more significantly, it left me free at weekends, with no reflections in a chalice.

I was due to return to Marham on the Friday in order to preach at Sandringham in the presence of the Queen and the Royal Family on the Sunday. The weather intervened, and East Anglia was cut off by huge snow drifts; but as helicopters were airlifting food around the county I was sure the Queen would understand. So I returned to my seat in the Library and shared my predicament with a fellow reader, Dr Donald Gray, the Rector of Liverpool, who later became the Rector of St Margaret's Church, Westminster, and Chaplain to the Speaker of the House of Commons, and who is now a colleague at St Mary's Church, Stamford, where I have officiated since my retirement from the Rectory of Caythorpe.

My farewell 'bash' at Marham was in two parts: the usual barrel of beer at Happy Hour in the Mess, but I also put on another barrel of beer in 55 Squadron hangar for all ranks. As I ducked my head beneath the wings of the Victors on my way to the lavatory, the sound of laughter and chatter echoing around the hangar, I reflected that this might be the last time I would experience the camaraderie which flows from membership of a squadron, and the thought saddened me.

Looking back over my time in East Anglia, I regard it as my 'bread and butter' period. By that I mean that it was a time when I began to apply all my ministerial experience up to that point, and so make 'loitering with intent' my chosen method of being a priest in the midst of a down-to-earth and hard-nosed community. By 'keeping the rumour of God alive', as my later colleague Fr Tony Smith put it, I tried to represent the love and care of Christ for those among whom I lived and worked.

CHAPTER SEVEN:

The Ministry of Defence

I travelled to Adastral House in September 1978 for the interview with the Chaplain-in-Chief. He explained that the Staff Chaplain had two major roles: first, he was the Personal Staff Officer (PSO) to the Chief; second, he was the Desk Officer for the Chaplains' Branch, and they came in that order. In the first role, he would work so closely with the Chaplain-in-Chief that he could advise the Assistant Chaplains-in-Chief in the Chief's absence. In the second role, he worked closely with the Civil Service Department through the Senior Executive Officer (SEO) on the Chief's Staff. The Chief's outer office was run by his Personal Secretary.

It was all very daunting, particularly when Hewitt Wilson had been Chaplain-in-Chief for nearly seven years, ran a tight ship in his governance of the Chaplains' Branch, and did not respond well to mediocrity in his clergy. He was a tall, well-built Irishman, who had played Rugby for Ireland at schoolboy level. It was a penetrating interview, and near the end he suddenly said, 'Do you remember our conversation about the frequency of the Eucharist at St Mawgan?' I replied that I was new then, but he continued, 'You stuck to your guns; I liked that. I can get any number of chaplains up here who are "Yes Men", but I want a man who will tell me what he thinks, and will have a row with me about it if he thinks he's right. In the end, I will make the decision, but let us have candour between us.' That attitude commanded my total respect, and I learned a huge amount about leadership and about myself in the year we served together. I also discovered that Hewitt was not the tyrant some chaplains imagined him to be, but a just and fair man of deep spirituality, who loved life and loved his chaplains.

It was arranged that I should start work in London on 3rd April 1979. Having handed over to my successor at Marham, I took a room in the Officers' Mess at RAF Northwood for the week before Easter, and began an acquaintance with the Metropolitan Line as I travelled to Holborn each day. That week my predecessor, Padre Mike Stokes, went through the files with me before going out to RAF Sek

Kong, near the Chinese border with Hong Kong. I had succeeded Mike at St Mawgan, so the hand-over was as smooth as silk.

RAF Northwood is a joint RAF/RN unit and is known by the Royal Navy as HMS Warrior. Consequently, there were many maritime air force officers who were already our friends living in the married quarters there. The friendly officer in Malta, who had phoned me with the news of my mother's death, was now the officer in charge of allocating the married quarters at Northwood. Now Squadron Leader, Ian Macgregor responded favourably to my request for a quarter, as a percentage of the houses at Northwood were allocated to Ministry of Defence officers.

I was given 2 Avior Drive, a large detached house about a five minute walk to the primary school for Mark and Simon, and a fifteen minute walk from the Underground station in Northwood itself. Next door lived an unaccompanied admiral; when I asked why an Able Seaman was hanging washing on the garden line I was told that an admiral is entitled to a boat crew. Northwood was that kind of unit.

One of the most difficult adjustments we had to make to our way of life in London was the absence of church life. At first I called on the Rector of Holy Trinity, Northwood, and offered my services on Sundays, but when the next week he produced a schedule for the month which had me preaching or officiating at the Eucharist every week, I realised that I had made a mistake, for, after a busy working week, I was spending Saturdays writing a sermon to preach the following day. At the end of the month I looked elsewhere, and we settled in a friendly church on the outskirts of Watford where I took the occasional service for the vicar.

Once Helen began full-time education, Joy was able to return to teaching, and secured a post in Vyners Grammar School in Hillingdon teaching History, and Geography to 'A' level. The following year Mark began as a pupil at Rickmansworth Grammar School, and walked with me to Northwood Underground station each morning, but caught the Watford train on the opposite platform. Simon and Helen were at the primary school at the end of Avior Drive.

During a half-term holiday I arranged for Mark and Simon to visit the House of Commons as a part of their education. I had known the Speaker, Mr George Thomas, when he was MP for Cardiff West and I was at Llandaff, so I wrote to him and asked for three tickets to see the House at work. He phoned me and told me to arrive in time to see the Speaker's procession after lunch, and one of his staff would escort us to the gallery, and then, when we saw him vacate the chair, we must come and join him for tea in Speaker's House.

We stood in the lobby and watched the procession make its way to the chamber, George giving Mark and Simon a huge wink as he passed. Later, he showed us the treasures in the cabinets in Speaker's House as the boys tucked into cakes and squash. He was the very best of politicians: a natural, uncomplicated man who had a passion for improving the lot of working folk. He despised cant and hypocrisy, preferring honesty and plain speaking. I have been with George Thomas in many situations and he was always the same man for all people.

I travelled each day on the Metropolitan Line. It was tedious and some people invented games to keep themselves amused. My game was subtle, and known only to me. I called it, 'Seat the Blonde.' Every morning my train was on time, a blonde in her early twenties got on at Preston Road. In three years I never spoke to her; I don't know her name or her occupation. I don't even know where she was going each morning on the 0725 from Preston Road, for her journey was not complete when I left the train at Kings Cross. This is how the game worked.

Usually, my train was almost empty at Northwood as it had only come from Watford just up the line. Commuters are creatures of habit; each morning they enter the train by the same door, as it's the door nearest the exit at their destination. This means that you get to know the regulars—not actually speak to them, of course—but you get to know their likes and dislikes, their preferences and their aversions.

Thus, I knew that the man with the grey moustache and pork pie hat always sat in an aisle seat, with his back to the direction of travel. The man with the black, lank hair and a wet expression always sat in the offside corner, facing the front. The little old lady, with NHS specs, would only sit in an aisle seat, but didn't mind which direction she faced, while the big American usually sat in the middle of the three-seat (off-side) bench, and read the New York Herald, with his arms spread wide across all three seats, instead of folding the paper. This infuriated the chap in the pork-pie hat, who sometimes, in wet weather, made his brolly drip down the middle of the front page of the New York Herald.

There were others, too, but you get the drift. All these boarded the train at various stations between Northwood and Preston Road. Now, on boarding the train at Northwood, I would decide where I wanted the blonde to sit when she boarded the train six stops later. I would then choose my seat with care, and spread my bag and my raincoat about the place. By gathering my belongings onto my lap at different strategic stops, I could allow or deny people their preferred seat, which would result in them moving further down the car to find a similar seat. They would glower at me, but no matter: I was interested only in getting the blonde to sit where I had decided she would sit. She was always the first to board at Preston Road, and I would remove my last obstacle, revealing the one empty seat, which she pounced upon. A harmless game, played no more than once a week, but it kept me amused on many a cold morning.

Adastral House, Holborn, 1980

When I wasn't engaged in seating the blonde, I read notes about the chaplains and their families, for before I could be of much use to the Chief I had to know the Chaplains' Branch in every detail. I soon decided to travel early before the rush hour in order to have a seat. More often than not Joy would drive me to Moor Park station, where I caught the 0720 fast train from Amersham to Kings Cross. The forty-five minute journey in the morning was useful time, for learning the names of Chaplains' wives and children, where chaplains had worked in the past and where they might go next. Later, I used the time to draft letters to be typed as soon as the Secretary arrived for work, so that the Chief could sign them before the morning postal collection.

Chaplaincy Services (RAF) was located on the third floor of Adastral House in Theobalds Road, Holborn, which now accommodates the offices of Warner Brothers TV. It was a happy community on the third floor: RAF Personnel Services occupied most of it, with Director, Women's Royal Air Force in the south corner between the Chief and the two Principal Chaplains. Roy and I had offices around the corner.

The Staff Chaplain was responsible for the recruitment of new chaplains, and this process began with the publication of the ITTs. My civil service colleague on the staff, Roy Widdup, was a splendid character. He had been in the civil service all his life and had risen through the ranks to become a Senior Executive Officer (SEO). He taught me an enormous amount about how the civil service worked; essential advice such as, 'If you have a strong case, by all means send a two-page Loose Minute; but if your case is weak, send a signal.' His office was next to mine, and we were forever borrowing cigarettes from each other, until, just after Christmas in 1979, I suddenly stopped smoking when I officiated at the funeral of Sue Delabilliere, the excellent member of the Silver Jubilee Committee at RAF Honington, who had died at a young age of brain cancer. She, too, had smoked cigarettes.

When Roy first mentioned the ITTs, I thought the poor chap was suffering from alcoholic poisoning, until he revealed that it was the six-monthly Into-Training Targets. It set the figure for the number of new recruits the Chaplains' Branch could accept within the forecast strength of the RAF for the next ten year period. These were essential reading, for I might recruit a chaplain this year, but in three years time there would be no room for him, thus creating hiatus and indigestion all round.

Roman Catholic priests, who were seconded to the RAF by their bishop, and CSFC clergy, applied alike to their denominational Principal Chaplain, who interviewed them and passed the papers to me for processing for me to assess whether they had a vacancy. I interviewed Anglican clergy, and if I thought they were worth pursuing I would arrange for them to attend again, with their wife, to meet the Chaplain-in-Chief for a more formal interview. If we had a vacancy and he wanted to recruit them, I would send the application forms to them and take up references from their bishop. The papers were then sent 'up the line' to the personnel department. It was a long process but it prevented mistakes.

I interviewed one chap whom, apart from his bushy beard and rough manner, I liked, and so did the Chief. He decided to recruit him but ran into difficulties with the ITTs and associated problems, and so he was unsuccessful. Six weeks later, as I picked up the Daily Mail at Northwood station, I froze in horror, for staring out from the front page was the man with the bushy beard under the headline, 'Serial Rapist Caught'. As I said, it was a long process but it prevented mistakes.

A squadron leader from the Recruitment Branch called one day to say that a sum of money was available to update the Chaplains' Branch recruiting brochure. I suggested at once a week in Cyprus to film the work of chaplains overseas. We flew from Brize Norton with a writer and a photographer and stayed at RAF Akrotiri. We took excellent staged photographs of Padre Brian Halfpenny visiting the RAF Hospital there, the CSFC chaplain taking a school assembly, and so on. While there, the recruiting team used the opportunity to take some photographs of other branches and trades for their portfolio, and so we arranged a location near the hospital known as 'Dreamer's Bay' for an action shoot featuring the RAF Regiment's new Scorpion Combat Reconnaissance Vehicle with its 76 mm, rifled gun.

The shoot was scripted in the morning, but when we assembled for the take after lunch a small Morris Minor was parked nearby, but as it was out of shot we pressed on. On cue, a five-ton truck raced to a halt and twelve armed men leaped out and took up a defensive position around a low bluff, while to the sound of an astonishing growl the Scorpion tracked vehicle roared up to the top and halted with its gun pointing straight at the Morris Minor. Our gaze followed the pointed gun and we saw two white faces peering from the back seat of the Morris Minor: one minute sweet canoodling, the next World War Three.

After the heat of early summer in Cyprus, Adastral House in the rain seemed full of even more routine bureaucracy than usual on my return: it was time to draft the September postings. There are two forms known intimately by every RAF officer: F1771 on which expenses were claimed, and F1369 or the Annual Confidential Report (ACR). I had always signed the first page of my ACR to confirm the details printed on it, but never saw it again; the ACR was totally confidential. It was a standard form for all officers. The first reporting officer for chaplains was the man's Station Commander. If, as sometimes happened, it was delegated to OC Admin Wing, the Chief always sent it back. Then it went to the Assistant Chaplain-in-Chief for comment, and on to the Air Officer Admin, and, for Wing Commander chaplains, to the Commander-in-Chief, before returning to the Chaplain-in-Chief for retention.

The Chaplain-in-Chief saw them before passing them to me for filing, and for the first time I saw what senior officers thought of chaplains and I became so proud of my colleagues. For the most part station commanders appreciated the work done by their chaplains and said so. I have long considered that parochial clergy ought to have an annual confidential report raised by their churchwardens and passed to the archdeacon for comment, and the bishop for retention. What a record of service they would amass.

A chaplain's promotion was after one year to squadron leader and then after fourteen years to wing commander. Promotion to the acting rank of group captain was on appointment to a Command position by the Chaplain-in-Chief. At the end of the station commander's annual report on a F1369 there was a line for the chaplain to be specially, highly or just recommended for promotion (or not recommended), and no promotion could be effected unless the station commander completed this section. It was the Staff Chaplain's job to note what each station commander signified and raise the paperwork to upgrade chaplains when appropriate. Happily, it was extremely rare to read, 'Not recommended.'

Also at the bottom of the first page of F1369 was a space for choice of next posting. It allowed the officer to indicate the sort of job he would like to move to after his current posting. In a small Branch like the Chaplains' it was rather pointless, and I always wrote, 'At the discretion of the Chaplain-in-Chief'. It was a large part of the Staff Chaplain's job to draft the posting of chaplains for the Chief to consider. I would spend hours poring over annual reports and increasing my knowledge of the chaplains. In order to give my colleagues a balanced career, I would consider whether it was time for a chaplain to work at a hospital, or at a training unit, or to have a turn overseas, or in a senior post training a new-entrant chaplain. The reason for moving men about stemmed from the necessity of finding a place for a man returning from overseas. When there were two or three of these about the same time there was a danger of posting half of the Branch. I considered that I had done my job well if there was very little room for change when I went through it with the Chief.

This happened four times a year and was followed by a meeting of the Assistant Chaplains-in-Chief, who each wanted to post chaplains they favoured to their own territory. I had to be on my toes to explain why chaplain A could not go to station X, and why chaplain B would be a disaster at station Z. Occasionally they came up with a good option, but I would not yield if it meant redrafting the entire plot; I would attempt to mollify them with a drink after the meeting.

The Chief's Personal Secretary retired towards the end of my first year having been with Hewitt for most of his time as Chief. He depended on her for the efficiency of his work a great deal, and was clearly anxious that her successor would be up to speed before he retired. His anxiety increased when a young, eighteen year old recruit, Miss Julie Pocock, was appointed straight from the Civil Service College. It was a big job for a young lass as she was responsible for booking train

Roy Widdup (SEO), Hewitt Wilson (the Chief), and BHL in the Chief's Office in 1980

and airline tickets, arranging for cars to be available to take the Chief to all parts of the UK as well as running the outer office and keeping the appointment book. At first Hewitt began to sound off to me about the civil service training regime, but as she grew into the job his confidence in her increased and Julie developed into a very competent personal secretary.

After I had spent only a year with Hewitt he retired after a long and distinguished Service career, and was succeeded by another Irishman, Padre Herbie Stuart. I walked with Hewitt to the front door of Adastral House as he left the building for the last time, and fumbling in his pocket he said, 'Tell Herbie this is my sole legacy to him', and he handed me the key to the Air Marshal's lavatory on the third floor. Herbie is a gentle, kind man with a twinkle in his eye and a mischievous smile never far from his lips. Yet, he had steel when it was required and he was no-one's fool. I must have been a great trial for him; I was constantly urging him to make decisions when he preferred to reflect longer before action. He once shouted at me to back off, 'You are always telling me to do things which I don't want to do!' I went back to my office with the knowledge that he was right. An hour later he put his head around my office door, and in his soft Irish accent and with an endearing grin, said, 'Can you spare a minute?' Everyone loved the man.

When a letter arrived inviting me to nominate a mid-career chaplain to represent the Chaplains' Branch at a service in St Paul's Cathedral to celebrate the 80th birthday of Her Majesty The Queen Mother, I knew just the chap. As I had to travel in uniform I requested a staff car, and on the appointed day, 4 August,1980, when the front desk called me down to my car, I discovered a huge Austin limousine parked outside Adastral House. 'That's not my car' I said to the receptionist, as the driver came over and said that it was, indeed, to take me to St Paul's. I gave him the windscreen security sticker I had received and I set off along the royal route in great style. As I drove slowly along Fleet Street the crowds waved wildly at me, so I gave a modest wave in return. As I alighted at the cathedral, I asked the driver whose car it was. He replied, 'Sir Arthur Hockaday, sir.' Sir Arthur was a delightful man who was the Second Permanent Under Secretary of State at the Ministry of Defence. When I met him socially some weeks later he explained that he had decided rather late in the day that he was able to attend the Queen Mother's service, and rather than recover his car, and cause mayhem in the transport department, he had carried his top hat in a bag, put on a plastic raincoat and travelled on the Tube. That was the thoughtful kind of man he was.

I am the chap who revised the 'Dress Regulations for Chaplains' single-handed. Apart from royal ceremonies, August in Adastral House was always stuffy. Even looking out of the window gave no pleasure, for my office overlooked the central well of the building. Most people on the third floor were on holiday. With Herbie on leave, life was tedious.

One hot afternoon the file containing 'Dress Regulations for the RAF' arrived in my in-tray; a periodic review was due. The Minute Sheet asked me to update the chapter on Chaplains. Idly, I turned the pages. Then I had an idea: I would write a spoof regulation. What fun I had. I called it, 'No.8(a) Dress, for Chaplains deployed to the Red Sea'. There has not been such a posting, then or now. I decided on a white, open-neck, short-sleeved shirt, with the rank slides on shoulder straps, white shorts, long white socks, black shoes, SD hat, and the Branch Brooch to be worn above the right breast pocket of the shirt. Feeling pleased, I tossed the file into the out-tray and tried a crossword.

When I returned from leave after Easter the following year the office copy of the 'Revised Dress Regulations for the Royal Air Force' arrived in the post. My misdemeanour hit me with the force of a brick wall. I had intended to delete my spoof at the proof-reading stage, but I was away when it came around, and I had forgotten all about it. For weeks I awaited the summons, but it never came; who reads Dress Regs? I was safe as long as no clever-dick chaplain demanded a white short-sleeved shirt, or long white socks from stores. It was still there, tucked away in the appropriate chapter of the publication years later.

One of the more arduous tasks in the Staff Chaplain's calendar was the organization of the Chaplain-in-Chief's Annual Conference of Chaplains. The conference was held at the RAF Chaplains' School, Amport House near Andover

Annual Chaplains Conference 1978

in June each year. The current house was built near the village of Amport in 1857 by the Marquis of Winchester and replaced two earlier houses built on the site. The gardens were laid out by Sir Edwin Lutyens as a scaled-down trial for his planned garden at the Viceroy's Palace in New Delhi, and were planted by Gertrude Jekyll. During World War II the house was taken over and used as the headquarters of Royal Air Force Maintenance Command. The Chaplains' School moved to Amport House in 1962, from Dowdswell Court in Cheltenham.

I had enjoyed attending these annual gatherings of priests since I joined the Service in 1970; apart from my time in Malta I had looked forward each year to a week of prayer in chapel, and joyous camaraderie in the superb environment of the House. The Conference was a meeting of friends, a sharing of jokes, some serious scholarship and a chance to discuss problems common to us all. Now, from January onwards the Conference hung like a cloud over the Staff Chaplain's desk as lecturers had to be booked, transport arrangements made, guests invited to the Thursday Dinner, authority given for the chaplains to be released from their stations, and a hundred other logistical problems to be overcome.

The Chief and I would travel down and meet the Assistant Chaplains-in-Chief for dinner on the Monday evening, and have the Quarterly Meeting and discussion of a postings plot on the Tuesday morning. After lunch the chaplains would arrive by train or car and the Conference began after dinner with Evensong and the Chaplain-in-Chief's 'Charge' to his chaplains in Amport village church, during which he would review the past year and focus on specific concerns he wished the chaplains to address. There followed two days of lectures in the morning, free afternoons, and a lecture on the Wednesday evening and the finale of the Dining-In Night on Thursday, when the loyal staff pulled out all the stops to make the dining room look enchanting and the dinner a feast. That evening was enhanced by the music of the Salon Orchestra of the RAF Central Band.

The most satisfying of the four conferences which I arranged was that held in June 1981. In his first conference as the Chief, Herbie Stuart chose as the theme, 'Proclaiming the Gospel.' The first lecturer was my former Oxford Principal, Fr Derek Allen, who addressed 'The Faith of the Proclaimer' and 'The Gospel he Proclaims' in two excellent sessions. He reminded us that we cannot fall in with everything that happens about us, and if ordination equipped us for this conflict, that was only the beginning; we were to go on receiving what was once given. He quoted Dr Austen Farrar, who spoke of the priest as 'a walking sacrament' who must be God's man first, before he can become the man for others.

The next day the lecturer was Professor David Jenkins, later to become the Bishop of Durham. He was brilliant and mercurial in his thinking. He asked the question, 'What is the shape of the Church and Society as implied by Queen's Regulations for the RAF?' and answered it with a thesis which he called 'The Sociology of QRs'. He summed it up by stating that chaplains are authorized by the church and recognized by the system. Then he declared this to be false sociology and false theology, for we are not in a post-Christian situation, but a pre-Christian situation, for the Kingdom has never finally arrived, and the Christendom episode, though very long and influential, is just an episode. He was outstanding as a thinker and as a lecturer.

The Chief had asked the Archbishop of Canterbury to attend the Dining-In Night as our Guest of Honour. All Anglican chaplains to the armed forces relate directly to the Archbishop for episcopal oversight, which he delegates to the three Service Archdeacons. He also appoints a Bishop with the title, 'The Archbishop of Canterbury's Episcopal Representative to HM Forces', who is addressed by the easier (though misleading) title of 'Bishop to the Forces', when in fact he is just a link with Canterbury. Archbishop Robert Runcie accepted the invitation, and I made sporadic visits to Lambeth Palace to tie up loose ends. I thought it would be good to fly him to Amport by helicopter, so I telephoned the PSO to the Chief of the Air Staff (CAS), Wing Commander (later Air Chief Marshal Sir) David Cousins, seeking his support in tasking an aircraft of the Queen's Flight. David phoned back in half an hour. It was all fixed but CAS would also appreciate an invitation. Herbie replied that he would be delighted for Air Chief Marshal (later Marshal of the RAF) Sir Michael Beetham to attend.

On the Thursday the red Wessex helicopter touched down on the south lawn at precisely 1900, as the Chaplain-in-Chief and the Principal of the Chaplains' School, resplendent in their Mess Dress uniforms, stepped forward to welcome the VIP guests. The lawns had been cut that afternoon and looked immaculate, but the downwash of the helicopter blades covered the welcoming party in fine green cuttings.

Archbishop Bob Runcie looked splendid in his Court Dress, complete with silk stockings and buckled shoes. In his speech after dinner he thanked the Chief for arranging the helicopter for he often worried about the car breaking down and his attire might be exposed to ridicule, 'Although, I'm told that I have better legs than Mrs. Thatcher', he added. He said that he was reminded of the first council of the Church at Nicea in 325 AD as recent scholarship had revealed that the only session of the Council attended by all the bishops was the banquet given by the Emperor Constantine.

He went onto say that he was proud of his responsibility for the chaplains to HM Forces, and that he would 'count it a very black day indeed if the Chaplains' Branch became a particular target for defence economies.' He continued: 'Force must permit a breathing space when moral values can be examined. Force on its own is totally demonic; it must be held in a moral context. The presence of somebody who represents thought about that moral content is invaluable. Some of your men and women, and their families, must sometimes feel exposed as there is a growing revulsion at the prospect of a nuclear holocaust. The reason for this movement is complex, and while I respect their views I cannot be a pacifist or a unilateralist. We need hard heads as well as soft hearts. Turn this to the protection of the vulnerable and you will understand why I want to support you in your ministry.' He received an enthusiastic and long ovation from all present.

The following year we studied the Brandt Report on poverty, and I had arranged for a professor from Sussex University to speak to us. The chaplain I asked to bring him from the railway station came up to me on his return and said,' You're having a laugh, yes? He has no socks on and he's wearing a tarbouche.' Sure enough, the young prof entered the room and began his first lecture wearing a red rimless fez. There was a stunned silence at his appearance, and all eyes swivelled to me, but I was equally astounded, especially when what he said seemed to make no sense. In the bar that evening chaplains were convinced that he was a student from Sussex engaged in a spoof for charity.

In April 1982 the situation in the Falkland Islands became very grave, and the Ministry of Defence adopted a far more urgent posture. As the British Task Force was commanded from the Joint Headquarters at Northwood, it was evident in the faces of my neighbours, whom I saw in the evenings, that everyone was working around the clock. On 21st May HMS Ardent was sunk in San Carlos Water; that evening we went to a friend's house for a drink, and when an admiral came in, still in uniform, Joy said how sad we were to hear of the loss of Ardent, and he said in a tired voice, 'How do you know about that? Has it been announced?' The men were so cagey for they knew the reality of the situation, but had no idea what was going out in the media.

As the conflict developed, the Chaplain-in-Chief arranged with Strike Command to send a chaplain to Ascension Island. As Padre Gareth Jones arrived on the island, he was immediately asked to attend to a casualty, and when medics took over he was summoned to care for a bereaved soldier. It was some hours before he could attend to his own needs, and report to the command centre to ask where he was to be billeted. A Royal Navy captain told him that there was no room and no rations for him, so he was to board the aircraft and get out. A group captain stood by wringing his hands but did nothing else. Gareth phoned me at Adastral House the following day, and when I asked how were things in the mid-Atlantic, he revealed he was phoning from Brize Norton. I thought Herbie was going to burst a blood vessel, but, having contacted Strike Command, there was not much we could do as Northwood staff seemed to have the final word and were thinking 'Navy'.

Chaplains mingle with guests after the Annual Dinner at Amport House, 1980.

During the autumn of 1980 I began to consider my next posting, and as the chaplain at Akrotiri in Cyprus was due to return to UK in 1982, when I would have completed three years in post, I enrolled for a class in Modern Greek, arranged for government employees, on Wednesday lunchtimes in the basement of the Inland Revenue offices in High Holborn. I had studied Classical Greek for my degree and New Testament Greek at Oxford, but demotic Greek is very different. It was a class of about twenty and we became a group of friends from several government departments.

In November 1981 the Chief began to ask about the next posting round and I offered him a plot, but kept Akrotiri up my sleeve. In January he insisted on knowing who I had in mind for Akrotiri, and when I coughed modestly he said, 'Greek lessons—I should have known.' We both laughed, and so I was posted to Cyprus in July, going on embarkation leave immediately after the Annual Conference in June.

Surprisingly, I had enjoyed my time as Staff Chaplain enormously, and discovered that I had a flair for administration hitherto unknown to me. The life of a chaplain among his people is often lonely in the way his working day is constructed. He meets many people for short intervals as he visits them at work or at home, and might enjoy their company, but in the end he returns to the solitude of his office as he prepares the next sermon, service or lesson. There is nothing unusual or heroic in this; it is a way of life for many other disciplines. But in addition, a chaplain who cares for his people is never satisfied that he has completed a day's work; there is always more he could have done.

As Staff Chaplain, I experienced none of this. It was a great joy to work as a team member with experts in their field. I have always enjoyed solving problems, and here I was given an endless supply of them to deal with. They were all the more serious as decisions made would affect the day-to-day life of my colleagues, hopefully, for the better. As I grew in confidence, I began to trust my own judgement and discovered that provided I had done my homework properly, I was likely to get things right. I also found that the Chaplain-in-Chief was prepared to ask for my advice on all matters affecting chaplaincy.

The staff chaplain had been described by one of my predecessors in the words which begin the Holy Communion in the Book of Common Prayer, as the one 'unto whom all hearts are open, all desires known, and from whom no secrets are hid.' And so it was.

CHAPTER EIGHT:

Once More to the Med

In June 1982, I was driving in a terrific heat wave from Titograd to Skopje with my son Mark, who was thirteen years old. We were attempting to skirt around Albania in a journey from Northwood to Cyprus. Joy, Simon and Helen were to follow by air once we had arrived and taken over the house. We were crossing a remote mountain range, which marks the border of Montenegro with Kosovo, on an earth road, making for Tilova Mitrovica, where the major road comes south from Belgrade and on through Macedonia into Greece. The previous night we had camped by a river near Ivangrad, where Mark had played football with a young goatherd as I cooked supper on the camping stove.

About 10.00, high up in the rugged mountains, with the sun beating down from a cloudless sky, we passed a junction with a track going off to the left, where an old man was squatting on his haunches by the roadside. We had all the windows open in an attempt to keep cool. As we passed, he waved his arms and shouted at us, and I caught the words, '... hole. Rashca, rashca!' From his demeanour I assumed he had a grievance against the British. My son, who had been closer to him, said, 'I think he was trying to tell us something, Dad.' 'Yes, and I know exactly what it was!' I replied tersely, as I concentrated on the alarming road surface.

A minute later we rounded a tight left-hand corner with no safety barrier between us and the deep ravine to the right, and my son yelled as I hit the brakes and steered into the cliff-face and away from the ravine. We skidded on the loose dirt and stopped just short of three rusty oil drums which blocked our path. A landslide had taken the road clean away into the deep valley below. It continued on its way along the side of the ravine about a hundred yards ahead of us. Some hole.

We had stopped just short of disaster and certain death. Shaken, I managed to turn the car around, keeping as close to the cliff face as possible. I paused by the smiling man squatting at the junction, and thanked him, as we took the other track, which led us northeast through Novi Pazar, where we were just able to squeeze past a crane hauling a bus out of a river, and over yet another wild mountain range to Raška, before we joined the major road, where I filled our near-empty fuel tank, and turned south toward Tilova Mitrovica, Pristina, Skopje, and on to Thessalonika.

In the weeks before the Annual Conference at Amport House, I had arranged for our furniture to go into storage, replaced it with RAF furniture, and Joy and I packed our deep-sea crates which were despatched to the docks. Everything that was left, apart from essential items to enable Joy to live for the next three weeks, had to go into the new duty-free Fiat Strada. With the car packed to the limit, including camping equipment, for Mark and I were to live in a tent as we journeyed to the Mediterranean, another deep-sea box was ordered for the pile of things left on the drive.

Cyprus is situated only forty miles south of Turkey, and sixty miles west of the Syrian coast, and is the only divided island in the whole of the Mediterranean. This division is a result of an attempted coup by Greece in 1974 followed by the occupation of the northern part of the island by Turkey. The United Nations maintains a buffer zone known as the 'Green Line'.

The Sovereign Base Areas (SBAs) of Akrotiri and Dhekelia are those parts of the island which have remained under British jurisdiction since the creation of an independent Republic of Cyprus in 1960. In addition to the Sovereign Bases themselves, the 1960 Treaty of Establishment also provides for the continued use by the British Government of certain facilities within the Republic of Cyprus, known as Retained Sites.

We docked in Limassol on Saturday 3rd July and were met at the port, off the car ferry from Piraeus, by the Chaplains' Assistant, Miss Dorothy Twiss, who was to be my colleague, and she navigated the way to our house at 11 Mulberry Mansions, Berengaria, in the outskirts of Limassol. Our 'mansion' turned out to be a long bungalow with a corrugated iron roof. It was a temporary home for us until a house was available at Akrotiri; Dorothy lived a few doors along the road. The following Thursday we met Joy, Simon and Helen off the VC10 from Brize Norton.

The British Forces married quarters site in Berengaria was a UK 'Retained Site' under the Treaty of Establishment, and so it was fenced and secured by army patrols and the SBA Police. The majority of the families were army and worked at Episkopi garrison. The only advantage to Joy and the children of living in Mulberry Mansions was the open-air swimming pool at the bottom of the garden. It was hopeless for me, as I spent the working day at RAF Akrotiri and having returned home for tea would be called out to attend to a problem at the base, or to a patient at Akrotiri Hospital, two or three times an evening, a journey of thirty minutes each way.

Joy was anxious to settle the children at Akrotiri before the school year began in September. Simon and Helen would then attend Akrotiri Primary School, but Mark would have to travel each day to St George's Secondary School, which is situated on a hillside to the west of Episkopi Garrison with superb views of the cliff coastline. We paid the schools a visit the week after Joy arrived on the island. Like all British Forces schools abroad, they come under the care of the Service Children's Education Authority. Although we had been allocated a house at Akrotiri, the previous occupant had returned to the UK with his wife and would not be handing it over until his return to the island in October. So we moved into a bungalow at 14 Lowe Avenue at RAF Akrotiri on 4th August as a further temporary measure.

When the school term started in September, Mark caught a bus from the married quarters to St George's school and Simon and Helen walked the few hundred yards to the Primary school. By the time we moved into 19 Humphrey Road at the beginning of October, Joy was teaching 'O' level geography classes in the Education Centre to airmen and Senior NCOs who wanted to improve their chances of promotion. It is one of the happy outcomes of Service life that later she met many of her students again at Cranwell as they came on officer cadet courses during my time as Senior Chaplain there. Life was settling down after the upheaval of the summer.

However, Joy was not left in peace for long, for the Headteacher of the Primary School was a member of the congregation, and when he discovered that she was a teacher he asked her to join his staff. Joy explained that she was a secondary school teacher and was not trained to teach primary children, but he was not deterred. One Sunday morning, in a moment of weakness, she said that if she taught anywhere in his school it would have to be the top class. He declared that to be excellent, and so Joy began to teach ten and eleven year old children and found that she enjoyed it. She never returned to the secondary sector.

It was at this time that both Mark and Simon developed interests which were to play a big part in forming their life's work. When in Northwood we had bought a Sinclair ZX81 computer for Mark, and he quickly became adept at using it. Before long he began writing programmes for it and sent one or two away to Sinclair for them to use. Now, in Akrotiri, when the schools were being equipped with a BBC computer, we bought one for Mark to use at home. Little did we know that this would one day lead to his degree course in Business Information Systems, after which he would set up his own very successful company working on contracts in Edinburgh, Calcutta, Barcelona and Istanbul. Similarly, Simon's primary school teacher interested him in joining the War Games Club, run by a corporal. He

St Paul's Church, RAF Akrotiri

enjoyed the evenings he spent there with his friends, and continued his interest at Cranwell. After graduation, together with three friends from university, he established a company to market games which they devised, and today he designs and publishes games in America.

RAF Akrotiri and the RAF Hospital are located at the southernmost tip of the island, and are protected by a security fence across the width of the peninsula guarded by the RAF Regiment, and also by SBA Police, who control entry to the base. The station Church of St Paul stands at the junction of the playing fields with the main camp road, opposite the Astra Cinema, and has a hall and offices attached to it around a small courtyard. The office next to mine was occupied by the Chaplains' Clerk, Miss Thelma Sassoon, a Greek–speaking lady of indeterminate age and a lugubrious aspect. Despite her lack of obvious energy, she was in fact very kind, willing and helpful, and under the absolute domination of her aged mother. She had an on-going battle with Kris, the wizened gardener who tended the parched flower beds around the church: he was determined to ignore any instruction from a woman.

After three years in a lounge suit and clerical collar in central London, it was good to be back in uniform again, with the infrastructure of an airfield around me. RAF Akrotiri was a strange collection of lodger units. There was a helicopter unit, No.84 Squadron, combining search and rescue commitments for the RAF with operational sorties in United Nations markings for UNFICYP over the Green Line. There was a Royal and Electrical Mechanical Engineers (REME) workshop, which was invaluable for all kinds of odd jobs for the churches and leisure clubs. The Royal Army Ordnance Corps (RAOC) had a depot on the station; the Army Air Corps had a repair unit for their Alouette helicopters; there was an American detachment flying the U2 aircraft; and the whole was guarded by No.34 Squadron, RAF Regiment.

The airfield was constantly busy, not only with scheduled flights by RAF VC10 passenger aircraft from Brize Norton and the Hercules aircraft from RAF Lyneham, but by all types of NATO aircraft busy in the Middle East or in transit from all parts of the world. In addition, for six to eight weeks at a time the RAF fighter squadrons from bases in the UK and Germany came to Akrotiri on Armament Practice Camps (APC) when they were guaranteed good flying weather all day every day. Station life was vibrant and non-stop.

From April until October the working day began at 0700 and finished at 1330, when it became too hot to work in the open, although the airfield, where the temperature was often well above 40°C, was open to air traffic until 1500 most days. I spent much of the time in uniform shirt and shorts. From the outset I put in

With Dorothy Twiss, speaking to Sqn Ldr David Bills, OC No.34 Sqn, RAF Regiment, Cyprus.

place my practice of starting the day in church with Holy Communion and Matins, but had to delay the start until 0703 as the U2 took off each day at 0700 and the noise was indescribable. I created a small chapel at the west end of the church with nine chairs set out; it was more intimate and contemplative than using the whole building for a handful of weekday worshippers and made their reflection in the chalice more clearly defined.

My predecessor, Padre Brian Halfpenny, had gathered an amiable and devout group of worshippers into a regular congregation, and Dorothy Twiss had kept this very much alive during the interregnum, but the continual posting of families back to the UK meant that constant endeavour was necessary to ensure that new arrivals were visited and nurtured. Throughout my time at Akrotiri we enjoyed a vibrant church life: we had pancake parties on Shrove Tuesday, church picnics on Mount Olympus following a Sung Eucharist in the little church at Troodos on the Feast of St Paul, and joined with the RC and the CSFC churches to commemorate the Battle of Britain each September. I had appointed two churchwardens: Warrant Officer Don Bessant and Flight Lieutenant David Henchie, who had served on No.7 Sqn during my time at RAF St Mawgan. We had a thriving Sunday School and a good choir of adults and children.

BHL (with refreshment to heel) fielding for The Men v. The Ladies, St Paul's Church, Akrotiri

While all that was good and fulfilling, it was not enough. Since the early years of my ministry I have held the conviction that God did not call me to the priesthood merely to minister to Christian folk and 'keep the home fires burning'. From the time I first worked with men, in the steel works and elsewhere, who had not understood the Gospel of

Christ or who had decided to reject it, I felt compelled to be available to these lost sheep that had gone astray. I chose that word, 'available' carefully, for I saw my role as loitering with intent and befriending folk; to go in with bell, book and candle is, in my view, forced entry leading to trespass. Christ never forced religion on anyone; the rich young man who asked what he had to do to inherit the Kingdom of Heaven was almost brushed aside with, 'Keep the Commandments.' When the man said that he had done that since his youth, Jesus realized he was serious and invited him to give his wealth away and join him in his pilgrimage, but it was too much to ask and the man walked away. Jesus must have been very sad, but didn't go pounding after him; he watched him go. I took my cue from Jesus of Nazareth: he talked to anyone who would listen and enjoyed the company not of the Temple hierarchy, but ordinary men and women from all walks of life who knew they were sinners and in need of redemption. Similarly, I have always found myself in the company of the tax-collector in the shadows at the back of the Temple praying, 'Lord, have mercy on me, sinner that I am.' That is not pious humility: I have never been more serious.

So I put myself about for Christ's sake. Of course I could be found in church encouraging and leading the people of God who came to worship him week by week, but I was also to be seen at Happy Hour in the Mess, in the Rugby Club as its President, putting out to sea with the Marine Craft Unit, driving up the mountain to get alongside those serving in Troodos, putting on a 'Pub Night' in the REME Families Club with Joy at the piano, and generally enjoying the fun and esprit de corps that Service life offers. Once a month Joy and I held a drinks party at home for about thirty people from all sections of the station. There

Joy bowling for The Ladies v. The Men, St Paul's Church, Akrotiri

is no doubt in my mind that, by making myself available to the Holy Spirit of God in all kinds of ways, I was used by him. I offer as evidence the following episode.

Every Wednesday morning at 1000 I held a service of Holy Communion in the little chapel at the back of the church. Usually half a dozen people would turn up, and one morning I had just started, when a young woman in her early twenties came in and sat at the back with her shopping basket. I had not seen her before, and, as she did not take communion, I made it to the door before her after the service, and engaged her in conversation. She apologized, and said that she had no idea why she was there, for she left home to go to the NAAFI shop. As the NAAFI was in a totally different direction, I could understand her confusion. She then confessed to knowing very little about the church and took her leave. I called at her home in the afternoon and I suggested that she might like to attend the adult confirmation classes I had just started.

She joined the weekly class and found them interesting, so I called in at the Pathology Lab in the hospital and asked her husband, Tim, who had been an altar server as a boy, to encourage her and, perhaps, accompany her. In due course, she was confirmed in St Paul's Church by the Bishop of Cyprus and the Gulf, and Tim joined the choir. Just before I left Akrotiri he came to see me about ordination, and he was ordained to the priesthood in 1992. In 2009 Elaine was also ordained priest.

I also renewed my enjoyment of broadcasting with BFBS Cyprus. I went to the studios in Episkopi to record my sessions of 'Pause for Thought', but I was also taught how to use a recoding desk at the small studio at Akrotiri, and did some interviews there. I recorded an interview with the Chaplain in Chief, Glyn Renowden, during his visit, but my finest hour was a fifteen minute interview with former Battle of Britain pilot, Wing Commander George Nelson-Edwards, who lived in retirement in Paphos. He was a retiring, shy man, but, once I encouraged him to talk, the interview flowed so naturally that, when I faded out to 'Spitfire Prelude and Fugue' by William Walton, I knew that I wouldn't have to do any editing whatsoever. Not only that, but, when I handed my work to the producer in Episkopi, he and I were astounded to discover that it ran for exactly fifteen minutes. It went out on Battle of Britain Sunday as it was.

The Anglican Diocese of Cyprus and the Gulf was founded in1976 and, when Padre Len Ashton retired from the post of Chaplain-in-Chief of the RAF, he was consecrated bishop to work in Jerusalem prior to his appointment as the first bishop of the new diocese. Len had welcomed me into the Royal Air Force, and, although he had no jurisdiction over me, he now made me a most welcome member of the Diocesan Synod. The first meeting I attended was in May 1983, and was residential in a hotel in Kakopetria, on the northern slope of the Troodos Mountain range.

The members of synod were a friendly group drawn from the Gulf States, Iraq, Yemen and the chaplaincies in Cyprus. Late one evening we all trouped up the rough track behind the hotel in pitch darkness, following Bishop Len who declared that 'the nightingales will sing at midnight.' He was such a naturally amiable man that they did sing, and I have never heard such a sweet sound filling the night sky in the secluded valley. He was always a welcome guest in our home. I was honoured to be asked by his family to preach at his funeral in Chesham on 30th January 2001, when I was Rector of Caythorpe.

As the RAF personnel of No.12 Signals Unit at Episkopi came under the pastoral care of the army chaplains at Episkopi Garrison, and No.33 Signals Unit at Ayios Nikolaos was cared for by the army chaplains at Dhekelia Garrison, my first task was to visit the units at Akrotiri. Once that was done I turned my attention to my other main area of ministry, No.280 Signals Unit at RAF Troodos, another Retained Site near the summit of Mount Olympus. From the moment I arrived in Cyprus, I had the use of a Service hire car. They were called 'Z cars', for the registration plate was prefixed with the letter Z, and as the mountain roads were rather challenging, I was glad that my Strada was safe at Akrotiri.

I was always exhilarated as I set off on the forty-five minute journey to RAF Troodos, especially during the hot summer months. As the road wound its way upward, the temperature dropped and the air became fresh. I would often stop at a small taverna at Saitas for fresh orange juice and an elderly man would emerge from the cottage and bring a small plate of meze 'on the house'. Troodos is a small tourist village just over a mile high, with pine-filled clear air; the Signals Unit was on a bluff above the village with a fine view of the Radar Site atop Mount Olympus. By the time I had parked the car and climbed the steps up to the Mess I was in need of refreshment, and a coffee in the operations room was always available. The officer corps was a mixture of Air Traffic and Fighter Controllers under the command of a squadron leader.

At lunchtime we adjourned to the Troodos Hotel so that the Senior NCOs could join us. The Hotel was geared to the tourist market and was not exactly 5-star, with its corrugated roof. The owner was a Cypriot by the glorious name of Phidias Papapetrou, and who looked ancient when I first met him. Everyone called him Papa, and he called me Papas, the Greek for Priest. He was a splendid rogue who looked after 'my boys', as he referred to the RAF lads, with a generosity which knew no bounds. It was a happy unit and Papa was very much a part of the RAF community in Troodos.

I remember one occasion when I said to him, 'Papa, the board outside the hotel reads "Papapetrou Brothers", but I have never met your brother.' As tears filled his old eyes, I realized that I had touched a nerve and apologized at once, but he said,

BHL with Papapetrou at the Troodos Hotel

quietly turning away from the others, 'Papas, I'll tell you. In the bad days of EOKA we would look after our boys, and my brother would return from the mountain and advise them not to go back to Limassol by this road but to take that way. One day he was found shot in the back in the forest, by terrorists.' I put my arm about his shoulders and waited for the sobs to cease. Then he added, 'Do you know, Papas, for very many years his widow got a cheque from the British Government at Christmas.' Then he added with a smile, 'Only a small cheque, you know, but still.'

The Mount Olympus site was usually accessible only with snow chains during winter, and, during my first winter in Cyprus, snow completely covered the perimeter security fence. For this reason a long tunnel led from the main gate into the operations room. During the Turkish intervention in 1974 the shift on duty could see on their radar screens missiles coming straight at them followed by huge explosions outside; the Turkish aircraft were firing at the Cypriot television and radio masts on the adjacent peak.

It was great fun to go inside the huge golf balls which protected the radar heads. These massive pieces of equipment were constantly revolving, but it was possible to jump on the step and enter the cabin as it turned. The trick was then to throw your hat across the cabin to see it describe an arc before it fell to the floor. The view outside was breathtaking, with the Taurus Mountains in Turkey clearly visible, as well as the snow-capped mountain peaks of Syria and Lebanon on a clear day. The distance covered by the radar returns was, however, classified.

The personnel at this Signals Unit were always glad to see their Padre, and I had a great respect and love for them. The married quarters were hirings from local landlords, most of them in Platres. In this delightful village at about four thousand feet the air was not as thin as at Troodos, but the steep alleys between the main streets were known as Cardiac One and Cardiac Two. Life was not easy in this remote mountain village in winter, but they worked hard at maintaining a unit identity in the community. In 1983 I joined the CO's team in 'The Hogsback', a race around the mountain, which started and ended in the Troodos Hotel. To prevent it becoming too serious, it was in fancy dress and the rule stated that you had to drink a pint of beer at the half way mark. The entire 'race' was in thick mist swirling through the pine trees. As the CO, the Senior Ops Officer and I were dressed in choir robes, and the Adjutant in a monk's habit, we emerged out of the mist like phantoms, when we came upon the unit Land Rover with the Mess Sergeant in Mess Dress serving the statutory beer.

The Mess Bar was on the first floor, and, when the snow was deep enough, it was customary to jump out of the window into the drift beneath. For this bravery you

The Hogshead Race, Troodos, 1883. (Sqn Ldr Tom Haig, CO No.280 Signals Unit, looks heavenward as Mike Ashley, the Adjutant, wears the cowl

were given a certificate signed by the CO to prove that you had jumped from over a mile high without a parachute. It was too good to miss; I landed comfortably and collected my certificate. The following week the CO dug his staff car out of the week's deposit of snow in the car park below the Mess, only to discover that now it had a dent in the roof where I had landed.

Nearly all my station commanders were promoted to Air Commodore or above, and three of them became Air Chief Marshals, which illustrates how well I brought them on. The Chaplains beaver away year after year, on station after station, caring for service personnel and their families, but the station commander becomes a king for three years, and then goes back to his chosen discipline. This means that he relies on his specialist officers. He will be competent at running the flying programme on a front-line station, or the maintenance portfolio on an engineering unit, but more often than not he has had precious little training in personnel matters.

I have known chaplains who called on the CO weekly, to tell him how busy they were. The station commander expected us to be busy, so why waste his time? I

The Ven. Herbie Stuart, Chaplain-in-Chief (left), BHL, Group Captain John Willis, Station Commander (right) at RAF Akrotiri

chose to seek a meeting when I had some matter to discuss with him, or a concern on the station to share with him. The chaplain is the only officer who can do it with confidence; indeed, the chaplain wears 'relative rank' to allow him to be prophetic, and if a policy decision is impacting badly on a station, he can discuss it with the station commander without embarrassment on either side.

I had the good fortune to have as my Station Commander at Akrotiri Group Captain (later Air Chief Marshal, Sir) John Willis. Short in stature, he was a giant in his personality. He lived with his wife, Meryl, in Luqa House and was known and respected by all ranks. There were often complaints from officers and their wives that the aircrew visiting Akrotiri for the annual Armament Practice Camps made a nuisance of themselves by their noisy late-night parties. He made it clear to all officers on the station that he welcomed the squadrons arriving for the APCs, as it was one of the major tasks for the station.

However, like all good leaders, he looked after his people in return for their loyalty. On one occasion an APC squadron returned to the Mess from a night out in Limassol and when the President of the Mess Committee (PMC), who was having a quiet drink with his wife, reminded one of the young officers that he was required to wear a tie in the mess, the junior officer complained to his wing commander, the squadron CO, who ordered all his officers to remove their ties. He outranked the squadron leader PMC, who had no option but to leave and telephone the Station Commander, who immediately put the squadron CO in close arrest and ordered the squadron to return at once to their quarters. After a one-sided interview with John Willis the following morning, the squadron CO was escorted to the next flight to UK for an interview with his Air Officer. John Willis had no difficulty with discipline on his station.

On one occasion I called on him about some matter and saluted as I entered his office and went to sit down. It is the rule to remove your hat when seated, so I put it on the floor beside my chair. John rose from his chair and, looking at my hat, said, 'What is that?' 'It's my hat, sir.' 'Good heavens, Brian, it's a trucker's hat.' It was true that my hat had been around the world with me since I was first commissioned, and the peak in particular was rather grubby, but it was comfortable, and I had seen far worse knocking about in the Mess cloakroom. He came round and gave my hat a kick which sent it rolling under his desk. We discussed the subject which I was dealing with, and when I rose to leave I had to crawl under his desk to retrieve my hat. His PA came in at that precise moment and I heard John say to her, 'Padre's saying his prayers again.'

A few days later I was recounting this affront in the Mess at Troodos to a group of highly amused controllers, and one young Flying Officer offered to fetch a can of instant reviver from his room. He returned with it, and placing my hat in the middle of the floor in the anteroom, he shook the can vigorously and sprayed the peak of my hat. He explained that it took at least twenty minutes to work, so we all adjourned to the bar for lunch. An hour later we trouped back into the anteroom and, behold, my hat was pristine; it shone in the afternoon sunlight. I was delighted, and proudly picked it up off the floor. Then a loud gasp went up, followed at once by hilarious laughter, for the peak had remained on the floor; the wretched detergent had dissolved the stitching.

The following week I arranged a funeral for the hat and OC Personnel Services issued a formal Administrative Order in which the Station Warrant Officer was to provide an 'Escort to the Hat', OC No 34 Sqn RAF Regiment was to provide a firing party, Met briefing was to be at 0845 on the day of the funeral of the Hat, the Station Pipe Band was to play a Lament, and the Station Commander was to give the eulogy to the Hat. John Willis was delighted to be asked to take part in this jamboree, but the whole thing was scuppered by an alert caused by an act of terrorism in Beirut, so I flung the hat from the cliff top into the sea as if placating Poseidon in the manner of mariners.

By accepting the Presidency of the Rugby Club I made friends with a complete cross-section of the station, RAF and Army. We had two teams who played every Wednesday and Saturday from September to April, although in September,

Provision of an Aumbry in St Paul's Church by the REME Workshops. April 1985. Left to right: BHL, WO Tony Watson REME, two Cypriot craftsmen, Padre Ray Hubble (Assistant Chaplain-in-Chief), CO REME Workshop.

October and April I was always badgering the fire section to empty their water bowsers over the rugby pitches. Warrant Officer Bill McKay ran the bar in the club together with his wife Jess. Bill was also a member of the team. The officer i/c was Warrant Officer Mike Ball, who ran the Alouette Helicopter maintenance hangar, the 1st team captain was a teacher in the primary school, a REME WO2 captained the 2nd team and the coach was Captain 'Tug' Wilson, RAOC. Tug had been seconded to the Royal Marine Commandos during the Falklands War and wore the coveted Green Beret. A young pilot on his first APC, and rather the worse for drink, came up to him in the Mess one evening and said, 'What do you do, mate?' Tug looked down his broken nose at him and replied in his gravelly voice, 'Normally, I rip heads off, what do you do, son?'

Each year the Rugby Club organized a 10-a-side competition, which, for some years, was sponsored by Pepsi-Cola. I received a phone call one morning on a very bad line, but through the squeaks and crackling I discerned a voice asking, 'Do you arrange the Pepsi Tens?' When I replied that I did and asked his name, all I heard was. 'Captain ... crackle, crackle .. and I wish to enter a team.' I asked where he was calling from and to my astonishment he said, 'Sinai.' 'Sinai?' 'Yes, we are in the Fijian Army on UN duty.' Having stressed that we could not pay travel expenses I welcomed them. Three days before the competition the guard post rang me to say that a group of dishevelled men were asking for me by name. I went down to meet them in a minibus and brought them to some barrack accommodation I had scrounged off the Station Warrant Officer. They had caught the ferry from Haifa, and had walked up from Limassol in the heat of the day. They were enormous chaps, and went through to the final match against the Royal Marines. The stadium was packed to see this brutal game, but the Fijians could throw the ball the complete width of the pitch, and won with style. Joy and I entertained them to meals at our house, and, as they boarded the coach we had arranged to take them to the port, they called for Joy and me to board the bus to present us each with a Fijian ceremonial skirt-like wrap, while they sang a moving farewell song in their native language.

Having the hospital in my spiritual care certainly brought memorable moments. Joy and I were at a Ladies Guest Night in the Officers' Mess when a mess steward came up behind Wing Commander Tom Rodgerson, the senior anaesthetist, just as the soup was being served, and whispered to him. Tom rose, bowed to the PMC, and left. Ten minutes later the same steward whispered to Squadron Leader Ian Lowles, the consultant in Obstetrics and Gynaecology, and he, too, left. I confided in the lady sitting next to me that there was clearly an emergency in the Labour Ward. A fine steak was just put before me when the steward whispered in my ear, 'You're wanted urgently at the hospital, sir.' Ten minutes later I was wearing a surgical mask in a side ward, about to officiate at an emergency baptism for a very premature baby in an incubator. I looked over at Tom, a devout Catholic, and Ian, a member of my congregation, both similarly masked, all of us dressed in our Mess Dress with the gold braid on our sleeves shining in the lights, while the Staff Nurse, who was a faithful Presbyterian, assisted me. Afterwards, I had a word with the child's mother, an Army wife from Dhekelia, before we returned to the Mess in time for the Port. I am pleased to relate that the baby developed into a healthy child.

On Sunday, 23rd October 1983 I made a visit to the hospital in a far more sombre mood. The Station Commander telephoned me at home just before 0900 and asked me to go to the Ops Room at once for an emergency briefing. We were told that at 0620 a truck had driven into the lobby of the US Marine Headquarters in Beirut, where the driver, a suicide bomber, detonated his explosives, which were equivalent to 12,000 pounds of TNT. The force of the explosion collapsed the four-story building into rubble, crushing many inside. It was likely that a large number of the very badly injured survivors would be flown to Akrotiri hospital. I was asked to gather a team of chaplains together later in the day, not to visit immediately but to await invitation from the hospital.

As it happened, Joy and I were entertaining the chaplain from HMS Fearless and the chaplain of St Barnabas' Church in Limassol, Padre Des Sheppard, a former Assistant Chaplain-in-Chief, for lunch at home. In the event, only twenty-three of the more serious casualties came to Akrotiri, the remainder were flown to the US Hospital at Ramstein in Bavaria. That evening I went to the ward and spoke with some severely injured men, but one was improving rapidly. He told me that he had been manning a machine-gun post on the roof of the building when he saw the truck smash through the perimeter fence and race into the entrance below him. The next thing he remembered was sitting on the floor in the car park; as each floor had collapsed on the one beneath he descended with them. I prayed quietly with him as he remembered his less fortunate comrades.

The tragedies of the war in Beirut and in Lebanon as a whole cast a shadow over life in the Middle East during my time in Cyprus. In the autumn of 1983 HMS Fearless, a Landing Platform Dock (LPD) class vessel, patrolled off the Lebanese coast. In 1968, she was the venue for talks between Harold Wilson and Ian Smith over the future of Rhodesia, but her task in 1983-4 was to evacuate British nationals from the beaches in the event of an emergency. To do this the ship could partially sink itself at the stern, flooding the internal dock and allowing her landing craft to sail out and embark refugees from the beach, before returning with them to enter the stern and come right up to the edge of the vehicle deck for disembarkation.

She had been replaced on patrol by a converted container ship by the time an evacuation was required. When that day came, the Station Commander established a reception and processing centre in the Passenger Terminal building, and put me in overall charge of it. OC Admin Wing had responsibility for documentation, and arranged a row of desks manned by his personnel clerks. I was the interface between the RAF and the assembled representatives of other European and North American embassies and high commissions, and a few airlines. Royal Navy helicopters were airlifting people from the beach at Beirut to the patrol vessel, from whence a RAF Chinook helicopter ferried them to RAF Akrotiri.

The first Chinook off-loaded a group of Palestinians in flowing white robes. Those with UK passports and an address of a relation in the UK were taken to Larnarca Airport and put on a British Airways flight to Heathrow. Later in the morning I saw a young couple coming off the aircraft and noticed that the girl was in distress. I took them to one side and discovered that they had gone shopping in Beirut, saw a queue and joined it. Before they could protest they were in a helicopter on route to Cyprus. She was eighteen and terrified that her mother would assume she was dead. They had no passport and only enough money for the groceries for which they thought they were queuing. We could not take anyone into Lebanon, so I arranged for them to be given a sum of money, and a flight to Heathrow with a return to Damascus; that was the best I could do, but it didn't stem the flow of tears.

Meanwhile, the Station Commander was anxious that I wasn't moving on the Palestinians. I explained that they had no money and only an address in Berlin which couldn't be verified. He made it clear that he expected progress on the matter. The father in charge of them all looked so depressed and worried that my heart went out to him, and I assured him that all would be well, though I had no idea how I could improve his lot. As their little children were now hungry and tired, I arranged for them to have a meal and accommodation in a barrack block overnight. When the father gave me a hug and then relayed this to his large family in a torrent of Arabic a seven year old boy jumped up, hugged me and kissed me on both cheeks saying, 'Thank you for making my father happy.'

The following morning I drove them to the Lufthansa office in Limassol and explained the circumstances to the Cypriot desk clerk, but she would only issue air tickets to Berlin if I could quote an authority from RAF Akrotiri. So I wrote down the reference number of my Akrotiri Rugby Club fixture file dated the previous day, and suggested she seek confirmation from the German Embassy. She issued the air tickets and I put the family into two taxis bound for the airport. I had a Berlin postcard from the family two weeks later, addressed to 'The Chef', thanking me for my help, and Lufthansa never came back to me. When the Station Commander asked me what had happened to the Palestinians, I told him that he didn't really want to know.

The conflict in Lebanon continued and in December 1983 HMS Fearless reappeared in the Eastern Mediterranean. When she anchored off the coast of

Akrotiri, Joy and I were invited with other officers to a cocktail party on board. We boarded the Landing Craft at Akrotiri Mole and sailed the short journey to Fearless. It was strange to sail inside the hull and clamber out on 'dry land' deep inside the vessel. The ship sailed out to sea for Christmas Day. Although many people did as we did and invited members of the ship's company to join us for lunch, they were missing their own families and preferred to be at sea.

The following day, about 1030 in the morning, while Joy and Helen had gone to water the flowers in church, the door bell rang. Mark, Simon and I were still festooned in torn wrapping paper around the breakfast table. There were folk singing carols outside the door, and, on opening it, I gazed on the unlikely sight of four Royal Navy Officers from Fearless going strong with 'Hark the Herald'. Padre John Rawlings and the Bosun had been to our home before, but the Captain and the First Officer were welcome new guests. The Captain explained that they would appreciate making a phone call to their wives in the privacy of a land line. I was delighted to help them and offered them the use of the telephone in our bedroom.

They went up in turn and made contact with their families while I opened the 'bar' on the patio. Joy and Helen returned and joined in the party. It was late in the afternoon before the Captain called for transport back to the ship. He was so grateful that he invited me to go to sea with them for a week in January, when HMS Fearless was to be the first RN vessel to go alongside in the New Port at Limassol, thus enabling a majority of the ship's company to go ashore to celebrate the New Year. She would be sailing early on 2nd January, so it was arranged that I should join the ship for dinner on New Year's Day 1984.

As the Commodore was not embarked, I was given his cabin, just aft of the bridge. There were some similarities in the daily pattern of the chaplain's work, but also huge differences in that there were no families to care for, and I discovered a structured discipline in eating and drinking habits centred on the Wardroom. On the Tuesday a RAF Wessex helicopter from No.84 Sqn at Akrotiri landed on the afterdeck, the pilots giving me a 'thumbs up' signal as they saw me watching their descent. Since October 1983 the "USS J F Kennedy" had been diverted from its planned Indian Ocean deployment to cruise off Lebanon, after the Beirut barracks bombing. The Wessex had come to collect the Captain of Fearless for a conference on board the American carrier. During lunch in the Wardroom my parishioners asked if I would like to along for the ride. We took off for RAF Akrotiri where the Commander British Forces and the Station Commander clambered on board, and we were off again. As we approached the carrier I was astounded at its size: we taxied along the deck for ages, passing lines of aircraft.

In June 1984 I completed fourteen years service and was promoted to the relative rank of Wing Commander, which was a good excuse for a party in the

Mess. It also raised the question of my future, for my sixteen-year commission came to an end in 1986. Padre Glyn Renowden, the younger brother of my lecturer in Philosophy at Lampeter, had become the Chaplain-in-Chief, and Ian Thomas was his Staff Chaplain. After two Irish Chiefs, we now had a Welshman with a Welsh Staff Chaplain. I was invited to apply for a Permanent Commission to age 55. I discussed it with Joy, who said that whatever I wanted to do was fine with her. So I applied and was successful.

Our busy, eventful and colourful life continued, as the end of my three-year tour of duty in the sun drew ever closer. Most of the Service friends we had made on our arrival had already returned to new jobs in the UK. In June 1985 we gave our farewell parties, and the Church and the Rugby Club entertained us in kebab houses to Gozomees' (goes home?), as my posting to the RAF College at Cranwell was announced. We had enjoyed evenings out at the kebab restaurants throughout our time in Cyprus. Our favourite was Sylvanas, just outside the piquet post overlooking the salt lake. When Helen was about eight years old I made her a book of cheques, and she would solemnly write one and take it with the bill to pay for our meal. Gregory, who owned Sylvanas, is a gentle and kind man, and he accepted the cheque and gave her a receipt as I paid him behind Helen's back. When we went to the restaurant while on holiday with Helen and her family in 2009, Greg remembered her at once, and we had a lovely evening.

Padre Ron Hesketh had succeeded me as Staff Chaplain and he took a leaf out of my book and followed me to Akrotiri. Having handed over to him the church inventory and the files, on our 19th wedding anniversary we 'marched out' of Humphrey Road and had a welcome weekend in a 5-star hotel in Limassol. As we climbed on board the VC10 in the noonday heat of July, the cabin crew had to prize our fingers away

The Ven Glyn Renowden, Chaplain-in-Chief, with his wife Mary at 'the Rectory', Akrotiri, with Helen and BHL

to close the door for takeoff; we had enjoyed a very happy tour in Cyprus; Joy and our children were as brown as berries and they had become competent swimmers, and Mark and Simon were to miss the sail-board we had bought.

When I had received my notice of posting to Cranwell I called on a former St Theodore's man, and a former RAF colleague, Padre Brian Henry, who was then the Dean of the Cathedral in Nicosia, He had been a chaplain at Cranwell and said, 'My dear Brian, Cranwell isn't a posting; it's a state of mind.'

CHAPTER NINE:

The College of Knowledge

ERRATA:

Page 26. Line one should read: "...left to vent his spleen ..."

Page 35: For *Jackson's* Te Deum, read *Vaughan Williams*.

Page 75. Caption should read, "...No. 809 Squadron ..."

Page 101: Last para. For 'oxygen' read 'pressurisation' system.

Page 137. Caption should read, "Hogsback Race, Troodos 1983".

Page 139: For '*Luga House*' read '*Akrotiri House*'.

Page207. Para 2: delete 'Admiral of the Fleet', insert 'Field Marshal'

; still crowded, for the Commandant was playing light
is also word that he had locked the door to prevent
gh I didn't see anyone trying the door handle to check

e, and I had another month to do in Cyprus, I had
nnual Conference at Amport House, and to make final
otorcaravan which Autohomes were building for me in
anwell, John Daimond, had moved out of his married
I drove up to Cranwell in a borrowed car to take over
return to UK. All tasks completed, John had taken me
ficent College Hall Officers' Mess at the RAF College.

vith a balding RAF Regiment Officer, and, for some
ne, we were both wearing bar mats over our heads. I
standing alongside me asking what we were talking
annot enter the discussion unless you wear one of
returned suitably clad, and addressed the Regiment
d Padre, what are you talking about?' I explained to
he, that we were attempting to find a definition for
al Eric Macey had been keeping up with his officers

in sipping the sherbet, yet, having remarked that as Commandant he ought to
know something about leadership, he hardly paused for thought before saying,
'Leadership is getting someone to do something, which they do not want to do,
willingly.' Curly and I were dumbfounded as he returned to the piano. I have not
since heard a better definition of a leader.

In July we returned as a family from Akrotiri, and the Fiat Strada came back on
a RN Supply Vessel. We moved in to the quarter I had taken over at 19 Plantation

Road, Cranwell, and received our furniture out of storage in Northwood. Although we faced a vast green sward opposite the house, Helen played in the front garden, and when I asked why she didn't cycle along the pavement outside she said she didn't feel safe, for there was no guarded perimeter fence like Cyprus, and she had heard that there were wicked men in England who hurt little girls. We never know what children pick up from the media. Once the new school year began, Mark and Simon started in Carre's Grammar School in Sleaford and Helen went to the Primary School at RAF Cranwell. It wasn't long before Joy was asked to undertake supply teaching there, but soon she accepted a permanent appointment at Brant Broughton Primary School, about fifteen minutes drive away, and became the Deputy Headteacher there.

On Monday, 5th August, I travelled to Bagshot to collect our new Merlin motorcaravan. It had five berths and a shower room, together with the extras I had asked for; items like the safe bolted under one of the front seats, an extractor fan over the cooker, sliding side windows with fly-screens, an 'ice-alert' on the dash board, and a roof-rack with ladder. It handled well on the journey home to Lincolnshire, and it was the source of many happy holidays. Joy enjoyed driving it, and on one journey home from South Wales, once the children were asleep, she took over the driving on the M4 while I went aft to sleep for a while. I awoke as we approached Nottingham.

In October we continued our practice of welcoming people to 'The Rectory' with the first of a series of monthly Sunday Lunches. Wing Commander Martyn Steer, the Station Commander, asked me to call on him after our November lunch and said that the Commandant had sat on a stool in the fireplace during the lunch. I began to explain that it was the design of the lounge which had caused him to do that because he wanted to talk to everyone, but Martyn interrupted me. 'I have drawn the keys to another house for you to look at with a view to moving. It is a residence and it has just been handed back from the contractors after a complete redecoration following water damage.' I protested that we had only just unpacked our deep-sea boxes in Plantation Road, but when Joy and I went to view 6 Bristol House Road, we loved it, and moved in on 14th November 1985.

I saw at once that I had two major problems in my ministry at Cranwell: the sharp division between officers and other ranks, and lack of time to visit either side of the divide. This division was not a policy decision; it was just the way of life at Cranwell. The raison d'être of the College was to train and commission officers for the Royal Air Force. Senior NCOs are a vital part of the training team, but the College was, de facto, officer territory. This is exacerbated further by the geography of the campus. The officers' married quarters are adjacent to College Hall, whereas the airmen's quarters are half a mile to the east. Therefore, for an airman or SNCO to visit the chaplain's home he or she would have to walk across open spaces into the officer's 'patch'. It didn't happen as often as it had at my previous stations.

Sadly, the same was true of the C of E College Chapel of St Michael, which was situated right next to College Hall. Its outward appearance resembles a Fenland Pumping Station, and inside it is a vast hall designed for the cadet's graduation services. It had a small but excellent pipe organ, and an even more excellent organist, Air Commodore Charles Suttle, who was a retired Senior Director of Studies at the college. He was a lovely gentle, Christian man. In the middle of August I experienced my first Graduation Service; No.86 Course had concluded their course of training. The church was full of exuberant young men and women on one side, and their proud parents on the other. The Course Chaplain, Padre Frank Hutchings, preached a very pleasing sermon.

At the following Sunday morning service the large chapel had only about twenty people in the congregation, and a small choir of adults. In time, I recruited some NCOs and children to join the choir, but it took dedication to the task and a persuasive manner. I frequently lamented the long-lost St Christopher's Church. Until about 1960, before the construction of the present college chapel, the graduation services were held in a hanger church on the site of the present church car park, and there was a small station church dedicated to St Christopher, together with an office for a chaplain, on the south side of the main camp road, away from 'officer territory'. With hindsight, it should have been retained as the families' church; it would have been perfect.

My other main problem was finding time to visit the families in their homes. I thought I had solved that problem when, after the August graduation, one of the chaplains on the Specialist Entry and Re-entrant Officers' (SERE) course (the successor to the PQRE course I had attended at Henlow) was posted as my assistant at Cranwell, but such was the demand of the training programme that we were both heavily involved in lecturing to cadets and junior officers. In addition to the Department of Initial Officer Training there was a very large Department of Specialist Ground Training, which offered courses to engineering officers as well as to supply and movement officers. After 'graduating' from College Hall, many young officers stayed at Cranwell for these specialist training courses. Some of the officers selected for aircrew training also stayed on and joined No1 Flying Training School based at Cranwell.

All these post-graduate courses included lectures from the chaplains, and for this reason there was a team of us working together; usually a senior and junior Anglican chaplain, a Free Church chaplain with an assistant from time to time, and a Roman Catholic chaplain. I was fortunate in my colleagues at Cranwell. A Methodist minister, Frank Hutchings, was my Free Church colleague and Tony

Smith, from the Liverpool diocese, was the Catholic member of the team. Tony became a close friend, and we shared a similar irresponsible sense of humour, which often left us helpless in abandoned laughter. In addition to the lecturing, we each had our respective churches to organize with all the usual church commitments. There was hardly any spare time for visiting families.

When I became the Chaplain-in-Chief I remembered the negative effect on the pastoral care of families brought about by the demands of the teaching programme and I established a College Staff Chaplain to co-ordinate the chaplains' involvement with the teaching programme, thus allowing the station chaplains more time to carry out pastoral duties in addition to teaching. I appointed Padre Ian Thomas as the first incumbent in the post.

I had a succession of assistant chaplains, first John Betteley, then John Paddock and finally Graham Brown. I insisted that we all met in church at 0700 for Matins followed by Holy Communion. Sometimes we would be joined by other officers for the latter service, but more often than not it was just the two of us at prayer as we remembered the various units and streets of the campus. With my unhappy experience at Halton as a new 'sprog' in mind, I also made sure they got out and about the college and 'the parish', and I was delighted for them when they were posted to their own station once they had learned the ropes. For myself, I yearned for the fun and fellowship we had enjoyed at Akrotiri, when the church was vibrant and my priesthood in demand, and the station felt like an extended family.

The majority of our time was, without doubt, spent in the Department of Initial Officer Training with the new recruits. The officer cadets were divided into four squadrons, lettered A to D, and an 'R' (for Recourse) Squadron. There was also the shorter SERE Course for doctors, dentists, lawyers, chaplains, nursing sisters and officers retuning to the RAF. The chaplains' clerk, Mrs Jill Hodson, a discreet and efficient lady, arranged for each entry to have one of us as its course chaplain in rotation. This was quite a commitment, but it offered a tremendous opportunity for a chaplain to get to know a group of spirited young men and women. About 70% of the cadets had come straight from university, 20% from school or other employment and the remainder was made up of senior NCOs and airmen applying for a commission. So the majority of each intake was in their twenties, and eager to learn.

I found it extraordinary, but excellent, that on their second day in the Royal Air Force, all officer cadets in a new entry had to go to the church of their denomination immediately after dinner. This meant that while the Free Church chaplain had about thirty-five and the RC chaplain about twenty, I had nearly a hundred. I guessed that the majority of them hadn't been in a church for years, if ever, for the noise in the church when they arrived about ten to eight was full of excited chatter. I always wore a cassock for this initial meeting with them, and as soon as I appeared in the pulpit there was instant silence. I would speak for about forty minutes on the role of the chaplain in their squadron, and the part played by the church in Cranwell, before Joy, assisted by Helen, would appear with coffee and biscuits for all and sundry. For the next thirty minutes I mingled with them and chatted informally.

After this brief welcome to the squadron, all the chaplains appeared before them in uniform on stage in the lecture theatre the next morning and talked more about the role of the chaplain in the RAF in general. We lectured to them regularly in smaller groups throughout their time at Cranwell, but the chaplain allocated to a squadron had a far deeper and more intimate relationship with the group. I inherited my predecessor's attachment to 'B Squadron', but then I was allocated 'A Squadron' and I stayed close to them throughout their eighteen-week course.

After the 'Meet and Greet' in church on the second evening, I spent time in the squadron offices getting to know the squadron leader CO and his staff of Flight Commanders. The cadets on A Squadron were divided into fifteen flights, each commanded by a flight lieutenant. As they worked and lived as a flight, the role of the flight commander was hugely important. These junior officers were drawn from all branches of the RAF: aircrew, supply officers, air traffic controllers, administrators and engineers. There were some flight commanders who were given the job too soon after their own time at Cranwell, and had neither the wisdom nor the Service experience to encourage and educate the cadets in the ways of the RAF. Happily this was rare, and did not apply to 'A Squadron' at this time.

Joy and I always attended the Mid-Course Function when the cadets developed social skills, such as close-hosting visitors to the squadron, the Revue near the end of the course when nothing and no-one escaped the cadet humour, and the Graduation Ball after the Graduation Parade. I attended their training Dining-In Nights, and their final Dining-In. At one of these I arrived at the entrance to the Mess to be greeted by the Squadron CO with the words, 'Brian, RAF Valley is closed by fog and my guest speaker is stranded. Will you be the Guest of Honour? No, I can't ask that...' 'Of course I will' I heard myself replying. I jotted some jokes on the back of the menu during the meal, and all was well. I couldn't let them down. Besides, they hadn't heard my jokes. However, when the Mess Manager filled my Port glass for the Loyal Toast to "The Commandant-in-Chief", for such is the relationship the College has with the Queen, I drew his attention to the wine draining out of my glass all over the table. Swiftly and with style he removed the glass, which had been neatly drilled at the dental centre, muttering 'little buggers' under his breath.

Sir Frank and Lady Whittle arriving for a Graduation Service at St Michael's College Chapel, Cranwell

The Graduation Parade was always a moving occasion. Relations and friends will have travelled from all over the country for the event, and the graduating cadets will have rehearsed until every move was perfect and the drill sergeants were satisfied. As the Reviewing Officer marches on, there is a flypast of Cranwell aircraft, but at the end of the parade one of the flight commanders, who has a connection with a fast-jet squadron, will have arranged a more informal flypast of a couple of Tornado or Phantom aircraft; at one graduation a Vulcan flew over very low indeed. Then, as the new officers march off in slow time, while the band plays 'Auld lang syne', the Drill Sergeants march quickly to form two lines either side of the steps to College Hall in order to be the first to salute their students as they march into the building as officers in the Royal Air Force.

The graduating cadets of No.93 Course had a special guest watching their parade on Thursday, 19th June 1986. Sir Frank Whittle had received the Order of Merit from Her Majesty the Queen and had returned to Cranwell with his wife for a short visit. I met them at the church door as they came from the parade for the Graduation Service. There had been a flypast by a couple of English Electric Lightnings which had climbed vertically above the parade; the noise rattled the chapel windows. I asked Sir Frank if he enjoyed the parade, and, putting his hands to his ears, he replied with a broad smile that if he'd known what he was starting he would have left it on the drawing board.

The chaplains were tasked with teaching the sexual ethics and Officers' Confidential Orders part of the syllabus. Officers' Confidential Orders had to be signed by every officer on posting to a new station. They dealt with relationships between officers and other ranks of the opposite sex, and propriety between the sexes in mess accommodation. As the majority of the cadets were in their early twenties, and had been sharing accommodation in university for some years, I felt the instruction was rather too late. However, I was holding forth on this subject in a warm lecture room one afternoon when I noticed the eyes glaze over in my audience. I stopped abruptly and they re-focussed on me as I asked, 'Am I getting through to you?' There was an uncomfortable silence before an attractive young lady stood up and said, 'Padre, I cannot speak for the rest, but I know where I stand on this subject and I have long decided what I will and will not permit in my life; I think the Air Force is going over the top on this.' The others nodded in agreement, and I smiled. I could only agree with them. I urged them to read and sign the Orders anyway to make life smooth for themselves, and moved on.

Primacy of importance must go to the Leadership Camps. Camp One was held reasonably close, and was a week of exercises to develop leadership skills. Each flight completed a series of exercises while being led by a different cadet each time. Camp Two was longer and held in various training areas in the UK, from Otterburn in Northumberland, to Stanford Primary Training Area in Norfolk, to Catterick and Salisbury Plain. Due to my other teaching commitments at Cranwell, I could never attend the whole camp, but joined them for three to four days. It was at the extended Camp Two that I observed the leaders and characters emerge in the group. For the cadets it was a serious part of the course; a bad lead in an exercise could affect your chances of completing the course. On the other hand, a good lead could attract the attention of the flight commander.

I was walking with the flight commander behind a flight in Northumberland and commented that the chap leading the exercise was doing rather well. The flight commander agreed, and said quietly to another member of the flight, 'In a moment or two throw a rage and refuse to co-operate any longer.' Suddenly there was a shout from this man, 'That's it. I've had enough of this nonsense. It's all so stupid.' When the leader attempted to calm him down, the chap aimed his rifle at the leader and said, 'Stand on your head and whistle Dixie. Do it!' He had no option but to obey, so convincing was his recalcitrant colleague. This sight was too much for the flight commander and me, and we collapsed in laughter. The flight commander called a halt to the exercise, for the young leader had already demonstrated his excellent leadership qualities.

I attended an 'A Squadron' camp at Catterick Training Area during a particularly wet period. The accommodation for the officers at Catterick Garrison was full and so they were travelling each night to RAF Leeming, about forty minutes away down the A1. Flight Sergeant Price, the Welsh squadron flight sergeant with a voice like Windsor Davies, said to me, before they left Cranwell, 'Leave it to me, Padre. I will erect a 12 by 12 in the field for you. You do not want to be on the road all night with the officers.' I trusted him.

My Vauxhall Cavalier staff car squelched its way along the forest tracks and I found the camp in a clearing, largely by the smell of frying bacon. Entering the large Directing Staff tent, I was handed a steaming cup of coffee by the good flight sergeant. Seated at a long table along one side of the tent, half a dozen flight commanders waved in greeting as they filled in their records of the last exercise. Alan Price led me across the clearing to a tent marked 'The Chapel' in white chalk. I gasped as my eyes took in a full size bed with mattress and white sheets, an arm chair, and a writing table. An electric light bulb connected to a generator swung from the ridge pole. I was speechless, but Alan said, 'Anyone can live rough in the field, Padre, but not the RAF Regiment.' At 0630, after a good night's sleep, I heard Alan Price's voice, 'Careful with the Padre's water.' There followed a rattling of the tent canvas, and a cadet brought in a bowl of hot water for my ablutions.

The sun shone the following day, the first time for a week, and walking through a clearing near the cadets' tents I saw in a glade two female cadets, one with her long blonde hair released from her beret and as she tilted her head back, the other girl emptied a jug of water over her. I smiled, and she said, 'Padre, you have no idea how human I feel to have clean hair again.' I thought of my own daughter, and

Officer Cadet Camp at Catterick Training Area

my heart went out to these young people who were prepared to go through these rigours in order to achieve their goal.

During one 'A Squadron' camp the CO had invited the squadron officers' wives to attend for a day to see what went on, and included Joy in the invitation. It was no free ride, for they were to pretend to be a group of journalists who had to be guarded. For Camp Two, the squadron cadets were divided in two: one, 'Blue Force', representing the allies, and the other, 'Red Force', being the enemy. NCOs of the RAF Regiment attached to the squadron acted as 'special forces', and had the maverick role of throwing spanners into works. The wives were duly attacked with lots of smoke grenades, Thunderflashes and rifle shots, herded into a hut and rescued, all before a splendid lunch under the trees of the Stanford Training Area.

At the far side of the south airfield at Cranwell was an arrangement of single-storey buildings which were arranged inside to mirror the layout of a general office in a station headquarters. This was the office simulator, and for a few weeks in their course the cadets had to learn the RAF way of organizing files and procedures of documentation. I was roped in to enjoy some role-playing; I was a grumpy farmer complaining about low-flying aircraft, a splendid local planning officer, and, on one famous occasion, a lorry driver with an appalling stammer who had driven into the entrance barrier. The latter ended in the entire office erupting with fits of laughter and rather destroyed the teaching value of the exercise.

I would look forward to this informal way of helping the cadets to develop officer qualities, and I was in my element out in the field on camp with them; but the formal lecture room teaching was not my metier, and I disliked it intensely. Nor was I sure that this was an effective way to educate potential leaders of the RAF. The strength of Cranwell was born in the days when the cadets were in residence for three years and when they 'graduated' they were officers and gentlemen. When I raised such matters with the Commandant he agreed, but reminded me that the financial constraints of the training budget did not permit the luxury enjoyed in former times, and the shorter course was the best that could be hoped for with the money available. Of course he was right, but I still felt that the three-year course was not a 'luxury', but an ideal to be sought, and that Cranwell had become a sausage factory, turning out young men and women who achieved an amazing development in the short time they were with us, but who still faced a rapid learning curve when they moved on to their next stage of training.

The Senior C of E Chaplain at Cranwell was responsible for arranging a rota of chaplains in the area to celebrate Holy Communion each Thursday in the Airman's Chapel in Lincoln Cathedral. In this way I began my association with the cathedral, which has lasted until the present. The Dean was Oliver Fiennes, a most able and charming man. He arranged an imaginative service to mark the 800th Anniversary of the Enthronement of Hugh as Bishop of Lincoln. Archbishop Robert Runcie preached a brilliant sermon in the company of the Roman Catholic Bishops of Nottingham and Bruges. The clergy of the diocese lined the central aisle, and I smuggled Fr Tony Smith into the procession, for St Hugh had been one of his denomination.

The Commandant asked me to call on him and I discovered that the new Chairman of the Lincolnshire County Council, Councillor Zena Scoley, wanted her chaplain to represent the links which the RAF had with the county and had asked for me. When he had assured me that there was no political overlay in the appointment, I phoned her and asked what it entailed. On learning that it meant turning up in robes to say prayers before the commencement of the four full meetings of the council each year, and attending various dinners and receptions, I agreed at once. Then I discovered that I would be asked to preach in the cathedral at the annual Civic Service in July. On the day, Joy and I gathered in the Judge's Lodgings, near the Castle, and I walked with Zena in solemn procession to the cathedral which was packed with voluntary organizations and the great and good of the county. It was all very wholesome and most enjoyable.

Thus Joy and I came to know the county at large, quite apart from the RAF. We discovered a county with standards in public life and charming people. Zena and her husband, Peter, farmed at Martin. They are a delightful couple. Zena was a formidable Chairman of the County Council as she is very articulate and possesses a gift for assimilating a mass of detailed arguments, and then drawing out the salient points. She put a tremendous amount of time and effort into the job, and I saw that she commanded respect from all parts of the chamber. Joy and I became good friends of the Chief Executive, Dudley Proctor, and his wife, Adrienne. He was recovering from an onslaught when he tried to remove the Lincoln Imp from official notepaper and vehicles. He felt bruised by the experience and swiftly reinstated the image.

I was in my office preparing a leaflet containing the services for Holy Week and Easter in 1986 when Fr Tony Smith, my RC colleague, came in and looked over my shoulder. 'Hmm, Palm Sunday Procession, we do that. Mass of the Last Supper on Maundy Thursday, we do that. New Fire of Easter and Paschal ceremonies, we do that. Why don't we do them together?' I looked up at him and saw that he was serious. 'We must involve Frank', I said, and Tony agreed. Our CSFC colleague, Frank Hutchings was over in a jiffy, and we mapped out an ecumenical Holy Week.

All three congregations met near the Station Headquarter building on Palm Sunday for the reading of the Palms Gospel and the prayers, then we set off in a silent procession through the grounds before the CSFC folk turned off to St Andrew's Church, while the remainder continued across the main road, where the

RC folk turned to St Peter's Church, leaving my folk to enter St Michael's. As we filed into our respective church our unity was maintained by each congregation singing the same hymn: 'All glory, laud and honour.'

On Thursday, after the evening Mass of the Last Supper, my congregation joined St Peter's in walking to St Andrew's Church for the ceremony of the feet-washing. On Good Friday we all came together in St Michael's church. Paschal Candles were not in Frank's Methodist tradition, so on Saturday evening the C of E and RC congregations gathered in the car park between the two churches, and John Betteley, my Assistant Chaplain, lit the New Fire of Easter. Flight Sergeant Price had prepared the brazier with items regimental, for it went up with a 'Whoosh' and nearly set fire to my colleague. Then Tony and I blessed the two Candles and greeted the people with the Easter greeting: 'Christ is risen', and they replied, 'He is risen indeed.' For some reason I repeated it louder, again and again, until spontaneous applause broke out. It was quite remarkable. In this jubilant frame of mind we retired to our separate churches to celebrate the Easter Mass.

After the 11.00 Sung Eucharist on Easter Sunday, 11th May 1986, I brought my Merlin motorcaravan to the church for Wing Commander Trevor Bush and Flight Lieutenant Stephen Wood, my churchwardens, to check the mileage. Simon

Ecumenical Palm Sunday procession at Cranwell, 1987

Founders' Day at the RAF College, 1986. BHL, Fr Tony Smith, Dean of Llandaff (Preacher), AVM Eric Macey (Commandant), Frank Hutchings, Trevor Hoggard, John Paddock

and I were about to set off on a journey to Istanbul, and the church was raising money for charity by asking people to guess the return mileage. Our route would take us via Salzburg, Zagreb, Belgrade, Skopje, Thessalonica, Alexandropolis, and Keşan and so join the infamous Londra Asfalti into Istanbul. I planned to arrive on Friday. The following Sunday we would celebrate Holy Communion in the Merlin at Gallipoli before taking the ferry across the Dardanelles to camp at Troy, and then on to Pergamum, Miletus, Ephesus, and Kusadasi. We had great fun and extraordinary experiences, which would form a volume in its own right. It was the jaunt of a lifetime, so I was obliged to repeat it with both Mark and Simon some years later when we had 'downsized' to a large frame tent and a Ford Sierra.

Four times a year there were Sundays when the resident cadets paraded to church behind the Queen's Colour for the Royal Air Force College. This happened on Founders Day at the beginning of February, the Old Cranwellians Reunion Sunday in June, Battle of Britain Sunday in September and Remembrance Sunday in November. These were grand affairs with the College Band and Corps of Trumpeters in attendance, and a packed church. We took it in turns to invite guest preachers, but the organization of the church service was down to me. The morning concluded with the cadets forming up on the parade ground prior to marching off with the band, and then everyone enjoyed cocktails in the Rotunda of College Hall.

After several of these Colour Sundays, as they were known, I realized that while the College had a March, there was no College Anthem which could be sung at these formal occasions, so I wrote a three-verse poem which I titled 'Superna Petimus', the College motto, meaning, 'We seek higher things.' I took the script to Flight Lieutenant (later Wing Commander) Robbie Wilkinson who was then the Director of Music for the Band of the RAF College, but later became the Principal Director of Music for the RAF. I told him that I wrote the first line with a fanfare of trumpets in mind, but left the rest to him. He produced an excellent musical setting for my words, and it was first performed in the College Chapel. It was later sung in London by the St Clement Danes Choir with Robbie conducting the Central Band of the RAF.

In February 1987 the College celebrated the 25th Anniversary of the Consecration of St Michael's Church. I invited all the surviving former Senior Chaplains to attend, and they made a fine sight as we processed to the church from College Hall. Bishop Len Ashton and the Chaplain-in-Chief wore copes, and I wore the damask cope, which the Chapel Embellishment Fund had presented to the Chapel to mark the occasion, and for which Mr Richard Green, who had succeeded Stephen Wood as churchwarden, had donated a hood embroidered by the Royal School of Needlework with the College Arms. Dom Gordon Beattie had by this time succeeded Fr Tony, and he considered the ceremony very proper.

Holy Saturday, 18th April 1987 was the day when I fulfilled a life-long ambition. Ever since I saw the Tiger Moth aircraft flying over Port Talbot in my youth I had longed to fly in one. Cranwell Flying Club owned one, T 5493, and Flight Lieutenant David Mabbett, one of the flight commanders and a member of my congregation, offered to take me up. We took

Preparing for Takeoff in a Tiger Moth at Cranwell

off from the grass strip which was North Airfield, and flew over Sleaford to Heckington, where I took the controls. Under Dave's instruction, I dived steeply to build up enough speed, then I pulled the stick back hard and over we went in a succession of loops. This was real 'Biggles' flying, with the wind in your face.

At the end of July 1987 Staff Chaplain Ian Thomas telephoned to say that the Chief wished to see me urgently. It reminded me of the similar call which marked the end of my tour at Marham. I travelled to London the following Monday, convinced that I was being moved from Cranwell after only two years. I knew that the senior chaplain at RAF Lyneham was due for a move, so perhaps I was to replace him. Having been the staff chaplain you always know the score, or, at least, you think you do. As I was shown into the office I noticed two Welsh flags arranged on the Chief's desk, and Ian smirking in the corner. Glyn Renowden, the Chaplain-in-Chief, came straight to the point. Padre Harry Bourne, the Assistant Chaplain-in-Chief at Headquarters RAF Germany, had asked to take Premature Voluntary Retirement (PVR) and so some chaplains would have to move at short notice. Then he said, 'I am promoting you to group captain, and you are to replace him in Germany in October.' I was stunned.

Gathering my wits, I replied that I was honoured to be asked, but with Simon sitting the first GCSE examinations the following June, it was not a good time to move the family, so if he had anyone else in mind I would be happy to stay at Cranwell for the time being. Glyn Renowden stood up behind his desk and said, 'Lucas, do as you are told. I will explain to the Commander-in-Chief that you will begin your tour unaccompanied.' There was no further discussion and the three of us adjourned to a local hotel for lunch.

I spent a week with Harry in Germany at the end of September, travelling down to Ramstein and the RAF families scattered around that area in Landstuhl and Kaiserslautern, and doing useful tasks such as booking a British Forces Germany driving test. In the event, the posting slipped a few weeks, and I travelled out in the motorcaravan on Monday, 2nd November. For some months prior to this posting, OC Station Services Squadron had been asking for my tour expiry date, for my quarter was due to be refurbished and he wanted to fit it into the schedule. When it was announced that I was posted to Germany, but leaving the family behind for the time being, I was asked to move into a smaller house further along the road. So to avoid friction, we made yet another move at Cranwell into 10 Bristol House Road in the third week of October. We didn't know it then, but it was to be our last married quarter.

CHAPTER TEN:

The 'A' Team

Having parked my Merlin motorcaravan at the rear of the RAF Officers' Mess, I was allocated a room until an appropriate suite became available. For a few days Harry Bourne and I went through the files and completed a hand-over. He was leaving the Royal Air Force the moment he left Rheindahlen early the following morning and was driving straight to his house in the UK. I felt that it was rather unsatisfactory for his military service to end with the clanging of the back gate, so, having ascertained that he was leaving at 0700, I was up in good time the following morning, and dressed in No.1 Dress Uniform. As Harry came out with his suitcase to climb into his car I was able to thank him for his ministry and salute him as he drove away into civilian life.

An Assistant Chaplain-in-Chief (ACC) is, indeed, an assistant to the Chief, but the bulk of his work is spent at a command headquarters leading the team of chaplains in that command and advising the Commander-in-Chief on chaplaincy matters. It carries a responsibility delegated from the Chief. Thus, apart from the quarterly meetings of the ACCs in the Chief's office in MOD, the rest of my time was spent in Germany. Unlike the majority of RAF chaplains, I had never served in RAF Germany, but I knew the chaplains stationed in the command and knew that I had a good team.

Rheindahlen was a Joint Headquarters, and was more like a medium-size town than a military base. It was so huge that there were German road signs with the three letters JHQ at the approaches. It was originally the HQ of the Northern Army Group, 2nd Allied Tactical Air Force (2ATAF), British Army on the Rhine (BAOR) and Royal Air Force Germany (RAFG). It was a mix of administrative buildings, living quarters, shops and other areas typical of civilian towns. There was a medical and dental centre, several primary schools, one secondary school, which had a boarding house, a travel agent, banks, a filling station, a restaurant and cafes.

Padre Bob Bailey was the RAF Chaplain, and he and his wife, Sue, were very active in the community. The whole complex was fenced in with check points at the three exits. Within a five-minute drive there was the RAF Hospital at Wegberg, where Padre Steven Collis and his wife, Cath, kept an open house. Steve also provided chaplaincy cover at Decimommanu, a NATO bombing range in Sardinia.

The Headquarters building itself was an enormous office block. The western end was the home of RAF Germany, the eastern end housed BAOR, and the central bulk of the building accommodated the NATO formations of the army group and the 2nd Tactical Air Force. The Command Chaplains' offices were on the second floor of the RAFG end. I had a secretary, Jackie, the wife of a warrant officer, and I shared a clerk, Helga, with my CSFC and RC colleagues. Helga was a German lady who possessed a great sense of humour. She had married a British serviceman, now retired, and they lived in nearby Möenchengladbach. The CSFC chaplain was Desmond Harvey, a delightful Presbyterian (who became ordained in the Church in Wales after his retirement). My RC colleague was Tony Smith from Cranwell. I couldn't have wished for better chaplains, and we made a very happy headquarters team. They were called Command Chaplains, but were primus inter pares with the few commissioned chaplains they had in the command; in most of the units they relied on officiating chaplains from the civilian church.

I realized at once that, in such a relatively small and tightly knit command, there was a danger of the Assistant Chaplain-in-Chief getting under the feet of the chaplains. As a chaplain, I would have resented that, and with such a team of thoroughbreds, I knew that that they would also find it irksome. So I determined that, apart from staff visits, which I was obliged to carry out once a year, I would keep out of their hair, and only visit stations when I was invited. I found it difficult; when a chaplain rang up to ask about something or other, and ended by saying that he had to go to a Confirmation Class, or Choir Practice, I had a wistful longing to be similarly engaged with folk. I had no reflections in a chalice of my own.

I did, however, have personal responsibility for dispersed groups of RAF personnel, in very attractive locations. Twice a year, in December and June, I visited the NATO Headquarters known as BALTAP (Baltic Approaches) in Viborg, Denmark. I would drive from Rheindahlen as far as Flensburg in North Germany, where I always stayed in a pub called the 'Swartzer Walfisch', the Black Whale, situated in a dark alley near the harbour, and as I arrived at night, I wouldn't have been in the least surprised to see Black Dog lurking in the shadows, or hear old Blind Pew tap-tap-tapping his way up the alley. The following day I continued my journey across the border to stay in the smart Missionet Hotel in Viborg. At the December visit the main street of Flensburg was always awash with Gluwein, and there were the usual Christmas parties and Carols, as well as the Communion Service, to be enjoyed at Viborg.

Twice a year I paid a visit to the RAF folk attached to the NAMMA and Eurofighter teams in Munich, where I borrowed a US chapel for Holy Communion services and Christenings. Once a year I flew with Steve Collis to Cagliari, in Sardinia, to visit Decimommanu. We stayed at a hotel near the Quartu Sant-Elena, which is where the majority of the RAF families were accommodated. On one occasion the Italian Base Commander gave a Pranzo in my honour. It was the most extraordinary meal I have ever enjoyed; it seemed to last for hours, as course after course was put before me. A kind Italian Air Force officer sitting next to me quietly advised me that I did not have to finish every course.

Once a month I travelled south to Landstuhl, near the huge US Air Force Base of Ramstein. There was a Royal Air Force unit headquarters under the command of a wing commander, and his team administered the RAF personnel and their families. The airmen and Senior NCOs and their families lived in large blocks of flats in Kaiserslautern, while the officers' families lived in a block of flats in Landstuhl. I would arrange a service of Holy Communion in one of the apartments in Kaiserslautern, and the following evening in St George's on the ground floor of the flats in Landstuhl. For the rest of the week, St George's was 'The George', a bar run by the officers as a community club for their families. Once a month Squadron Leader Peter Hereford rearranged the room to serve as a chapel for an hour, and he would put a notice advertising the Communion Service in the lift. It was at 1800, so some of the officers would arrive in uniform straight from Ramstein.

During the day I visited sections at Ramstein, including the BX (Base Exchange, a US kind of NAAFI) where everything to make the American serviceman feel at home could be bought, from Weber barbeques to Ski and Golf equipment, and all at duty-free prices. Little wonder that RAF personnel stationed there had a permanent smile. The steaks which were served for lunch in the Officers' Club would feed a family of four in UK. I always included a visit to the RAF personnel at Birkenfeld, about thirty minutes away, where the nature of their work was classified, so we met in a small community hall. One of the wives would also arrange a coffee morning at each of these locations, so that I could meet as many families as possible. I always had to take a big box of NAAFI bread for them, as well as Baked Beans.

This was all very well, but what was my role? There was no job description for the Assistant Chaplain-in-Chief. I was responsible to the Commander-in-Chief, RAF Germany, for the provision of chaplaincy services to the command, and to the Chaplain-in-Chief for ensuring that such provision was properly carried out. All that didn't help me very much; it merely expressed the line management. I had observed other Assistant Chaplains-in-Chief over the years, noting their strengths and their weaknesses; well, what were my strengths, and what were my weaknesses?

I am well aware that I am not a theologian; if the chaplains are looking for a biblical scholar, I am not their man. Neither can I be called a 'man of prayer', though I pray all the time. On the other hand, I know Christ, and his love for me. If the chaplains are looking for a priest who stands on firm foundations, then I might be of help. I determine to love my chaplains and their families, and to be myself. I resolve not to be dazzled by the scrambled egg on my hat, but to remember always the Chaplains' Branch motto: 'Ministrare non Ministrari', which may be translated as, 'To serve not to be served.' The chaplains know of my adherence to catholic doctrine as laid out in the formularies of the Church of England, but it was my purpose to enable them to conduct worship according to their own tradition, as long as it was mainstream Anglican.

Having saluted my farewell to Harry Bourne on the Thursday after my arrival, the following day I travelled with two officers from the Personnel Staff to the Bellaria Hotel in Bad Tolz, a spa nestling in the Alps to the south of Munich, for the weekend of Remembrance Sunday. It was the responsibility of the Assistant Chaplain-in-Chief to officiate at the annual Remembrance Service in the Commonwealth War Graves cemetery at nearby Durnbach. The great majority of those buried in this cemetery are airmen shot down over Bavaria and Austria, and brought from their scattered graves by the Army Graves Service. The remainder are men who were killed while escaping from prisoner of war camps in the same areas, or who died towards the end of the War on forced marches from the camps to more remote areas. The huge cemetery contains 2,934 Commonwealth dead of the Second World War, 93 of whom are unidentified.

The Commonwealth War Graves Cemetery in Durnbach, near Bad Tolz in Bavaria.

The UK Consul-General was to read the lesson in German, and the Lande President of Bavaria would read the same lesson in English. The British Defence Attaché from Bonn, an air commodore, would lay a wreath on behalf of the Air Force Board. We had a rehearsal on the Saturday and the Sunday dawned bright and crisp, with fresh snow in the clearings in the forests. The American Air Force provided a contingent of men, so did the Canadian Air Force, and they were joined by the RAF Regiment and the Luftwaffe Band.

On Remembrance Sunday we all went first to a German war cemetery at Gmund, where the same four contingents paraded, and a salute was fired by a German Alpine Pioneers Corps, using ancient muskets which covered us all in ash. The service at Durnbach was very moving and went smoothly. It was attended by several hundred people from Munich and the surrounding towns, and very many wreaths were laid. About half way through a smartly turned-out officer in army uniform stepped forward from the back of the crowd, laid a wreath and saluted, then disappeared into the crowd again. I learned afterward that he was a Major in the Special Air Service, and appeared each year as if from smoke. The evening was spent with the air commodore in an Italian restaurant in Bad Tolz and we returned to Rheindahlen the following morning.

The first week on my own was spent passing the British Forces Germany (BFG) Driving Test, obtaining BFG licence plates for the Merlin, and having my official photograph taken for the Commander-in-Chief's file. Then on the Friday I was invited by Padre Noel James to join him at Happy Hour. Noel and his wife Mollie were at RAF Bruggen; both were from South Wales and were generous in their hospitality.

Before November was out I flew to Berlin to install a new chaplain at RAF Gatow. I remembered from my own experience, that the last thing you wanted to do when arriving in a new station, especially overseas, was to host the boss from command headquarters. So apart from a rehearsal on the Thursday morning, I took my meals in the mess and spent the rest of the day exploring the museums of Berlin, and the scandal of the Wall. The Installation in the evening was well attended and the Station Commander formally presented Ian Greenhalgh, so that the direct link with the station executive was made clear. After a Dining-In night at RAF Gatow on the Friday, I returned to Rheindahlen on the Saturday. On Sunday I drove to UK and home.

My purpose in returning to UK was to attend to another part of the job, that of being an Assistant Chaplain-in-Chief (ACC). When I was Staff Chaplain I had to produce a postings plot for the quarterly meetings of the Assistant Chaplains-in-Chief; now I was on the other side, wickedly trying to unstitch the work of the Staff Chaplain. But Ian Thomas had done his work well and it was watertight. We met in the Chief's office in Adastral House, and I found it strange going back to the familiar corridor as a visitor. I was greeted by my colleagues from the other two commands, Brian Halfpenny at Strike and Roger Kenward at Support, as well as John Daimond, the Principal at Amport House and Mike Stokes, the Resident Chaplain at St Clement Danes, who had been my predecessor as Staff Chaplain.

We sat around the table, and worked through the agenda, discussing matters ranging from recruitment to synodical government of the church. Each ACC presented a report from his area of responsibility, before we adjourned to St Clement Danes church for Holy Communion at 1230. After lunch we turned to the approval of the posting plot. It was an opportunity to become actively involved in defining policy for the Chaplains' Branch. It was a chance to fly a kite for your particular 'good idea'. Usually, it was quickly shot down by the Chief or one of your colleagues, but if you had prepared well and were skilful in debate, you could often make your kite dip and dance and stay airborne long enough to be accepted.

That November was not exceptional in the amount of travelling: it was the norm. Early in December I returned to Germany and paid a visit to RAF Gutersloh, and RAF Jever, before travelling to Viborg in Denmark, then visiting Padre Phil and Christine Mortimer at RAF Laarbruch, and fitting in a weekend in Ramstein, before moving into a suite of rooms in the Mess and then returning home for Christmas.

It was in February that I held my first formal meeting of the RAF Germany chaplains. Padre Douglas Sirr, who was the chaplain at the Headquarters Allied Forces, Europe, in Brunssum, Belgium acted as the host, in a Headquarters building which had once housed the offices of a coal mine, or so I was told. It was during this meeting that the chaplains called themselves the A Team; and so they were. Douglas was a large, gentle Irishman, and both he and his wife, June, were loved and respected by us all. I subsequently held these meetings quarterly to report back on the proceedings of the ACC's meeting in London and to impart any strictures of my own and to discuss matters pertaining to our work in Germany.

In these ways my life in Germany was occupied fully; working for and caring for the chaplains in my care, with an occasional rebuke when required. New station commanders were obliged to call on the Assistant Chaplain-in-Chief as a part of their arrival procedure in the Command. This was an opportunity to get to know them, but far more important was the chance to explain to them how to relate with their station chaplains, what to expect from them and how to ensure that their chaplains had the necessary funding and resources to carry out their ministry.

I missed the family, particularly at weekends when I wasn't involved at any of the station churches. The chaplains were kind, and said that I had only to ask to be invited instantly to participate; but I remembered my decision to keep out of their hair and let them exercise their own ministry. I would drive south to the Ahr Valley, or park the motorcaravan along the Mosel, and sit on the grassy bank and watch the river wind its way in its deep valley towards Piesport. If the weather was poor I would spend the weekend reading or listening to music in my rooms, sometimes calling on Fr Tony Smith for a 'sundowner'. Group Captain Alan Bridges, who had commanded RAF Wittering near Peterborough, and was now a staff officer at the headquarters, lived across the corridor from my suite. He, too, was good fun and excellent company.

Wednesday, 27th April 1988, saw the chaplains assemble outside the Mess at Rheidahlen at 0830 to board a minibus bound for Gutersloh and Braunschweig, near Hanover. I had arranged a quarterly meeting of the chaplains at RAF Gatow in Berlin. Padre Tom Goode, who was the chaplain at RAF Gutersloh, the nearest Royal Air Force base to the East German border, was arranging lunch for us in his Mess, and Padre John Roberts, the BFBS chaplain, was tasked with collecting cans of beer (code name 'Prisoners') for the train journey; for after lunch we were travelling to Braunschweig to board a military train in time-warp, which was operated by the Army and which ran every day through East Germany linking Berlin with the West.

The day before I had attended Joy's mother's funeral in South Wales, and had driven my Merlin through the night to arrive in Rheindahlen at 0645, just in time for a shower before greeting the team. Once we left Rheindahlen, our driver made such progress that we arrived near Gutersloh with time to spare, so we made a halt at an alehouse for refreshment, and so arrived at Gutersloh at the appointed time. After a good lunch, we climbed aboard the bus, John Roberts dragging a suitcase full of 'Prisoners' behind him, and we set off again to join the train.

'The Berliner' was the name of the British Military train. My comment about time-warp was because it was redolent of the Orient Express in its heyday, with Wagon-Lits Pullman saloons and dining car. But it had a British Army organization, so the officers' coach was allocated in order of rank: the first compartment was solely for me, the next for the two wing commander chaplains, and the next compartment for the squadron leaders, and Nick Heron had one to himself as the new flight lieutenant chaplain. But as I insisted on having custody of the 'Prisoners', everyone crammed into my compartment. The doors on all coaches were locked and chained to prevent East Germans forcing an entry to escape to the West, and the train was patrolled by soldiers of the Berlin Infantry Battalion.

At Helmstedt, the last station in West Germany, the locomotive was uncoupled and an East German engine coupled up for the journey through East Germany to Potsdam. At this point the Train Warrant Officer came to collect our Identity

Cards for inspection by the Russian authorities at Marienborn. He was offered, and accepted, a beer as we talked about his work on the train. Suddenly, as the train slowed, he remembered that he had yet to collect documents from the remainder of the passengers, and he dashed off. At Marienborn the train came to a halt in the middle track of the station while the Officer in Charge of the train, a Captain, with the Warrant Officer and an interpreter, disembarked and marched smartly along the platform. As they arrived at the guard room, two Soviet soldiers emerged; the party all saluted together, and went inside the office closing the door behind them. I am told that there was usually much bonhomie and Vodka behind the closed door, but this was never evident to the passengers on the train.

Sometime after the train had passed Magdeburg we were called for dinner, and we passed along the corridor to the Dining Car, with its tables laid with crisp white napery. Dinner was served in four courses and was excellent; we had to pay for the wine from a very good list. As we enjoyed the meal, more wine was ordered, and the only other diner, a man about my age, was included in our fun. By now, the chaplains were in high spirits, and there was a whoop of joy when our friend, the Warrant Officer, came in with a tray held high bearing glasses of a ruby liquid and calling out, 'Potsdam Port on the Royal Corps of Transport.' Sure enough, the train had stopped at Potsdam for the East German locomotive to be exchanged for

The 'A Team' at RAF Gatow, Berlin. Left to right: Ian Greenhalgh, Tom Goode, Noel James, John Roberts, BHL, Nick Heron, Ian Thomas, Steve Collis, Martin Loveless, Douglas Sirr. (Absent—Bob Bailey & Philip Mortimer)

a West German engine for the final run into Berlin. We toasted the Royal Corps of Transport.

Still the train waited, and there was another roar of applause as Padre Noel James came in bearing a tray of glasses and calling out, 'Potsdam Drambuie on the RAF Chaplains' Branch.' 'That's my boy,' I thought, as we toasted the Branch, including our fellow traveller. 'The Berliner' left the 'corridor' just after Potsdam and, passing through the Wall, made its way to Charlottenberg Station in Berlin, where we disembarked. Our fellow traveller turned out to be the Colonel responsible for the operation of the train, and as he weaved his way along the platform called back, 'Best journey I've ever had on the train.' There was more sobriety during the journey back on the Friday; but not much.

I made many visits to Berlin during my tour, usually by air, although when my son Simon came out for a short visit, I took him on the train for him to appreciate a divided country as we made our way through the Soviet zone. Berlin was divided into four zones which were occupied by France, USA, UK and Russia, and as a member of an occupying power I was permitted to cross from West onto East Berlin via Checkpoint Charlie provided I wore RAF uniform. My car was always held in the checkpoint with the windows closed, while the East German guards kept asking for my papers. We were forbidden to show them any document; we just stared ahead, until they lifted the barrier, for we had a right to enter any of the zones. I was moved by the monochrome buildings in the Soviet Zone, and the queues for such meagre offerings in the shops.

On many visits to Berlin my programme included a tour of the city by a German on the Public Relations staff named Werner. He would drive visitors to see the sights and chat in an easy manner about what they were doing and how long they were staying in Berlin. On one occasion he took me to see the Glienicke Bridge, which spans the Havel River to connect Berlin with Potsdam in the Soviet zone. In 1962, the U.S. released the Russian spy Colonel Rudolf Abel in an exchange in the centre of this bridge for pilot Gary Powers, who had been captured by the USSR following the U-2 Crisis of 1960. As we stepped onto the bridge a West German guard stood before us ordering us to keep off the bridge. Werner brushed him aside, saying loudly as he pointed at me, 'Officer of the occupying forces.' I felt most uneasy at his description of me, but the guard melted away, and we strode to the white line which marked the border between East and West Germany. When I returned to the city after the Wall had been demolished and Germany was re-unified, I asked for Werner, only to be told by the Station Commander that he had been arrested as a double agent.

Later that spring, Padre Glyn Renowden and his wife, Mary, paid a staff visit to the Command and I arranged a programme for him. When we were alone in the office he asked me what arrangements I had made to bring the family out. I explained that I had a married quarter booked for July, after Simon's exams. He then revealed that I was pencilled in the postings plot to return early from Germany the following year to look after Support Command, and that I might not wish to move the family for such a short period. It was a very kind thing to do, for Joy and the children would have moved to Rheindahlen in July, only to return the following April to Brampton, near Huntingdon. I cancelled my application for a married quarter and the Chief advised the Commander-in-Chief.

When the quartering authorities at Cranwell discovered my change of plan, the pressure increased for me to hand over the house to which I was no longer entitled. I returned to UK for the Annual Conference, and while at home Joy and I made the decision to buy a house of our own. During another visit I obtained a mortgage from the bank and one weekend I drove home and we toured the local area looking for a detached, freehold house. We found our present home on the market, had a look at it, and shook hands with the vendor. The following day I telephoned the estate agent from the Mess in Rheindahlen, and made a formal offer for the property. It is not the best way to buy a house, but my time in UK was limited. We moved in to 6 Arnhem Drive, Caythorpe, in September 1988, and I returned to Germany to complete my tour of duty.

Surprisingly soon it was November again, and time to return to Bavaria for the 1988 Remembrance Sunday weekend. I decided to add a few days leave to the beginning of the weekend. The Merlin had been sold to raise additional funds to cover our house purchase, so I drove in my new Ford Orion to Vienna for a few days. When I arrived at Bad Tolz on the Friday, to join the rest of the team, I walked into the Hotel Bellaria to be greeted by the owner, 'Herr Bürgermeister has arrived', and a glass of Jägermeister was waiting for me on the bar. The previous year I had enjoyed that particular schnapps, but could never remember the name, so I called it Bürgermeister; hence my nickname in that hotel.

After the Saturday rehearsal, I drove Squadron Leader Bob Hunt, his wife, Angela, and Flight Lieutenant Hugh Henderson to see the castle at Neuschwanstein, built by the mad King Ludwig ll. Then we caught the relay of cable cars to the top of the Zugspitze, at 9721 feet, the highest peak in the Bavarian Alps. The Remembrance Service at Durnbach went very well, except that the weather was in severe contrast with the year before, and rain poured down on the parade. After lunch in the German Army Caserne in Munich, we were invited to drinks by one of the Munich based officers. Later that evening we retired to the Italian restaurant with the Defence Attaché for a convivial evening.

As soon as I awoke on the Monday morning, I knew I was in trouble. I had become blind in my right eye. Trembling, I shaved and dressed, and went outside into the daylight. There was only a narrow slit of light at the top of my right eye, the rest was black. I had to drive back to north Germany, so I drove as far as the corner and realized it was hopeless, and re-parked my car. I went back into the hotel, met Bob Hunt coming down for breakfast and explained what had happened. Hugh Henderson had travelled down with them, so it was agreed that Hugh would drive me in my car back to Rheindahlen.

We set off, and, once we had skirted Munich, I telephoned my office from an autobahn rest area, and asked Helga to alert Wegberg Hospital that I was on my way. Hugh was marvellous and we made good time. I arrived at the ophthalmic department at 1600. Ten minutes later I was being examined by the surgeon, who diagnosed at once that my retina had torn at the top of my eye and was hanging down. He allowed me to go to my room in the Mess to collect personal kit, but warned me to walk softly. Hugh came with me and drove me back to the hospital, where I was admitted, and then he returned the car to my garage behind the Mess.

My eyes were bandaged and for the next four days I had to lie on my back, in the hope that the retina would fall back into place ready for the surgery. At least I had a private ward, so I was in peaceful quiet. For the second time in Germany, and this time more forcibly, I was reminded of Blind Pew of Treasure Island infamy. The four days extended a little, as specialized equipment had to be flown out from a UK hospital. I was not allowed visitors except that each evening Padre Steve Collis came in to read Evening Prayer with me, and I joined in the prayers I knew by heart. I shall always be in his debt for that great kindness, for it kept me in touch with the church at large and with my spiritual self. At last all was ready, but the evening before the operation to attempt to save my sight, after Steve had left, I experienced a huge sense of loneliness, such as I never wish to know again. By reciting the Jesus Prayer over and over, I drifted into sleep.

When I awoke in my little ward, everything was black, and raising my hand I felt the bandages, and relaxed. Mr Morgan, the surgeon, was of the opinion that he had been successful, but would not know until the eyes had settled. So it was another week of blackout and lying on my back. One of my worries was that the Bishop to the Forces was visiting Germany, and I should be escorting him, but I had delegated that to Douglas Sirr when I phoned Helga from the autobahn. It was shortly after the operation that he came with Douglas to visit me, and though I couldn't see them, it was good to have a chat about his visit and to praise 'my' chaplains. Brian Halfpenny, who had recently succeeded Glyn Renowden as Chaplain-in-Chief, also paid a visit, and although he was only allowed five minutes, it was a great lift to my morale. Meanwhile, Mr Morgan came from time to time to have a look at my eyes, but without opening the lids.

I was usually awake by the time the BBC World Service handed over to Radio 4, and I grew to love the tune 'Sailing By', which marked the switch-over, because at that time every morning the same two young nurses came in to change my eye dressings. They were always cheerful and joked with me as with great tenderness they would bathe my eyelids and then replace the blackout. They came in one morning, after some weeks, and announced that Mr Morgan had said while my left eye should remain bandaged to avoid eye movement, they could remove the dressing on my right eye and I could try to open it. All three of us held our breath as I slowly opened the eye. 'Oh!' I said, 'You are beautiful!' 'I'm not that good, Padre', she joked. 'Yes you are, I can see you', I replied. And so I could; not very well, but I could make out her face and her hair; everything was in black and white, but I could see. The euphoria didn't last as the blackout had to return to the right eye, but a day or two later the bandages were removed from my left eye, and life could resume in a limited way. I could dress and sit up during the day.

And then the reaction set in. I was totally unprepared for it. It was a Friday evening, when, without warning, I was overwhelmed by a terrible sense of dread. Dark thoughts closed in; I had lost any useful sight in one eye, so I could no longer drive a car; if I couldn't drive, I could no longer do my job as an ACC; so I would be out of work, and I had just taken on a mortgage for our home, with no prospect of repaying it now. Round and round the thoughts buzzed in my head, and I found myself gripping the edge of the writing desk, staring into a kind of abyss. It was all very real and very frightening.

Deliberately, I stood up and looked into the mirror. It was not a pretty sight, but it was still me. And I forced myself to realize that I was becoming depressed, and that it was a luxury I could not afford. So I determined that on the morrow, I would break out and go to the mess for a pint of beer; I wanted to see the real world going about its business and I would be content.

I slept well that night. Every four hours during the day a sergeant nurse came in to administer eye drops and medicine, and the following morning he said that the doctor had said that I could wrap up warm and take a short walk in the grounds if the weather was dry. It was now the end of November, but there was a wintry sun outside the window, so I didn't have to break out, it would be legal; the escape would be to leave the hospital grounds to cut across a field to the security post. If I left straight after the medication, I would have nearly four hours to get to the Mess and back.

Well, I made it. Luckily there was nobody in the bar as I drank my pint of beer; In any case they might not have recognized my bandaged face. I went to my rooms to collect a few things, which I tucked in the pockets of my greatcoat, and made my way back. The sergeant sniffed as he administered the drugs, and he was about to

Small Change at RAF Gatow.
Padre Ian Greenhalgh (left) arrives,
Padre Stephen Greenhalgh (right) departs.

say something, but changed his mind and grinned. The following week I became the subject of a complaint from Matron. My secretary, Jackie, had been replaced by Mary, an Administrative Officer before her marriage, and very efficient. I had arranged for her to bring files from my in-tray, hidden under the fruit basket she brought in every morning. It didn't fool Matron, and Mary was forbidden to visit. So I asked for a telephone to be installed, and conducted my work by phone. I think Matron was glad when I was discharged shortly afterwards, to return on sick leave to UK. Padre Ian Thomas had completed his tour as Staff Chaplain and had joined the A Team; with his wife, Margaret, he was at nearby RAF Wildenrath, and as I was not allowed to fly, Ian drove me to Ostend, where I caught the fast hydrofoil passenger ferry to Dover, and then travelled by train to Grantham, where I was met by Joy and Helen.

It was good to be home for Christmas, surrounded by a loving family. Slowly, my sight improved, and after a few weeks colour vision returned to my right eye and by early January 1989 I was ready to return to work. It was later that month when I returned to Rheindahlen and resumed my duties. At the next quarterly meeting of chaplains I was still wearing a patch over my right eye, and I was cheered by quips such as, 'I don't think the Assistant Chaplain-in-Chief is seeing both sides of my argument,' and, 'Shall I write the Minutes on the left hand half of the page?'

In due course, I had the stitches removed and normal service was resumed with my eyesight. There is a slight distortion in vertical lines where the retina did not lie perfectly flat, and I have an encircling band around the eye, but I was soon able to drive again and live normally. The round of visits continued unabated; the staff work in the headquarters was undiminished, and the A Team worked hard and played hard. The standard of pastoral work carried out by the chaplains on their stations was excellent, and I thanked God for them.

I cannot conclude the chapter on Germany without relating my involvement with the Band. The Band of RAF Germany had arranged to play in the English Church in Nice for a Battle of Britain Sunday in September 1988. When I remarked that if it was a church service then I ought to be involved, it was agreed that I should join the team. So it was arranged that I would join the Senior Personnel Staff Officer, Group Captain David Smith, and stay with Madame Marcya Harrison at her home near Nice for the weekend. Marcya was the widow of an RAF officer, and lived with her daughter, Maureen, on a hillside above Contes; her Mas included a ruined mediaeval castle atop the hill.

The weekend was a success, and the following year a more ambitious visit was planned. Mme Harrison invited the Mayors of Menton, Nice, Cannes, Grasse, Frejus and many others, to contribute to the cost of bringing the 'famous L'Ochestre de la RAF' to perform in their town. For ten days in July the Band played nightly in town squares to rapturous applause. AVM Mike Dicken permitted me to travel to Germany, and together with Group Captain Jim Rennie from RAF Rheindahlen, I carried out the public relations side of the tour; mingling with the audience and filling the air with bonhomie.

The former Chaplain-in-Chief's forecast of my tour length being shortened proved to be accurate, and at the end of April I handed over the job to my successor and returned home. Apart from the separation from family, and the lack of a church and altar (and therefore a chalice) of my own, it was a splendid tour. I discovered a flair for leadership, and that my style was to lead from the front. There is an inherent risk in this, for not every Christian soul can understand why a priest would lead the singing in the bar, or spend so much time with non-church folk. I take that risk daily, because I want to go where Christ is. And all the members of the A Team would join me in that—and did.

CHAPTER ELEVEN:

Command Chaplain

The timing of my posting was not brilliant, for the Highways Agency was busy removing roundabouts and constructing flyovers along the route of the A1. It was the first week of May 1989 and I was travelling south along the A1 to the Headquarters RAF Support Command at RAF Brampton to take over the post of Assistant Chaplain-in-Chief (ACC) from the Reverend Roger Kenward, who was retiring. In short, for the whole of my tour my journey to the office from home in Caythorpe was fraught with delay.

My office at Brampton was the bedroom of a former married quarter on base, a short walk from the headquarters building and the Officers' Mess, which was the splendid old manor house named Brampton Park. I shared the house with my two colleagues, Ray Brown, the Free Church Assistant Principal Chaplain (APC), later succeeded by Tom Lowe, and Tony Harris, the RC Assistant Principal Chaplain. Maggie Maywhort was my PA, and was a splendid character. We all got on very well together and the house was usually filled with laughter; even when Maggie's 'mophead' dog committed a disgraceful act on my office carpet, my anger was short-lived due to Maggie's unusually sombre face.

Support was a big, integrated command, and took its name from the support it gave to the front line in Strike Command by its Training and Maintenance groups. It comprised nearly 200 units at home and overseas, in addition to Directly Administered Units. It was a gear change in responsibility after RAF Germany. Far more commissioned chaplains served in this command, largely due to the concentration of chaplains at the training establishments like Cranwell, Halton and Cosford. Shortly after I arrived, I welcomed a new Commander-in-Chief as Air Marshal (later Air Chief Marshal, Sir) Mike Graydon arrived from a NATO job.

Soon after taking over the post at Support Command I was appointed an Honorary Chaplain to Her Majesty the Queen, adding the letters QHC after my name. It sounds vastly important, but is, in fact, a sinecure. My uniform looked more decorative, with the Royal Cypher on my epaulettes and gold threaded aiguillettes suspended from my right shoulder. A chaplain to the monarch also wears a cassock in Royal Scarlet, and as I have always worn a soutane style cassock, I now looked like a cardinal. When I tried it on for the first time in my bedroom, Joy exclaimed, 'You are not going out in that are you?' It did look rather startling after wearing black for so long.

On 5 November 1989 Joy and I travelled to Birmingham where I was taking the stage in the City Hall to officiate at the Midlands Festival of Remembrance. It was quite a 'do', and we joined the Lord Mayor for a Civic Reception afterwards. It was at events such as this that I began to experience the affection of the general public for the veterans of two World Wars who turned out immaculately to pay their respects to their comrades who did not make it home.

Support was the Lead Command for the New Management Strategy (NMS), which was testing the efficacy of delegated budgets from Air Force Board level down to the individual formations. The idea was that with funding came responsibility to deliver the required performance. This also gave senior commanders the opportunity to consider where savings might be made in their management structure. This was the one of the first of the cost-cutting exercises that has bedevilled government departments ever since.

Early in 1990, I was asked by the Air Officer Administration, Air Vice-Marshal Mike Dicken, to prepare a plan for a revised structure of the Command Chaplains as a part of the post Cold War 'Peace Dividend'. I considered that the so-called Peace Dividend was forty years of peace, but I drafted a structure whereby the two APCs (wing commander posts) would be 'double-hatted' as station chaplains, leaving the ACC (group captain post) at the headquarters. This reduced the number of headquarters posts by only two. He didn't appear to be hugely impressed, but said that it would do for the time being. As I did not have the authority to make such changes, I explained that it was only my idea, and advised him to seek approval from the Chaplain-in-Chief. As it was at that stage only a 'paper exercise', nothing came of it.

Once I had settled into the Command Headquarters, I began to arrange visits to see the chaplains in the field; literally in the case of RAF Hullavington, the Wiltshire airfield where I had once walked with my Dad and uncles under the wings of Lancaster bombers. The chaplain there, Padre Bernard Rumbold, had arranged for me to lunch somewhere on the vast airfield. The mobile Field Catering Unit was based there and was always glad of VIP visitors on whom they could try out their skills. It was an excellent lunch which could not have been bettered in an Officers' Mess. Then Bernard surpassed himself by taking me to the Balloon Section.

The officer in charge had a huge, though only partly inflated, balloon in a hangar. They resembled the wartime barrage balloons, and were used for training parachutists, who made their first descent from a tethered balloon at 500 feet. I am told that it was far worse than jumping out of an aircraft at a significantly higher altitude, because you had time to think about it before you stepped into space. The NCO asked if I would like to go inside the balloon. I was intrigued and pulled on a white, anti-static overall over my uniform shirt and trousers. With the hood pulled up, and wearing gloves, the sergeant held open a nozzle, exactly like the end where you blow into a party balloon, only larger. As he did this, the air inside tried to get out, so I had to wriggle and force my way into the envelope against a significant air pressure. Suddenly I popped into the balloon. I would not have been in the least surprised if I had found myself in Narnia. I laughed aloud and my voice echoed from all the geodetic surfaces making up the skin of the balloon. There was a rush of air, and Bernard joined me. Conversation was difficult because of the multiple echoes, and it was like walking in a huge bouncy castle.

It was a sad day when, as Chaplain-in-Chief, I returned in 1995 to take part in the formal closure of this venerable RAF station, and, as a link with my boyhood, I arranged for my Aunt Edna, who still lived in Castle Combe, to be present.

RAF Shawbury, in Shropshire, was the centre of training for rotary-wing aircraft, which I had always called helicopters, and was a fascinating visit in my

The Balloon Section, RAF Hullavington. BHL, the Section Commander, Padre Rumbold

itinerary around the chaplaincies in the Command. I was interested in establishing a Commissioned Chaplain at Shawbury, instead of the local Vicar, who was the Officiating Chaplain. I wanted to see the station for myself and talk to the Station Commander about it. As I was experiencing a distinct lack of flying, I made sure that a flight was included on the visit programme. I had always enjoyed helicopter flights, for there is a relationship with the terrain below; the relatively slow forward speed enables you to wave to folk walking on the hills, or working in the fields.

So, after lunch, I was airborne in a Gazelle helicopter. It is a delightful little aircraft with excellent visibility. We flew across country to the disused airfield of RAF Tern Hill, where the pilot encouraged me to try flying the Gazelle. He showed me how to alter the pitch of the rotary blades and how to make it go forward, move up and down and from side to side, and then it was my turn. I discovered that it is absolutely impossible to fly a helicopter. I made it go forward and climb slightly; but then it decided to slip sideways. When I corrected that, it went backwards— an aircraft shouldn't go backwards. Flying it was like rubbing your stomach and tapping your head at the same time. I confessed over the intercom that I had lost control; the pilot agreed and took over. When I asked him what would happen if the engine failed, he calmly switched it off. In a voice several octaves higher I said that an oral answer would suffice, but we descended like a sycamore leaf, with the wing auto-rotating, until we landed, rather more forcefully than if we were under power. Then, off we went again on the return flight to Shawbury. I had enjoyed my flight, and my admiration soared for the aircrew who wage war in rotary wing aircraft.

I began to experience the enormous expertise we had available to the defence of the realm in Support Command. On a visit to RAF Sealand, near Hawarden in North Wales, I watched silently as a young Leading Aircraftsman unplaited a loom of wires, which linked the 'cloud and clonk' forward-looking radar dish, in the nose of a Tornado aircraft, with the instrument panel. I've forgotten how many wires he separated, but I believe they exceeded a hundred. He checked each one for breaks, and then replaited the loom ready to be installed in an aircraft. I asked him how long he took to complete one loom. He told me that he started on Monday morning and finished on Friday afternoon. Then on Monday he would take another off the shelf and repeat the process. I remarked that the lives of aircrew depended on the high quality of his work, and I asked if the aircrew ever came to see what he was doing, but he replied that he had never seen any in the hangar.

When I returned to the Headquarters, I called on the Commander-in-Chief, and made the point that the tireless patience and care of this eighteen-year old airman was ensuring the safety of Tornado aircrew, and it would be good for his morale, and instructive for them, if, occasionally, a crew would pay a visit to see what he was doing for them. Air Marshal Graydon agreed, and I later had a copy of a letter he sent to the C-in-C at Strike Command suggesting this, but I heard nothing more about the matter.

It might have been at Sealand, but was most likely RAF St Athan in South Wales, that I experienced more dramatic expertise. A sergeant was busy at his workbench, which was littered with expensive-looking bits of equipment. When I asked him what he was about, he said that he was repairing a circuit board. Fearing that he was going to engage me in a discussion about wiggly amps, I told him that I couldn't tell the difference between a circuit board and an ironing board. He explained that it was a deep, ten-layer board (it looked as thick as a wafer biscuit to me), and that there was a break in the circuit seven 'decks' down. I looked suitably impressed, but unmoved, until he offered me the microscope he was working with. He showed me which wheel to turn to obtain a critical focus, and I applied my eyes to the instrument.

It was a blur of lines, but suddenly, as I twirled the little wheel, I was looking down on a large city from above. It was like the beginning of the film, West Side Story. I gasped aloud with surprise. 'Ah', he said alongside me, 'You've seen my world.' I slowly turned another wheel on the microscope, and I began to descend into the 'city' beneath me. He had drilled a hole through each layer so that he could look for the break, and I carefully lowered myself through it, down and down, until I reached the layer where he was working. Then, I saw the break; a wire had become detached and he was about to solder it, a blob of solder had been placed there already. With great regret, I began my ascent to the surface, and when at last I looked up, I had to hold on to the bench to steady myself. 'Sergeant,' I said, 'I have seen your world, and it is beautiful.' He beamed in genuine pleasure, and explained that formerly they had discarded broken circuit boards, but under the New Management Strategy it was found to be more cost-effective to repair them.

While paying a visit to RAF Farnborough, I had noticed a strange-looking Hercules aircraft parked on the pan. It had a long, thin proboscis painted with red and white stripes, and a curious aerodynamic device mounted above the flight deck. I was told it was operated by the Meteorological Research Flight and was called 'Snoopy' and was offered a flight when I was free to come down again.

When I was able to accept the invitation a few months later, I clambered aboard Hercules XV208, and sat at the back of the flight deck. The sortie objective was 'to study the physics of low stratus and fog in the South West approaches, with a view to increasing our understanding of the phenomenon.' The sortie was carried out between the Bristol Channel and 8 degrees west. The flight of four hours duration was in a series of profile descents from precise heights to the lowest permitted altitude. I was free to walk about the aircraft and when I asked what the camera above the pilots was for, I was advised to knock on the door of a steel room just aft of the flight deck. I ventured inside this box and discovered a young Met Officer working at a bank of instruments. Just above her desk was a screen with a picture of the view ahead of the aircraft. 'It's supposed to help me to orientate', she said, 'But I'm too busy to look at it.' As I left the crew at the end of the flight, I reflected yet again on the rich and invaluable wealth of expertise available to the nation in the Royal Air Force.

In these ways, slowly but surely, I built up a good working knowledge of the Command and a friendship with the chaplains serving in it. I also came to know their wives and children, their hopes and difficulties. Unlike other sections, the chaplain worked alone on a station more often than not. His office was usually in the station church, remote from other workplaces. This was ideal for confidential interviews, but it had its drawbacks, one of which could be loneliness. Some coped with this by linking with local clergy groups such as Rural Deaneries, but civilian clergy do not always understand easily our working conditions, or how we identify closely with our people. Our concerns are not theirs, and vice versa. My intention when visiting a chaplain was not to check up on him, but to sit alongside him and listen, to be a source of encouragement, a critical friend at times and an advocate when required.

When I gave a short address at the installation of a new chaplain, I always explained the ministry of a priest to the people, and encouraged them to make use of his ministry to enable them to grow in faith. I also required the station commander to sit next to the new chaplain and present the man to me for installation, which expressed the close working relationship they should enjoy.

More than anything, I was aware of how isolated were the chaplains' wives. They had extraordinary expectations laid upon them by a relatively self-reliant community, from the social round of the officers' mess to the organization of any charity known to mankind, and all this often miles from the nearest town. On top of which, they had a home and family to look after. They, too, needed moral support. Some enjoyed attending the annual conference arranged for chaplains' wives at Amport House by the Chief's wife, if not for the formal sessions in the lecture room, then for the garden in which to walk and think and be themselves for a while, away from the constant, busy, demanding routine of family life.

The quarterly meeting I had held with the chaplains in RAF Germany was not possible in the UK because of the scattered nature of the command, and Strike Command was even more fragmented; the practice had been to hold a command conference at Amport House every other year. The next Support conference was due at the end of January 1991, by which time more urgent business demanded my attention, for on 2nd August 1990, Iraq invaded Kuwait in an unprovoked and violent attack.

Within days, RAF squadrons were sent to protect north-east Saudi Arabia, for there was a fear that Saddam Hussein would seize other Gulf States for their oil reserves. The United Nations quickly imposed sanctions against Iraq and empowered the use of armed force to enforce them. General Sir Peter de la Billiere was appointed the Commander of the British Forces in the Gulf in what was called Operation Granby. Sir Peter's brother, Commander Fred de Labiliere, had been the splendid President of the Mess when I was at Honington, and I had enjoyed Sir Peter's company and found him a quiet, courteous and caring man.

Brian Halfpenny, who had become Chaplain-in-Chief in 1988, summoned his five Assistant Chaplains-in-Chief (ACCs) to a conference in his office in Adastral House. The main item was to determine which chaplains we were going to send to war, for it was becoming clearer by the day that this would be the outcome of the diplomatic frenzy. The second concern, and equally important, was how we intended offering support to the casualties and their families.

Padre John Daimond, ACC Strike Command, felt strongly that his chaplains should go to war with the squadrons on their stations. I could see the force of that argument, but those stations were also full of anxious families, who needed a calming and reassuring presence of a chaplain they knew and trusted, to keep them up to date with news, and not rumour, from the front line. I argued that we should send chaplains from Support Command. We discussed it for some time and I won the day when the Chief said he was of the same view as me, and I was encouraged later, when John Daimond told me that Strike Command station commanders were grateful that we were leaving their chaplains with them. The Chief was meeting with the Principal Chaplains RC and CSFC later that day and felt sure that they would agree with our decision.

By this time we had well over forty thousand servicemen in the Gulf area, and given the possibility of Iraq conducting a dirty war in terms of chemical and biological weapons, a huge number of casualties were feared, possibly running into tens of thousands. The RAF hospitals were units in Support Command, so I agreed to discuss the reception of casualties with the hospital COs and report back in due course. We were not alone in considering casualties. On 30th November, UN Security Council Resolution 678 took effect, setting the 15th January 1991 as the final date for the Iraqis to leave Kuwait. Clearly events were moving fast, and not long after that the Chief of Chaplains of the United States Air Force phoned from Washington to say that the Chaplain-in-Chief had suggested my name as a source of help. He said that in his view war in the Gulf was inevitable, so the US Air Force was setting up two 1,000-bed hospitals, and one 500-bed unit, in the UK, and could I provide chaplaincy cover for them for the first fourteen days of hostilities, until National Guard chaplains could be mobilised to take over. I agreed to find three chaplains for him, but he choked on the phone: 'Three? Three? We establish a chaplain for every 50 beds.' I felt a bit miffed at his scorn, and said I would do what I could. He gave me the name of a 'Bird Colonel' who commanded the US Hospital, Bicester, and who would fill me in on the details.

A few days later I drove down to Bicester and had lunch with the US Air Force colonel in the hospital mess. After lunch we drove over to RAF Little Rissington, where one of the 1,000-bed units had been established. We parked between two of the big aircraft hangers, each containing 500 beds, and he explained that the transport aircraft would taxi to this point, triage having been carried out during the flight from the gulf. The casualties would then be transferred to the hangar with the care best suited to their injuries.

We walked to the hangar on the left as he apologised that there would be no power switched on inside. He unlocked a small door to one side and we entered the darkened hangar. As my eyes became accustomed to the gloom, I caught my breath in shock. All I could see were the white pillows on each 'gurney' (stretcher), row after row, and line after line, stretching away to the farthest end of the vast hangar. And there was another such hangar next door. And this was repeated at another location, with the 500 beds before me also replicated at RAF Nocton Hall, in Lincolnshire. It was at that moment, standing in the gloom, that the enormity of the undertaking in the Gulf dawned on me.

We moved into the rooms which run along the length of a hangar, usually accommodating crew rooms, and operations rooms. Now they were intensive care wards, eight beds clustered around a core of electronic instruments which the average NHS hospital would give anything to possess. There must have been about forty-eight such beds in this one hangar. The Americans had not been idle since the Iraq invasion of Kuwait.

I managed to allocate five chaplains from the Command, one to each 500 bed unit. It was the best I could do. Meanwhile, I was receiving several telephone calls a day from parish clergy all over the UK offering help in informing next of kin when casualties were known. Those who were near a military hospital offered to assist the hospital chaplain in any way we wished. This willingness to join in was unexpected but most gratefully received.

Meanwhile, we had chaplains in the Saudi Arabian desert and at Dhahran with the Tornado squadrons, and in Bahrein. It was at this time that I received a signal from Chaplaincy Services informing me that the Foreign and Commonwealth Office had ordered that chaplains were not to wear Christian symbols in Saudi Arabia. Furthermore, they were to be issued with new Identity Cards showing them wearing a uniform collar and tie. I had never heard anything so absurd in my life, and rang the Chief to say that I refused to pass the order on to the chaplains, as it was quite illegal, and contrary to the codicils of the Geneva Convention for chaplains to be anything other than men in Holy Orders and to be known as such to the enemy, and that in any case, I was not under FCO command. Either we went to war as chaplains, or we did not go at all, and did he want me to inform the Department of Pre-emptive Cringe (as someone had described the Foreign Office), and was the Medical Branch to discard their snake and staff badge because of its possible Hebrew connotation? Perhaps I got a bit carried away, but I felt most strongly about it, and I went to see AVM Mike Dicken, Air Officer Admin at the Command Headquarters. He agreed, and said he would take it up. Eventually, my point was recognized, and chaplains could wear the Branch Brooch on the uniform and the Red Cross armband, but had to have new ID cards which did not show the clerical collar.

On 16th January 1991 Desert Storm began. It was to be an American-led war, with General Norman Schwarzkopf in overall tactical command. The first phases were to be fought in the air, followed by the land war. RAF Tornado GR1, Tornado F3, Jaguar, Buccaneer, Nimrod, and tanker aircraft, all played a huge part in the offensive, and by 21 January 7,000 sorties had been flown, ensuring air superiority. The land war began on 24 February, but only five days later a ceasefire was announced: the allied objective had been achieved, and Saddam Hussein had been evicted from Kuwait, leaving a trail of wanton destruction in his wake. The RAF had lost six Tornado aircraft and one of the navigators who died in the desert was Flight Lieutenant Max Collier, an old friend from my 'Youth Club', No.7 Squadron, at RAF St Mawgan, in 1971. Some of the aircrew who ejected and survived were paraded on Iraqi television and humiliated.

On 20 February, I took time off from the Headquarters to travel to Cardiff to deliver a lecture in the University of Wales Hospital on Suffering and Redemption, which was highly influenced by some of the experiences of chaplains in the Gulf War. Then, in the first week in March, I made a brief visit to RAF Akrotiri, and while there I paid a visit to the RAF Hospital to meet the aircrew who had been captured and badly treated by Iraqi forces and who had been released from captivity the day before. They were now receiving medical attention and recuperation before their return to UK. One of them, Flight Lieutenant Robbie Stewart, lived in a village near my home, and Joy and his wife were friends, so I promised to visit her that evening on my return. Joy and I did just that, as soon as I arrived back from Gatwick. I told her, 'I saw Robbie this morning, and he really is free and alright, apart from a broken leg.'

On Thursday 16 May 1991, the Dean and Chapter of Norwich Cathedral held a Service of Thanksgiving for Peace in the Arabian Peninsula, and invited me to preach the sermon. The beautiful old cathedral was packed. I took as my text, 'David walked out to meet the Philistine with his sling in his hand', from the First

Book of Samuel. I began by taking on The Revd Philip Crowe, the Principal of Salisbury & Wells Theological College, who had said on Radio 4 in 'Thought for the Day', on 30 April that 'to thank God for anything to do with the Gulf War is blasphemy.' I thought he was wrong about that, and said so. I quote from my sermon:

> 'He didn't say why or how he came to that conclusion, but if it's because in thanking God we involve God in some way in the outcome of war, then he's missed the point. We thank God today not because we believe God was on our side and ensured a right result; we thank him because that is how we feel about the outcome—a deep gratitude that the potential horror of enormous casualties did not materialise, and we want to share our relief and happiness about that with God, who cares for us as we care for ourselves.

> In this Service, we thank God for the men and women who acted on our behalf in liberating the oppressed men, women and children in Kuwait. And not only those who served in the Arabian Peninsula, but those throughout the United Kingdom who worked long hours, and endured separation and stress to ensure success; all those throughout this County of Norfolk who sent messages and gifts of support, and those who prepared to care for the injured. The armed forces stood on a pyramid of commitment.'

The whole service had a rightness about it, and it was very encouraging to see the public support for what had been achieved.

The Chaplain-in-Chief asked me to call on him in Adastral House. We met in his office on 27 February, and Brian Halfpenny told me that the Air Force Board had received approval from both HM The Queen and the Archbishop of Canterbury to appoint me as Chaplain-in-Chief and Archdeacon of the Royal Air Force when he retired in July. I could tell Joy, but otherwise, the appointment was embargoed until an official announcement would be made a month or so later.

Presented to their Majesties King and Queen of Sweden in the Royal Palace, Stockholm

Joy and I arrive by air for the Chaplains' Wives Conference at Amport House

An Audience with Pope Jean-Paul ll in the Vatican

Amport House—the RAF Chaplains' School

Annual Conference of Chaplains at Amport House.
Front Row: T. Goode, B. McAvoy, AVM David Cousins, BHL, Bishop of Sherborne, R. Turner, P. Bishop

About to depart Waterkloof Air Base, South Africa. Padre Potgeiter, BHL and the pilot of the Beechcraft King Air 90

187

The Retired Rector greets the New Boy at Fulbeck, 1996.
Left to right: Julian Fane, Denis Oliver, Canon Mitchell, BHL, Mary Siddans

Parishioners at a Summer's Evening Party in the Rectory, Caythorpe, July 1999

The West Façade, Amiens Cathedral, France

A section of the vault of Albi Cathedral, Tarn, France

Mediaeval glass depicting St Vincent refusing to worship an idol. Bourges Cathedral, France

A lunch at the Savage Club to mark the 55th anniversary of the death of Brother Savage the late Sir Henry Wood. David Howe reading with BHL looking over his shoulder

Savage Club Founders' Dinner to mark the Club's 150th Anniversary. (BHL top left)

Easter Sunday at St Nicholas' Church, Normanton

Mark, Helen, BHL, Joy and Simon at home in Caythorpe

CHAPTER TWELVE:

Leader of the Pack

At 0940 on Thursday, 25 July 1991, Brian Halfpenny shook hands with me in the office and said, 'That's it; it's all yours. Good luck, Chief.' After he had left, I sat in the chair behind the desk and gazed around the office I knew so well. It hadn't changed since I had been Staff Chaplain to Hewitt Wilson all those years ago: the locked door behind the wardrobe, which ensured that the only entrance was through the outer office; the huge desk, with trays for 'In', 'Pending' and 'Out' files. They were empty, but that was unusual, and would not last an hour. Then my eyes settled on the photographs of my predecessors lining the left-hand wall. All fifteen seemed to be looking at the new boy with interest. Some of the early ones appeared formidable; there was John Jagoe, who, when the Archbishop of Canterbury told him that on his retirement as Chief he was to be the Bishop of Bermuda, protested that there must be better men than him, and the Archbishop replied, 'There are, Jagoe, but I have other jobs for them.' Then there was the smiling Frank Cox, who would return from an extended visit to the Far East and astound his staff chaplain, Hewitt Wilson, by arriving in the office at 0830, straight from the airport, to write his 'thank-you' letters. Len, Hewitt, Herbie, Glyn, and Brian: they had all sat at this very desk and worked day in and day out to serve the chaplains under their command, and to bring the Branch through good times and bad. The words, 'It's all yours', echoed in the quiet room.

Then my Personal Secretary, Barbara Boughey, came in with a pile of files and letters to be signed, which she dropped in the 'In' tray. 'Cup of coffee, Chief?' she asked, and my new life began.

While I was ready to give a good account of myself as Chaplain-in-Chief, it had come as a bit of a surprise; John Daimond was senior to me, and I had expected him to be appointed, but clearly the Air Secretary had assessed the requirements of the job and decided that I had the required qualities. The Air Force Board of the Defence Council grades the Chaplain-in-Chief as an Air Vice-Marshal; the Church grants him the style and dignity of an Archdeacon.

I had been collated as Archdeacon of the Royal Air Force by the Archbishop of Canterbury, George Carey, during a service of Holy Eucharist in Lambeth Palace Chapel two days earlier on the 23rd July, when Joy and I were able to celebrate our Silver Wedding anniversary in style. The Archbishop celebrated at the Eucharist, and preached a short sermon which compared the duty of an Archdeacon to those in his care with the joy of a loving home and marriage; he was excellent. The Air Member for Personnel, Air Chief Marshal Sir Roger Palin, representing the Air Force Board, presented me to the Archbishop for Collation, and afterwards joined members of my family and office staff at a reception given by the Archbishop and Mrs Carey in the state rooms of the Palace.

The Licence granted to the Archdeacon for the RAF is unusual in that is signed and sealed by the Archbishops of both Canterbury and York. The Licence is unique, too, in that it gives to the Chaplain-in-Chief the authority usually reserved to a bishop, namely: 'to exercise within Our Provinces the spiritual supervision and direction of the Chaplains to the Royal Air Force, and the general superintendence of the work of the Church of England among the officers and men of the Royal Air Force.' It was a commission which I took very seriously, and which I constantly bore in mind when dealing with chaplains and their congregations.

The last two months had been rather a whirligig. Sitting in that familiar office on my first morning, I thought of the chaplains now under my jurisdiction. With one or two exceptions, they were working hard and effectively. I heard splendid reports of them from station commanders and air marshals alike, so I was not concerned about the spiritual life of the RAF; that was in good hands.

I knew that change was imminent, for it was in the air all about me, but I had prepared a short list of tasks which I considered urgent and which I wanted to tackle straight away. First, I had to appoint a Staff Chaplain. Second, I wanted to make sure that the chaplains had the right tools for the job, especially those at teaching establishments. Third, bearing in mind the New Management Strategy, which I had begun to work with at Support Command, I wanted to understand my budget allocation and make sure that it was being used to the best advantage in the Branch. Then I wanted to learn how to defend it. This was in no way usurping my budget manager, but I wanted to set the priorities myself, before I left him to implement them.

Little did I know it on that serene morning in my new office, but my work as Chaplain-in-Chief was to be determined largely by what Harold Macmillan, when asked what had influenced his time as Prime Minister, described as, 'Events, dear boy, Events.'

The previous month, when my appointment had already been announced, I had joined my predecessor in appointing two new Assistant Chaplains-in-Chief. John Daimond had decided to retire early when he was not appointed Chief, and the Resident Chaplain at St Clement Danes, the excellent and much-loved Douglas Sirr, who was about to move to Germany as the Command Chaplain, had died suddenly before he could take up the post. The Command Chaplain Germany was a difficult post to fill, because it was known that the command would cease to exist in a few years and there would then be no appropriate post for the man we were about to promote. Padre Philip Mortimer was the ideal candidate: he was slightly older than his colleagues, and possessed a fine grasp of the priestly life and sound Yorkshire common sense. In addition, he was trusted and valued by his peers, but, as important in this case, he had only a few years left to serve before he retired. Philip's retirement and the closure of RAF Germany would be co-terminus. The other vacancy was the post of Principal of the RAF Chaplains' School at Amport House, for Brian McAvoy had moved to succeed me at Support Command.

Peter Bishop, as the Staff Chaplain, was taking a note of our deliberations, so I asked him to organize some coffee for us. While he was out of the room I proposed that he should be promoted to the post of Principal of Amport House. I don't think it had crossed my predecessor's mind, but he readily agreed that Peter ought to start gaining experience of command. When he returned to the room he was told to start 'clearing his desk' on his return to London, but he took hold of the wrong end of the stick and spilt the coffee. So one of my first tasks was to appoint a Staff Chaplain by October, when Peter Bishop would move to Amport.

I decided to appoint a more junior man, who would use the experience gained in the post throughout his career, as I had done. I chose Dermot McKavanagh, a bachelor and an Irishman, who had been honoured recently by the Queen. An airman working in a hangar on his unit had climbed into the cockpit of a jet aircraft and removed the safety pins from the ejector seat. He would allow only Padre Dermot to come near, for he was trusted by the airman. Dermot was obliged to lean over the side of the cockpit to talk to the man confidentially. At any moment the man could have pulled the handle and decapitated the chaplain as his seat shot out of the aircraft. After a long time in conversation, Dermot persuaded the airman to replace the safety pins and leave the aircraft. For this pastoral care in the face of danger Dermot was awarded The Queen's Commendation for Brave Conduct, the only chaplain to wear the Oak Leaf ribbon on his uniform. When I interviewed him in Adastral House and offered him the post he was surprised and delighted at the same time.

With my Staff Chaplain Dermot McKavanagh in Gibraltar

With a Staff Chaplain in place, I could now turn my attention to my accommodation. I had been offered an Air Officer's residence at Maidenhead, but as Helen was settled in her sixth form in Grantham, and I would be travelling a good deal of the time, we decided that we would continue to live in Caythorpe and I would have a pied-à-terre in central London. Since taking up the appointment I had lived in a suite of rooms in the Officers' Mess at RAF Uxbridge, and renewed my daily acquaintance with the Metropolitan Line, but when my predecessor vacated the flat he rented in Fitzrovia in September, I arranged to take over the lease. The apartment in 49 Hallam Street was a twenty minute walk from Adastral House, but only a two-minute walk from Oxford Circus, something of great interest to my daughter Helen and Joy. I was happy and comfortable in my abode.

It was time to address the second of my urgent tasks: to make sure that the chaplains had the right tools for the job. One of my responsibilities was the functional control of the RAF Chaplains' School at Amport House near Andover. In this idyllic setting, Padre Philip Sladen had begun work in writing a Beliefs and Values syllabus for the Chaplains' Branch, which was validated by Professor John Hull of Birmingham University. The essential tool for the job for chaplains at training establishments was a comprehensive and authoritative syllabus. This had been close to my heart since my unhappy experience at RAF Halton in 1970. When Philip had completed his work, the programme included visual aids for each lecture and was graded for use at the initial training courses for airmen at RAF stations such as Swinderby, Halton, and Cosford, up to Officer Cadets at Cranwell.

In addition to conferences for chaplains, courses such as Pastoral Care, Bereavement and Loss, Marital Listening, Personal Awareness (formerly called 'Moral Leadership'), Family Dynamics, Financial Management and factors governing Military Ethics were offered at Amport House to airmen, NCOs and officers. They were taught either by chaplains on the staff or by experts 'bought in' for a particular course. While the Chaplain-in-Chief formally authorized the courses, the day to day running of the School was delegated to a senior chaplain who was appointed as the Principal, with the status of an Assistant Chaplain-in-Chief.

The next fairly important tool is a church building. Several station churches were in a poor state of repair, and, with my active encouragement, station commanders found money to refurbish or build new churches on their stations. RAF Boulmer, in Northumbria, was the first new church which I dedicated, much to the delight of the young station chaplain, Nick Barry. A larger church, to be used by all denominations, was designed for RAF Lossiemouth in Scotland. There was great excitement when I laid the Foundation Stone, and even more when I returned with the two Principal Chaplains for the dedication of the completed building. The third urgent task I had identified was to understand my budget, and I turned to it with relish. Under the terms of the New Management Strategy, the Air Force Board was required to devolve budgetary management as far as possible down the chain of command to unit level. This was a clever move on the part of the Treasury, because, in future, to achieve cuts in defence spending, the Treasury could just impose a percentage cut across the board and the budget allocations would be adjusted accordingly. This became known as 'salami-slicing'.

Funding for the Chaplains' Branch was delegated from AMP's Top Level Budget, so I attended a Screening Meeting with my HEO and Budget Manager, Doug Collard, and, as with all my colleagues on AMP's Management Board, I had to make a strong case for each line of my funding requirement. I was given a £4.3 million allocation to run the Branch, and for the first time, the Chaplain-in-Chief could see the cost of running the variety of operations within his command.

The new church at RAF Lossiemouth. The PSA Project Manager presents BHL with the Trowel used to lay the Foundation Stone on 17th September 1992

Happily, the first year was merely a paper exercise to give departments a chance to prepare to run their budget 'live'. I was glad that I had taken the time to understand the detail of my budget, and how best to implement it, for it stood me in good stead for the rest of my time at the top.

Meanwhile, a row had broken out in RAF Germany. A friend from Cyprus days, Air Vice Marshal 'Black' Robertson, was Deputy Commander Germany, and he telephoned to say that the C-in-C, Air Marshal (later Air Chief Marshal Sir) Andrew Wilson, (known throughout the RAF as 'Sandy' Wilson), had ordered that each married Staff Officer should be accompanied by his wife, and that as Philip Mortimer was not, I would have to replace him. I explained that there were good family reasons why Philip was not accompanied, but that his wife would come out as often as she could. I offered to fly out to speak with the C-in-C, but 'Black' said he would deal with it, yet there were a few more phone calls due to my intransigence.

A few weeks later, at the RAF Staff College, Bracknell, I came face to face with the C-in-C Germany in a corridor before lunch. 'I believe you wish to pick a bone with me, sir', I said, and introduced myself as the Chaplain-in-Chief. He gave me both barrels about his insistence on accompanied staff officers, and then I explained that Philip Mortimer was the best chaplain for the post, and that if he insisted, I would bring him home, but would not replace him, and then we could both explain to the Chief of the Air Staff why there was no Command Chaplain in Germany. We stood in silence for a minute or two as he fixed me with his basilisk gaze. Then he said, 'Is that your final word?' 'It is, sir', I said quietly. 'Well, Chaplain-in-Chief, you had better buy me a beer', he said, and we adjourned to the bar and became firm friends from that day. The following year he had the good grace to say that Philip Mortimer was one of the best chaplains he could wish for as his adviser in the Command Headquarters.

A very memorable event occurred in November 1991, on the Feast of St Hugh, the Bishop of Lincoln under King Henry ll, when I was installed as a Prebendary and Canon of Lincoln Cathedral during Choral Evensong. The Dean, Brandon Jackson, in an ancient ceremony, led me by the hand to the stall of the unendowed Prebendary of St Botolph in the magnificent St Hugh's Quire. As I took my seat I saw, across the packed Quire, Bishop Eryl and Jean Thomas; my first Vicar and mentor had travelled from Wales to be at my Installation. It is an honour accorded by the Bishop to successive Chaplains-in-Chief, so continuing the close relationship between the RAF and the County of Lincolnshire dating from the Second World War, when the county was almost one huge airfield for bomber aircraft.

While on Church matters, I should explain that Anglican chaplains in the armed forces are under the jurisdiction of the Archbishop of Canterbury, but he appoints a Suffragen Bishop as his representative. When I took up my appointment the Bishop of Maidstone, David Smith, was his man. He was very generous with his time, and met regularly with the three Service archdeacons: the Chaplain-of-the-Fleet, the Deputy Chaplain-General and me. When David became the diocesan Bishop of Bradford, the Archbishop appointed the Bishop of Sherborne, John Kirkham, to succeed him. He and I got on well at once, and we became good friends. For matters of moment I saw the Archbishop in Lambeth Palace, and I was able to share concerns with George Carey in the quiet of his study; but I worked routinely through John. He invited me to preach one December to the Guild of the Nineteen Lubricators in a service at St Margaret's Church, Westminster. I accepted due to the novelty of the title, and discovered a congregation of household names, such as Jimmy Hill, who were all engaged in charitable endeavour. I enjoyed the experience, and so did they for I was invited again.

When Archdeacon Mike Henley, the Chaplain of the Fleet, retired to play golf at St Andrews, I became the senior of the Service archdeacons, and Bishop John invited me to lunch at his Club, for he wanted my view on a suggestion

With Bishop John Kirkham at Amport

that he should became a full-time Bishop to the Forces. I advised him to dismiss the idea from his mind for several reasons. First, it would be an unbalanced episcopate, for he would never ordain a man under his jurisdiction, as potential ordinands left the armed forces and trained in the diocese where they lived. Second, he would not be able to recruit and employ chaplains, nor could he see their files, as that was the job of the Ministry of Defence through the uniformed archdeacon, who also had responsibility from the Archbishop for the spiritual direction of the clergy. Third, there would be no money available for a salary or for accommodation. In short, there was no requirement for such a post. I felt that such a kind and honest man deserved my candour, and, although it might not have been what he hoped to hear, he appeared grateful for it.

Another of my responsibilities was the church of St Clement Danes in the Strand. It belongs to the Diocese of London, but was offered to the RAF after the war as the Central Church of the Royal Air Force and a home for the Books of Remembrance. It was a bombed shell when the RAF took over responsibility for it, and subscriptions from all over the air force paid to restore it to its former glory. The Chaplain-in-Chief is the Priest-in-Charge, but had always appointed one of his senior chaplains, with the status of Assistant Chaplain-in-Chief, as the Resident Chaplain.

A major event in the diary when I became the Chief was the unveiling and dedication of the statue outside St Clement Danes Church on 31st May 1992, of Air Chief Marshal Sir Arthur Harris, the wartime Commander-in-Chief, Bomber Command. Her Majesty Queen Elizabeth, the Queen Mother, was to unveil it and then I was to dedicate it, having first preached at a service in the church, to which all the veterans of Bomber Command were invited. My mentor in all of this was the driving force behind the memorial, Marshal of the Royal Air Force Sir Michael Beetham, and we had many meetings together to ensure that the event would be smart and dignified and worthy of the sacrifice made by the 55,000 men who served in the command and who did not return from battle. Sir Michael had been Chief of the Air Staff when I was Staff Chaplain, and I had discovered then that he is a remarkable man, and his attention to every detail is impressive.

On the day, the church was packed with Veterans of Bomber Command, representatives from the armed forces of the NATO Alliance, and the Royal Air Force in particular. I received The Queen Mother at the west end of the church and escorted her to her place at the head of the nave. I began my sermon by making the point that a statue can often be misunderstood. I told the tale of the young son of an army officer stationed in Khartoum, who was taken by his mother each day to see the statue of General Gordon on horseback. Each day the little boy would say, 'Hello Gordon.' When the time came to return to England, the mother took the lad to say 'Goodbye' to Gordon. As he waved and said 'Goodbye, Gordon, I am going to England now,' he asked his mother, 'Who is that on Gordon's back?' I then addressed the veterans, reminding them of the leadership of Sir Arthur Harris before speaking to them about their former colleagues' sacrifice and duty, concepts which they readily understood. As we processed through the church at the conclusion, I indicated the presence of Sir Leonard Cheshire, and the Queen Mother went straight across to his wheelchair to thank him for attending.

We retired to the Vestry, where we were joined by her Private Secretary, the Lady-in-Waiting and Sir Michael Beetham, while the congregation vacated the church and assembled around the statue ready for the unveiling. While she enjoyed a refreshing glass of gin and Dubonnet, she told me that during the war she had gone with the King to visit the East End of London and noticed an old lady looking miserable and leaning on her gate. She said, 'I went over to her and remarked on the terrible destruction caused by Herr Hitler, to which the lady replied, "Bugger Hitler".'

When we joined the assembly outside, Sir Michael invited the Queen Mother to unveil the statue of Sir Arthur Harris, and after the applause had died as the covering fell away to reveal the statue, I began the dedication of the memorial and said the blessing as a Lancaster aircraft roared low overhead. Sir Michael later invited me to become the Honorary Chaplain to the Bomber Command Association, a post I accepted gladly and hold to this day.

The Director of Music and Organist, Martindale Sidwell, had been in post since the church was restored to use after the war. He was a fine, if fiery, musician and was responsible for the high standard of the musical tradition at the church, which was recognized as possessing one of the premier choirs in London. Nevertheless, I soon came to the view that it was time he retired. I consulted with the Trustees and we agreed that he should be informed by me. There was no easy way to do it after such a long and distinguished service. It was one of the harder things I have ever had to do. I then discovered that there was no pension plan in place for him, so I proposed to the Trustees that we offer him a cheque equal to a year's salary, which was readily agreed. Happily, we remained the very best of friends and brother members of the Savage Club, and he continued to sit in the congregation on Sunday mornings and offer ruthless criticism to his protégé and successor, Peter Long.

Another memorable service in the church was held on Friday, 25th March 1994, to commemorate the fiftieth anniversary of the Great Escape from Stalag Luft lll in Sagan, Germany, in 1944. I had read Paul Brickhill's book about it when I was a teenager, and I was very moved at the account of the fifty POWs who were murdered by the Gestapo after their recapture.

When I arrived at the church, it was absolutely packed; flags of the Dominion and Allied Forces which were involved in the escape were draped from the balconies of the church, and the Central Band of the RAF was playing the catchy signature tune from the 1963 film of the escape. It was a magnificent occasion, and the choir of St Clement Danes was on top form, as they sang Parry's, 'I was glad' as the introit anthem. When I climbed the stairs into Grinling Gibbons' fine pulpit, the sight was almost overwhelming. Dame Vera Lynn sang, 'We'll meet again', during the service, and the entire congregation joined her in the reprise. When we talked together after the service I suggested that it must have been the first time for her to have received no applause after her performance, due to the memorial nature of the service. She agreed that it was a first.

The paramount concern throughout my entire time as the Chaplain-in-Chief was the continuous restructuring of the armed forces under the spending cuts of the John Major government, but in my Assistant Chaplains-in-Chief, Brian McAvoy at Support Command, Robin Turner at Strike Command, Philip Mortimer at RAF Germany, Tom Goode at St Clement Danes and Peter Bishop at Amport House, I felt that I had a team I could rely on in the turbulent waters ahead.

Within the first few weeks of my appointment I was in the lift at Adastral House, Holborn, on the way up to my Office on the third floor, with the Director General Training (RAF), Air Vice Marshal John Willis, who had been my Station Commander in Akrotiri. He asked casually how my plans for restructuring the Chaplains' Branch were coming on, for he was in overall charge of drawing up the revised structure of the Air Force Department under the terms of the Prospect Study. My blank stare answered his question. He informed me that mine was the only branch yet to submit a draft; I had two weeks to meet the deadline. He agreed to give me a briefing that afternoon.

The Second Permanent under Secretary of State for Defence, informally referred to as 2nd PUS, was conducting this study called Prospect, which proposed decentralizing MOD from London. It required the Air Member for Personnel and the Air Member for Supply & Organization to relocate as Commanders-in-Chief outside London. Two new commands would form: Personnel & Training Command and Logistics Command. Support Command would then disband together with RAF Germany. If the Prospect Study was accepted by the Government, then my department would become a part of Personnel & Training Command at RAF Innsworth in Gloucester.

At the same time, the revised structure had to take into account the reduction in the size of the RAF under the Options for Change Report. Within the two weeks I had drawn up a draft revision of the management structure, which I submitted to John Willis for comment. On 12th September 1991, I called a meeting in my office with the Revd Ray Brown, the Principal Chaplain (CSFC), Monsignor Mike Cassidy, the Principal Chaplain (RC), and laid my draft proposals before them. The three of us were friends and shared our thoughts with honesty and candour, and we were in agreement about the way ahead. It was the first of such meetings which would chart the tortuous route of agreeing a branch management structure.

I had inherited an establishment of 106 chaplains, including the two Principal Chaplains and myself, which were allocated, according to the percentage of their serving personnel, to the three denominational elements. I took the view that while particular denominational pastoral care was essential at station and unit level, it was relatively unimportant at management level; one didn't have to be Baptist or an Anglican to be an effective manager at a command headquarters, provided that someone at that level would provide denominational support to the chaplain in the field. I began to plan accordingly.

As I continued my drafting and re-drafting, I decided that I would use the opportunity to change the titles of the senior chaplains to match those of other branches in the RAF. The Head of Branch was usually a Director General, assisted by one or more Directors, who, in turn, delegated work to a Deputy Director. I remembered that, in the Civil Service Department, the Branch was referred to as 'Chaplaincy Services (RAF)', so that completed my title: Director General Chaplaincy Services, or DGCS (RAF). The two Principal Chaplains became Director CS 1 and Director CS 2, and the Assistant Chaplains-in-Chief and Assistant Principal Chaplains became Deputy Directors CS. That was the easy and cosmetic part; but at the same time, the Options for Change study, following the end of the Cold War, was demanding massive savings in the defence budget. There was a clamour for a 'Peace Dividend'. The posts shed under Prospect had to offer a real saving, and there was talk of a redundancy programme. I tried to argue that the so-called Peace Dividend was surely the peace this country was enjoying, but no one seemed to listen. So, for the time being, I preferred to work alone; I felt that a committee would cloud the thinking, and might 'frighten the horses'.

At a confidential meeting of Senior Commanders, convened at the RAF Staff College, Bracknell, in December 1991, it was disclosed that total manpower in the RAF was to reduce from 88,000 to 75,000 by 1995. Eleven stations were to close in the following two years, Phantom and Buccaneer aircraft were to be withdrawn together with the Bloodhound missile by 1993, and four RAF Regiment squadrons were to disband. Two of my former squadrons were disbanded: Nos. 42 and 55. It was clear that the Options for Change programme was going to be ruthless in its demand for savings. Uncertainty and rumour was everywhere to be found.

In an attempt to assert some order into the proceedings, early in 1992, a Manpower Structure Study was set up which became known as The Roberts Report. Air Vice Marshal Andrew Roberts had been at St Mawgan when I was the chaplain there in 1971, and, being a very fine organist, had often used the church instrument as a practice organ. We had kept in touch over the years at Coastal Command reunions, and he often called at my home in Caythorpe when he was in the area. In one such meeting I challenged him about the scope of his study. He explained that the task was to establish the pattern for future manpower requirements for the RAF, and in pursuit of that, he would be examining every corner of the Service to discern areas where things might be done differently, more efficiently and hopefully in a more cost effective way. He looked me straight in the eyes and said, 'Brian, there will be no sacred cows.' For the first time, I wondered whether I would be able to secure the continuance of a commissioned Chaplains' Branch in the face of such powerful Treasury determination to cut cost.

When it was my turn to face the 'inquisition' from a member of the Roberts Study Team, I asked Peter Bishop to join me as two minds addressing the questions would, I thought, be helpful. The first question required me to defend the need for a Chaplains' Branch at all, and from there every detail of our operation was minutely examined. At the end of a bruising morning, we felt that we had given a good account of ourselves, and Peter and I retired to a local wine bar.

When, in the first few weeks of my appointment, Air Vice Marshal John Willis was explaining to me the terms of the Prospect Study, he assumed that I would be relocating my department from London to the RAF Chaplains' School at Amport House. I said that on the contrary, I would go where the Air Member for Personnel (AMP) went, as I was one of his specialist officers. John accepted that argument, and wired the Chaplains' Branch into the command structure for the proposed new command under AMP at Innsworth, Gloucester. I had feared that if the Chaplain-in-Chief's headquarters was at Amport House it would make a neat branch to lop off when the going got tough financially. After the Roberts Study interview I was glad that I had insisted on sticking close to AMP. When the Report was published, several sacred cows were sacrificed and it recommended that the RAF should reduce to fewer than 60,000 personnel, but the Chaplain's Branch emerged unscathed.

The Roberts Study was an RAF initiative, but by 1993 the Government was looking for further savings in the Defence budget, and set up the Defence Cost Study (DCS). In fact, it was made up of nineteen separate studies including training, organization, medical, and chaplaincy, and its worst aspect was the imposition of two redundancy programmes in the RAF alone. My former C-in-C at Support Command, Air Chief Marshal Sir Michael Graydon, was now the Chief of the Air Staff and was batting for the RAF. Once again I had an interview with a member of the Study Team, in which I had to give detailed evidence in support of the continuance of the Chaplains' Branch. When the report on the Defence Cost Study was published, it was evident that the Roberts Study was a much better structured plan for the RAF. Even so, as a result of the DCS we suffered from redundancy programmes and the massacre of the Medical Branch.

All the Departments and Branches in the RAF were bending before the winds of change, and there was an air of every man for himself. I took comfort in the concept of 'All of One Company', to use a phrase gaining currency in briefings. It was time to bring the Chaplaincy firmly into the core of the RAF, not in any executive sense, for I considered that relative rank was appropriate for clergy. However, since its formation in 1918, the Chaplains' Branch had worn a distinctive cap badge on an officer's SD hat: it was a crown above the branch brooch. We had all worn it with pride, but I decided that it was no longer the time to stand out from the crowd.

I wrote to the Air Force Board making a case for the distinctive Chaplains' Branch cap badge to be abolished, and for all chaplains to wear the standard Officer cap badge instead, as an expression of the fact that we are 'all of one company'. There was also a saving to be made on the supply of the former unique cap badges. It took a while to get it on the agenda of an Air Force Board meeting, for there were more pressing matters requiring a decision, but at last it was discussed and met with a favourable response. For some reason AMP sought opinion from retired Chaplains-in-Chief, and so I informed the commissioned chaplains what was in hand, and because I did not want to disclose all the reasons for my proposal, it was met with a mixed response, which did not affect my decision in the slightest. When Royal Assent was received, a Defence Council Instruction went out informing the RAF at large of the change in cap badge, and a small part of the Branch passed into history.

Many chaplains were sad about the loss of a distinctive cap badge but I declined to enter into any discussion on the matter, for a sense of danger is bad for morale. I hoped that as matters became clearer the chaplains would understood the good reason for being 'all of one company'.

When I realised the scale of the imminent closure of the overseas stations, I decided that for the recruitment and retention of good chaplains I required another overseas chaplaincy, but in an age of austerity it was a tall order. So Dermot McKavanagh came with me on a visit to RAF Germany; we stayed in the Officers' Mess in Rheindahlen for the few days before we flew to Berlin with Philip Mortimer. The following day, the C-in-C, Air Marshal Sandy Wilson and his wife Mary, invited us to lunch with the Germany chaplains and their wives, at his residence, Air House. It was a happy occasion and after the chaplains had departed, the C-in-C and I had a private meeting. When I explained the reason for my visit, and that I considered there was justification for the establishment of an Anglican RAF chaplain in the huge US Base at Ramstein, where other denominations were adequately represented, he encouraged me to staff it in the usual way, indicating that it would find a favourable reception from him. He asked my plans for Berlin and on discovering we were to stay in the Mess, he ordered his Staff Officer to open 'High House' for us and to make his staff car available during our stay. 'High House' was a splendid mansion on the bank of the Havel, and had been the Berlin residence of the RAF Commander-in-Chief since the war. The three of us spent three days there before returning to London and Philip to Rheindahlen.

Such visits were oases in a wilderness of staff work. The loudest noise in the ministry of Defence was the sound of papers being torn up as new directives came from the Government. Everyone was working hard, often to the point of exhaustion.

As the Air Member for Personnel's Management Board assembled in his outer office for the last meeting before Christmas 1992, AMP asked me to come into his office with the Air Secretary. Closing the door behind him, Sir Roger congratulated me and told me that I had been appointed a Companion of the Most Honourable Order of the Bath in the New Year Honours List. That was not unique, for all previous Chaplains-in-Chief had been accorded the honour before they retired, but this was only seventeen months into my time as Chief.

Each year in July the Order holds an evening Party in Westminster Abbey after it is closed to visitors. One year Joy was unable to join me so Helen accompanied me, as she was now eighteen. We were in the Henry VII chapel, which is the chapel of the Order, when an usher called, 'Make way for the Great Master', as the Prince of Wales came in with the Dean. He made his way along the chapel chatting with the Knights and Companions, but before very long his bodyguard told the Dean that he had to get the Prince away to another function. As they began to leave, the Dean saw me and said, 'You will know the Chaplain-in-Chief, sir,' They stopped by my side as we shook hands, then I said, 'Your Royal Highness, may I present my daughter, Helen, who is standing in for her mum this evening.' Prince Charles turned to my daughter and said, 'That's a culture shock, Helen; I do it myself sometimes.'

Whenever I hear a military band playing Elgar's Variation, 'Nimrod', I am reminded of two of the most moving occasions in my life. On Remembrance Sunday the head of each of the armed forces chaplaincies take it in turn to accompany the Bishop of London, as Dean of the Chapels Royal, on the parade at the Cenotaph. As it was my turn in 1991, I served long enough to do it again in 1994. While I went to a robing room, shared with the Bishop, Joy was taken to a balcony overlooking the Cenotaph. As the Bishop, my friend and contemporary at St Stephen's House, David Hope, and I followed the Choir of the Chapels Royal out into Whitehall, the Massed Bands were playing 'Nimrod'. The whole event is public ceremonial at its most solemn and devout. I was reunited with Joy afterwards in one of the state rooms of the Home Office at a reception for visiting Ambassadors and High Commissioners hosted by Douglas Hurd, the Foreign Secretary. There was an interval following the reception, and we adjourned with Fr Willie Booth, the Domestic Chaplain to the Queen, to his apartment in St James' Palace, where I changed into a lounge suit, before continuing to Barton Street for lunch with the Bishop of London. I enjoyed a long conversation with a delightful lady named Elizabeth, and when I asked what her husband did, she said, 'He's still Lord Chancellor', as she pointed across the room to Lord Mackay of Clashfern. Meanwhile, Joy was speaking to a tall, slim man, who introduced himself as Dick, and said, 'You must be the new Chaplain-in-Chief.' I said that I was and asked him, 'What do you do, Dick?' 'Well, when I left the office on Friday I was the Chief of Defence Staff.' I apologised to Admiral of the Fleet Sir Richard Vincent, and took everyone at face value after that; lounge suits have a lot to answer for.

My turn came again in 1994 and by then I had grown into the job; I asked no-one their role if I hadn't met them. Joy astounded me at the Foreign Office reception when a friendly fellow came up to say hello. I faintly recognised him as he chatted away, and then Joy said, 'You must feel at times like a headmaster.' 'You are so right, Joy,' he replied. Later, Joy revealed that we had been speaking to Lord Bernard Weatherill, the former Mr Speaker; she had recognised his voice and the portcullis motif on his tie had confirmed it for her.

That year we had a delightful lunch party at the Bishop of London's House. David Hope had also grown into the job and it was relaxed and much hilarity was to be heard, not least from our table. Eric Evans, the impish Dean of St Paul's Cathedral sat at one end, with Joy on his right and me on his left—'the Welsh End', he called it. Douglas Hurd sat next to Joy, with Lady Mackay next to me. The conversation was scintillating and the Foreign Office anecdotes had us all in tears of laughter. To those who did not know him, Douglas Hurd appeared to be a cold fish, but nothing was further from the truth. I expect Malcolm Rifkind, the Secretary of State for Defence, was present, but I didn't see him or hear his voice. Earlier in the day, I had slipped away from the robing room set aside for David Hope and myself in the Home Office and returned to my staff car on Horse Guards Parade to get a cloak. On the walk back, I fell into step beside Malcolm Rifkind and said, 'Good morning, Secretary of State. It looks like rain.' He merely grunted and walked on. It was the rudest of encounters I have experienced.

The three service archdeacons were also ex officio members of the General Synod of the Church of England, which met three times a year for three or four days: in February and November in Church House, Westminster, and in July a residential session at York University. I addressed Synod on 30th November 1994, following the Archbishop of York in a debate on the 'Responsibility in Arms Transfer Policy', a Report by the Board of Social Responsibility, moved by the Bishop of Coventry.

I began by referring to paragraph 7 of the Report, where it acknowledged the part played by the Prime Minister in 1992 in increasing the transparency of arms transfer—'knowing who is selling what to whom.' I continued, 'However, knowing that the Exocet missile homing in on your tail-pipe was sold to the Argentineans by the French did not solve the problem for the [RAF] pilot under attack in the Falkland war.' I argued that it is sometimes almost impossible to determine the use to which our armament will be put following sale, especially when research and development costs these days make it necessary to work collaboratively with our allies. I concluded with an amusing anecdote which had the Synod in a gale of laughter and which, I hoped, would persuade them to accept my argument. It concerned a request from a local radio station inviting me to choose something as a Christmas gift. Without wishing to be greedy, I replied that I was partial to crystallized fruits. 'Synod can imagine my confusion on Christmas Eve, when I heard the continuity announcer explain that the radio station had done a survey on what people wished for Christmas, and the Bishop of Coventry had asked that the government ensure that Britain's arms policy was ethically responsible, while the Archdeacon of the RAF would like a small box of crystallized fruits.' [Pause for laughter to subside]. 'I wish to assure Synod that I have changed my mind, and now urge you to take note of the Report and to support the motion at Item 10.'

[Note: The speech can be read in full in the Report of Proceedings, General Synod Winter Sessions 1994, p.716–718].

At another meeting of the General Synod the decision had been taken to ordain women to the priesthood. I had voted against it on the grounds that the Church of England could no longer claim catholic orthodoxy in its doctrine if it adopted this practice. I knew that there were many of my chaplains who would be in some difficulty when the decision was made, so I invited them to an overnight meeting at Amport House, when I could explain my decision to remain in the Church of England for the time being as I felt I ought to recognize that the Holy Spirit must have some part in all of this, and they could have their say about their own position.

The news of this meeting became known throughout the Branch, and chaplains who readily accepted the decision of Synod asked if they could join their colleagues who were hurt by it. After a moment's thought, I consented, and about thirty chaplains attended. The meeting was a most moving experience. For when, after my introduction, I encouraged them to speak their mind, chaplain after chaplain felt able to bare his soul, and the care and compassion of the others was tangible. I was proud to lead such an honest band of brothers.

My predecessor had presided over the establishment of a synod for the Anglican Church in the RAF, and called it the RAF Archdeaconry Synod. The Royal Navy and the Army did likewise. The Synod assembled at Amport House on a Friday afternoon and dispersed after lunch on the Sunday.

One of the functions I created for my Synod was to decide where the major charitable giving should be directed each year. On two Sundays a month, each Anglican chaplaincy throughout the RAF sent the Offertory to the Chaplain-in-Chief's Discretionary Fund. This was disbursed to various good causes at the sole discretion of the Chief. For example, one year I had been doing a live broadcast from the BBC studios in Lincoln when I met the new secretary of the Lincoln Cathedral Music Appeal. She explained that she was hoping to raise money by getting large organizations to sponsor a chorister in perpetuity. She said that the cost per chorister was daunting at £35,000, but she hoped that someone would start the ball rolling. I knew that I had more than that in the Discretionary Fund, so I said that I would sponsor a chorister there and then. Thus 'The RAF Archdeaconry Chorister' was the first of many.

After that, I asked for a short list of charities from members of Synod in advance of a meeting, and the Synod Standing Committee would select two or three and ask the proposer to give a presentation at the meeting. When we chose 'The Weston Spirit' as the charity one year, we invited four young beneficiaries to address Synod; I shall never forget the occasion as many members of Synod were in tears at the life stories related by the youngsters. I had the privilege of presenting the cheque to Simon Weston at a later ceremony, and heard from him many other such tales.

To the Weston Spirit with love from the RAF Archdeaconry Synod

The cheque presentations were usually high profile for the charity to gain some publicity, so I had lunch with the Princess of Wales and appeared on stage with Princess Margaret, to name-drop but two.

A former RAF maritime wing commander had resumed his career as an artist when he retired, and had painted several air officers and had completed a stunning painting of Concorde taking off from Bahrein for the boardroom at the headquarters of British Aerospace, when he announced that he wished to paint the Chaplain-in-Chief. So after five tedious sittings, Stanley Baldock painted me in my robes in my stall in St Clement Danes. Given his Coastal Command background there was only one place I considered suitable for the unveiling ceremony, and that was in the bar at 'Auntie Pearl's' in Mawgan Porth, where I had spent so many happy hours when the fog stopped flying at St Mawgan. It was a riotous party with many of my old friends present.

Meanwhile, back in my office, having shared my skeletal draft of a new branch management structure with the Principal Chaplains in February 1993, I set up a working group to put some flesh on the skeleton and produce a report which could be sent to the Air Force Board. It was a good report, although I was not prepared to permit the idea of shared visiting of all personnel on a station irrespective of denomination, nor was I prepared to accept the proposal to disestablish my Staff Chaplain. With such amendments, I called a meeting of the Branch Management Team, and formally discussed the report line by line. At the end of the morning

I put it to the vote, and the Roman Catholic member of the working group voted against it. I said that I was not prepared to submit it to AMP unless all three denominations agreed to the terms of the report. After lunch I took a further vote and the report was agreed.

Air Chief Marshal Sir 'Sandy' Wilson had succeeded Sir Roger Palin as Air Member for Personnel, and so I took the final document to him in his office in Whitehall. I explained how I thought the structure would work in the new Lead Command arrangement, whereby one command took the lead and provided a service for the whole of the RAF. My Branch Management Team, established at the proposed Personnel & Training Command to be set up at RAF Innsworth, would provide a chaplaincy service common to both Strike and Logistics Commands. He agreed to staff it through the Policy & Plans department.

When, at last, it was discussed at length by the Board, the Commander-in-Chief Strike Command, Air Chief Marshal Sir John Thomson, was unwilling to lose his Command Chaplain; he wanted his chaplaincy adviser at hand. I went to see him in his office at HQ Strike Command and we talked about it for nearly an hour, without agreement. I liked him immensely; he was a man of integrity and candour, and had a fine sense of humour. He was a man with religious conviction and wished to retain 'his' Command Chaplain for the best of reasons. So we agreed to differ, and to discuss it with the Chief of the Air Staff.

When we both went to see the Chief of the Air Staff he informed us that 2nd PUS, Sir Moray Stewart, had asked for the Chaplains' Branch paper to be put on hold until the outcome of the Options for Change Study was known, so he would not overrule a Commander-in-Chief while this exercise was being staffed. That is why, when the new structure was at last implemented at the end of March 1994, one of the command chaplains remained at HQ Strike Command in High Wycombe while the rest of us went to Innsworth in Gloucester.

On the 10th July 1994, while I was in York at a residential session of the General Synod of the Church of England, I received a telephone call informing me that Air Chief Marshal Sir John Thomson had died. The brilliant, caring and generous man had, I believe, suffered a sudden brain haemorrhage. When I held the first (and only) Chaplains' Branch Ladies Guest Night at RAF North Luffenham Officers' Mess, to celebrate the 75th anniversary of the formation of the Branch, Sir John and Lady Jan Thomson were the Guests of Honour, and he was a great encouragement to all present.

When the decision was finally made to implement the proposals of the Prospect Study, I began to plan for the removal of my headquarters to Gloucester. Not only that, but arrangements had to be made to move to the management structure at the same time, for it was hoped that it would be approved by the time we relocated.

Dermot McKavanagh had been an excellent colleague at MOD, and had kept me well informed about the concerns of chaplains, and morale generally. However, with the huge turbulence in the office management ahead, I required a man who understood a systematic approach to organization. Such a man was Padre Brian Smith, who became my Staff Chaplain in June 1993, when Dermot succeeded him at RAF Lyneham. The relocation to Innsworth of a unified department with three hitherto separate filing registries was quite a task, and I gave the oversight of the transition to Padre Brian McAvoy, in addition to his duties at St Clement Danes.

That was just as well, for I needed my new Staff Chaplain for a more urgent priority which had come out of the blue. From time to time a paper listing a series of Alternative Assumptions defining which areas in the Defence Estate could be sold for profit. Towards the end of 1993, to my horror, I saw Amport House at the top of the list. Malcolm Rifkind MP, the Secretary of State for Defence, wanted to sell Amport House. I tasked Brian Smith with a journey to the MOD Main Building in Whitehall to return only when he had persuaded the author of the List to remove Amport House. Brian returned the following day; he had traced the source to a young, 'fast-track' graduate civil servant, who was not interested in the work done at Amport, but only that it was worth £3.5 million. The work of the Chaplains' School was held in high regard throughout the RAF, and I was determined that the School would continue at Amport House, and I prepared to do battle for it.

I got on well with the Second Permanent Under Secretary of State, Sir Moray Stewart, who was by this time instructing me in the search for an alternative venue for the School, and I told him that I had no intention of abandoning Amport, and that I would fight Malcolm Rifkind all the way to the wire. He persuaded me to look at Eltham Palace, the former RN Staff College at Greenwich, and the old army barracks at Guildford, which turned out to be a split site. I deemed none of these locations suitable for the Chaplains' School.

While all this was going on, I was 'in attendance' at a conference for retired Air Officers at the RAF Staff College, Bracknell, when I heard the Chief of the Air Staff say, 'After lunch I shall call upon the Chaplain-in-Chief to give an update on Amport House, to be followed by the Commandant at Cranwell who will give an overview of developments at the College.' There wasn't time to prepare anything, so after an enjoyable lunch I mounted the stage and gave a short burst about the Secretary of State being unprepared for a Barbary Welshman who voted against the ordination of women, and that it was becoming increasingly likely that we should retain Amport House as an RAF unit housing the Chaplains' School. It was received with roars of approval, loud cheers and laughter. Then Air Vice Marshal (later Air Chief Marshal Sir) David Cousins took my place and said, to more laughter, 'I shall spend the rest of my career making sure that I do not follow Brian Lucas on the platform.'

In the end we won the battle for Amport House, because I discovered that there were in the local area three other houses of similar size to Amport, which had been on the market for up to five years, and they did not have a listed garden for the buyer to worry about. Also, the School staff put together a robust in-house study, and I ensured that all this became known at the National Audit Office.

While the battle for Amport was being fought, my colleague the Chaplain-General of the Army, Jim Harkness, a Church of Scotland minister, was obliged to vacate his Chaplains' Depot at Bagshot Park. I encouraged Jim to join us at Amport, for we had always offered the Royal Navy Chaplains' Department use of Amport, and to establish a Tri-Service School would cement the future of the place. The Chaplain General said that he would prefer to remain independent, but Sir Moray Stewart was unmoved, and the Defence Cost Study (DCS) ruled that there should be only one chaplains' school. When I retired as Chaplain-in-Chief, the move had been agreed and we were working on the title of the joint establishment. I was keen on 'Defence Chaplaincy School' for the irony of the initials (DCS), but we settled on 'Tri-Service Chaplains' School', which has since became 'The Armed Forces Chaplaincy Centre', a part of the Defence Academy of the United Kingdom. The current advertisement reads, 'Whatever the time of year, the house and magnificent park and gardens offer a peaceful setting for the work that takes place at the AFCC.' Without my successful fight, it could have been very different.

Adastral House was beginning to take on the appearance of a removal depositary as the many departments were packing up for either Gloucester or Cambridgeshire, or, in a few cases, oblivion. My headquarters was no exception as the date of March 1994 drew nearer.

Towards the end of 1993 my Personal Secretary, Barbara Boughey, took extended sick leave, and I had to resort to an agency. One or two ladies came but I did not detain them long, until the agency sent Yvonne Nye. Apart from routine dictation and typing tasks, her job entailed keeping my diary, arranging interviews, booking airline tickets, train reservations and staff cars, and generally running my outer office. She was also the interface between the MOD headquarters building and my office, which sometimes demanded tact and diplomacy. The quality and quantity of Yvonne's work output was impressive, and I wanted her to apply for a permanent job as my PS, but she did not wish to transfer to Gloucester, and so I interviewed a civil servant from Innsworth by the name of Joy. She was a pleasant lady and when I appointed her, she came to London for a few weeks before the move, to take over from Yvonne. At Gloucester I would be surrounded by Joy—both at home and at work. Joy was a loyal and valued Personal Secretary, but I missed Yvonne's efficiency.

Diane, my Higher Executive Officer (HEO), who had succeeded Doug Collard, decided to retire rather than transfer to Gloucester, and so I appointed Trevor Oliver, an HEO at Innsworth who was looking for a new post. He also came to London for a few weeks to take over from Diane. He accompanied me on a budget screening meeting and was soon up to speed. He became a great asset to the Branch Headquarters, both during and after the move. All my successors thanked me for him.

With Trevor's appointment, I had a new team in place ready for life at the brave new world of Personnel & Training Command. Personally, the move was costly, for instead of a Lodging Allowance for my flat, a new five-bedroom Residence for the Chaplain-in-Chief was being built at the new Headquarters site. The rent for this would be deducted from my monthly pay. Towards the end of 1993, Joy came up from Caythorpe to Adastral House to discuss curtain fabrics and bathroom tiles with the building contractor. Events were moving apace.

The actual move to Gloucester came in the last week of March 1994. On Friday, 18th I held a 'Farewell to London' party in my office, and invited all the clerical staff who had worked at the Headquarters over the years to attend. The following week the office was cleared, then I cleared my flat ready to hand it over. On the Monday I moved into 18 Nicolson Close, Innsworth, which, against the regulations, I named 'The Archdeaconry'.

The Archdeaconry at RAF Innsworth 1994

My personal staff at RAF Innsworth 1994-95: Mark (Driver), June (Housekeeper), Trevor (Higher Executive Officer), BHL, Joy (Personal Secretary), Brian (Staff Chaplain).

The fact that I was now part of a Command Headquarters meant that I was back in uniform, for in London we all wore lounge suits. I felt that I had returned home. My personal staff was also enlarged, for I was allocated a comfortable Rover staff car and a uniformed driver, SAC Mark Newman. In addition, I was provided with a Steward for the house, although Mrs June Jackson acted more as a housekeeper for me.

To mark the formation of the new command, Sir 'Sandy' Wilson, as the Commander-in-Chief, arranged a Dining-In Night for all station commanders in the Command, and said to all his Board Members that he did not want to see any of the guests paying for drinks, for after dinner he was putting on a few barrels of beer behind the bar. Quite late on I saw a group captain reaching into his pocket, and told him that drinks were 'on the house'. He informed me that the free beer had run out, so I had a word with the bar staff and then climbed on top of the bar counter, called for silence and announced to the assembled officers that, 'There is a barrel of beer on the Chaplains' Branch'. The news was received with loud cheers, especially when the C-in-C had to help me to get down.

In the meantime, the Treasury was demanding yet more savings from the defence budget, and a study known as Options 1A(R) was introduced. I had already managed to bring the number of Anglican chaplains down to 57 without any redundancy or imposing a temporary ban on recruiting. Both of my senior colleagues were new to the cut and thrust of duelling with the Treasury: Mgr Tony Smith had been appointed Principal Roman Catholic Chaplain (with 10 chaplains) at the beginning of January 1994, and John Sheddon to the post of Principal Church of Scotland & Free Church Chaplain (with 17 chaplains) in the August of that year.

Following the redundancy programmes, the establishment of the RAF had decreased to 52,000, with the consequential decrease in the number of chaplains. I was greatly encouraged, however, when the study to determine the RAF's Core Requirement was published. This gave a figure for the number of personnel required to go to war, and the number of chaplains was established as 82. The commanders of the air force wanted their chaplains alongside them in time of conflict. I had read all the annual reports on the chaplains, and I was not in the least surprised, for station commanders and Air Officers were lavish in their praise for what the chaplains were delivering at station and unit level.

At the beginning of 1995, everyone in MOD was working flat out to achieve the new budgetary targets. Senior officers were tiring of fighting for every piece in the jigsaw of defence planning. I called on the Chief of the Air Staff at the end of another busy day and Sir Michael Graydon looked quizzically at me when I was ushered into his office. I reminded him of his station commander days, when his padre might pop in for an informal chat. 'I am your Padre, there is no agendum', I said. He smiled and poured two glasses of whisky, and we talked for a while about the pressure we were all enduring, and he more than most.

From that meeting came an idea: I decided to hold a House-Party at Amport House for the senior Air Marshals who all needed to relax and have a bit of jollity. I put the idea to Sir Michael and he accepted it with alacrity. So it came about that Joy and I hosted a black-tie dinner for five Air Chief Marshals, five Air Marshals and four Air Vice-Marshals, all accompanied by their wives, on Friday, 24th March 1995. I arranged for the Woodwind Quintet of the RAF Central Band to play before and during dinner, and the Choir of St Clement Danes sang Grace and entertained the guests in the Long Gallery after dinner.

I proposed a toast to the Royal Air Force in which I bade farewell to Sandy Wilson, who was retiring, and to John Willis, who was taking up the appointment of Vice Chief of the Defence Staff, and Mike Graydon replied. It was a lovely, informal evening, and while some enjoyed the singing of the choir, others played snooker, and the bar was kept busy until the small hours. All the guests were accommodated overnight and after breakfast on the Saturday, CAS used the opportunity to hold a meeting of his senior commanders in the quietness and security of Amport House, while the Principal gave the Air Vice Marshals not involved in the meeting, and the wives, a tour of the gardens. It was a brief respite from the daily onslaught.

The Chaplains' Branch Victorious Cricket Team, June 1995 Captain: Padre Tony Fletcher

In the June before my retirement there was another famous victory at Amport. Each year the Chaplains of the Army and RAF play each other at cricket. The army had won throughout my time as Chief. In 1995 the match was at Amport and the RAF Captain, Tony Fletcher, promised me the Cup. Despite losing a lot of blood from a well-aimed ball, he led our team to victory.

Officers on a full commission retired at the age of 55, but my tour had been extended to allow me to implement the move to Gloucester. My new retirement date had been agreed as 1st November 1995, All Saints Day, which meant that I would have completed four and a half years as Chaplain-in-Chief. I could have stayed longer, but while I enjoyed what I was doing, I was increasingly aware that I was working my body close to its limit. When my annual and terminal leave was taken into account, Monday 28th August 1995 was agreed as the date my successor would take over.

The Principal of Amport House, Robin Turner, was chosen as my successor and not long after his name had been announced I became aware that John Sheddon and Tony Smith had very different ideas about the future of the chaplaincy, so much so that at one of our Heads of Denomination meetings I adjourned the meeting 'until serenity returned'. Meanwhile, my old friend David Cousins had been appointed as Commander-in-Chief and AMP, and he was dealing with the new study, Options 1A(R), which required me to lose two of the four command chaplains, and with my four years experience of restructuring under the principle of 'best man for the job', I was quite certain of the two candidates. However, I knew that my two senior colleagues would oppose my decision, and with only a month to go before my retirement, I decided to avoid a row, and so enable my successor to have a clear run at the downsizing of the headquarters. When I began to discuss the planned structure of the Branch during the hand over, I discovered that he had already formed his plans about the future, so I wished him 'Good Luck in the name of the Lord'.

FROM: AIR MARSHAL D COUSINS CB AFC BA RAF

AIR MEMBER FOR PERSONNEL
AND
AIR OFFICER COMMANDING-IN-CHIEF

PTC/190/10/AMP

HEADQUARTERS
PERSONNEL AND TRAINING COMMAND
ROYAL AIR FORCE INNSWORTH
GLOUCESTER GL3 1EZ

Telephone: (01452) 712612 Ext 5001

Air Vice-Marshal B H Lucas CB QHC BA RAF
Chaplain-in-Chief
Headquarters Personnel & Training Command
Royal Air Force
INNSWORTH
Gloucester
GL3 1EZ

21 August 1995

My Dear Brian.

To mark your retirement from the Royal Air Force I know that the Under Secretary of State for Defence will be writing to you shortly to convey, on behalf of Her Majesty The Queen, an expression of her personal thanks for your long and valuable service.

This is really a letter I was dreading writing, for Innsworth without Brian Lucas will be a hollower place! Could I simply add my own very sincere thanks and those of my Air Force Board colleagues, for all that you have done for the Royal Air Force throughout your career. You have served with enormous distinction and flair. Your pragmatic and human touch in administering to the pastoral needs of our great Service are a model for all who will follow you.

In all this you have been most wonderfully supported by Joy and this letter would be incomplete if I did not also pay tribute to her. You are a very special couple who have enriched the lives of those with whom you have worked and played. You will both be enormously missed. Bless you both. Please do stay in touch. And thank you for your support to me in recent years. I told you I would have trouble writing this!

Yours as ever.

David. C

CHAPTER THIRTEEN:

If It's Monday, It's Moscow

As I descended the steps of the Boeing 767 at Rome's Leonardo da Vinci airport, an officer of the Carabinieri approached me and asked, 'Father Lucas?' I nodded and he beckoned me to follow him across the tarmac. As I glanced back I saw that the other passengers were following a steward in a different direction, and were all staring at me as if I were a criminal. I did feel rather uneasy as we approached a blank door in the airport building. I followed him through it and at once he indicated a suitcase and said, 'Yours?' Again, I nodded, and he said 'Bring it.' It bore a black cross VIP tag, so it would have been off-loaded first.

His English was excellent, for he held his hand out and said, 'Passport, please.' I gave it to him, and as we passed through a glass door he waved it at a man in an office and returned it to me. Going through yet another door we found ourselves in the sunlight and on the pavement where a military car was waiting. I asked where we were going, but received no reply, he just opened the back door for me, stowed my case in the boot, and climbing into the front passenger seat, we set off along the 22-mile motorway to the city centre of Rome. My arrival process had taken four minutes.

As we came to the end of the motorway two Carabinieri motorcyclists joined us, one on each side of the car and just ahead of it, and with blue lights flashing and sirens wailing I arrived at my hotel in no time at all, as we scythed through the traffic in the busy city boulevards. He opened the door for me to alight, gave my suitcase to a porter, and, with a smart salute, he was gone. I have to say that it is the only way to arrive at a hotel; for the rest of my stay I had the undivided attention of the entire staff. 'Ice for your gin and tonic, Monsignor, will one bucket be enough?'

For very many years, the chief chaplains in the air forces of the NATO Alliance had met together every May for a conference hosted in turn. A few years before I became Chief, the navies and armies of the Alliance realised that they were missing a trick, and organized tri-service meetings of chief chaplains every year in February. In 1991 the Italian armed forces invited us to a conference, which is why I had flown to Rome. It was my first visit to the city so I arrived the Friday before the conference to see the tourist sites. When Ray Brown and Tony Harris, together with my army and navy colleagues, arrived on the Monday, they travelled by military bus to the hotel, and had to fetch their own ice.

I went to St Peter's Basilica for Sunday morning Mass on the feast of Candlemas. Approaching the church I saw that police were checking tickets for entry to the basilica as Pope John Paul ll was presiding at Pontifical High Mass. I had no ticket, but I was wearing a clerical collar, so as I approached the barrier it was pulled aside and I was waved through.

I managed to find a place near the back of the packed church, but when the procession entered from the west end of the south aisle, everyone turned around, so I was near the 'front'. A procession of priests, followed by monks and nuns carrying enormous candles, was, in turn, followed by a procession of bishops and then cardinals, and bringing up the rear, his Holiness the Pope. He seemed so small in this vast crowd that he appeared to be 'trapped' in the office of the Papacy, and I said a silent prayer for him. Then the atmosphere was ruined when an exuberant nun standing next to me allowed her candle to set fire to the hair of the woman in front, and there was much patting of her head to put out the flames. Slowly the smell of burnt hair lacquer gave way to the welcome fragrance of incense, and the Mass went on.

It was a high-profile conference, organized by an officious archbishop from the Vatican, with the help of a splendid English-speaking chaplain to the Alpine Corps, Fr Frank Troy. On the Wednesday we were invited to breakfast with the President of the Italian Republic at the Presidential Palace, but the highlight was a guided tour of the Vatican later in the week. When we arrived at the Sistine Chapel, after some time marvelling at the painting, the guide opened a small door in the west wall and we entered the Papal private apartments. There were more treasures to see before we sat in a small audience chamber and John Paul ll came in to welcome us.

He spoke to us about chaplaincy for nearly thirty minutes before greeting us individually for a short conversation. Here was the man who had played such a pivotal part in bringing freedom to Eastern Europe through his unwavering support for the Solidarity movement in Gdansk. Here was the man who, at the Mass inaugurating his pontificate, had grasped his crozier like a sword and lifting it up had made the sign of a solemn benediction over the vast crowd in St Peter's Square. Throughout our private meeting, during which he spoke fluent English, I held eye contact with him and it seemed that he was looking into my soul, something I had experienced only once before when I first met Metropolitan Anthony Bloom.

On the flight back to London I sat on the flight deck of the British Airways Boeing 767 for much of the journey and the Captain told me to stay for the landing; we chatted until the aircraft came to its stand at the terminal.

I always looked forward to these meetings of Heads of Chaplaincies because we came from such diverse backgrounds and in many countries the priests and bishops were civilians and were not fully integrated into the military organization at home. I found the formal sessions rather tedious, especially when they were arranged by civilian clergy from Eastern Europe, but outside the conference hall we became excellent friends and enjoyed exchanging ideas in the jollity of evening meals and informal gatherings. In this way I learned a great deal about the scope of NATO.

I was usually accompanied by my colleagues Ray Brown and Tony Harris, and, when they both retired, by John Sheddon and Tony Smith. We went to Stockholm, where I was presented to the King and Queen of Sweden; to Copenhagen; to Washington, where we had lunch one day in the Pentagon with the Deputy Secretary of State; to Budapest, where Tony Harris, Ray Brown and I became lost wandering about the streets at midnight in sub-zero temperatures. When the Hellenic Air Force invited us to Athens, Tony Smith, John Sheddon and I travelled a week early, took some leave, and hired a car. We drove north, via Delphi, as far as the monasteries of Meteora, before returning along the east coast and into the

In conference with US Air Force Chief Chaplain Donald Harlin in Washington

With two Ukrainian Officers in Budapest

Peloponnese to Epidaurus. On the last evening before the conference began, we drank ouzo by the Temple at Sounion as the sun went down.

When Jim Harkness, the Chaplain General of the Army, retired, I succeeded him on the small Planning Group for the 6th annual European/North American Chief of Chaplains Conference. In September 1994, I spent three days in Warsaw at the home of Bishop Glodz (later Archbishop of Gdansk) drawing up the conference programme, and I insisted that Auschwitz be included.

The following February my colleagues from all over Europe and North America assembled for a busy week. I was particularly pleased that at the reception to mark the beginning of the conference, I was introduced to His Excellency Lech Wałęsa, the charismatic leader who co-founded Solidarity, the Soviet bloc's first independent trade union. He is a man of medium height, but he had achieved mighty works. I would have wished to talk with him for longer, but receptions seldom permit it to happen.

Auschwitz was added at the end of the conference for those who had time to make the long journey to the south of Poland. Everyone wanted to go, so a few coaches set off on the Friday to a Mass at the famous Pauline monastery of Jasna Góraat, the home of the Black Madonna painting in Częstochowa. Then we travelled the short distance to Auschwitz and toured the former concentration camp in awe and silence. I found it immensely depressing, but I was glad that I had asked to visit the place. I had also asked to spend a few days in the ancient city of Krakow. While the rest of the party returned to Warsaw airport for their flights home, Tony Smith and John Sheddon, together with the German Bundeswehr Chief Lutheran chaplain, Peter Blaschke, and I were driven by minibus to Krakow where we were to stay in the Royal Hotel, just 200 metres from Wawel Castle in the old part of the city. We were accompanied by the Parish Priest and by the Senior Military Chaplain from the Krakow barracks.

Over the soup at dinner that night, the kindly parish priest leaned across the table and said to me, 'Your Queen Victoria, she is well?' When I confessed that she was, in fact, dead, he became agitated. 'Dead? When did she die?' I explained that it was quite a while ago. He was astounded, and continued, 'Why were we not told?' I tried to form some explanation which would not insult the communist tendencies of anyone listening, but he went on, 'How did she die?' By this time Tony Smith was holding his napkin to his mouth in an attempt to stifle his laughter, and Peter Blaschke was utterly bemused. Then it dawned on me that he was referring not to Victoria but, perhaps, the Queen Mother. 'Ah!' I said, 'Do you mean Queen Elizabeth, for she is well?' 'No, she is your Queen, I mean Victoria.' As my now

With Bishop Glodz in Warsaw 1995

My favourite mode of travel awaiting my arrival at Dusseldorf Airport

cold soup was removed, I explained that the Queen and her elderly mother had the same name, and were both alive and well, but he was still giving me unsure looks even when the coffee arrived.

I kept up my busy schedule of visits to RAF stations throughout the UK, often to dedicate new Squadron Standards. HRH The Duke of Edinburgh presented such a standard to No.206 Squadron at RAF Kinloss. It had rained all night and was still raining as I robed and was driven to the Parade Square, where the squadron was already standing at ease. The Chaplain-in-Chief stands to the right of the dais and moves forward for the Dedication; then the person presenting the standard comes down from the dais, hands the new standard to the Standard Bearer and inspects the parade. I was sheltered from the rain by an airman holding a large umbrella over me, but those on parade were getting wetter by the second, and when Prince Philip left the shelter of the dais, he, too, was quickly very wet.

When the parade had marched off, he came to where I was standing and accused me, 'It's all your fault, Chaplain-in-Chief, you must pray harder.' I replied quickly, 'If you are free at 2 o'clock, sir, I am burying the Met Officer; you are welcome to attend.' At this, he laughed, 'You're right; they don't look out of the bloody window, do they.'

I paid a visit to RAF Lyneham on Monday 25th November 1991, because the station used the village church as its chapel, and I wanted to see for myself how the arrangement was working. I also had a Hercules flight lined up. A few days before my visit the station had received Mr Terry Waite back from captivity in Beirut, so I asked to call on him in his quarters in the Officers' Mess after lunch. I was escorted to the private corridor, which was closely guarded, and as I went on to his rooms a gale of laughter echoed up the corridor from his dining room. I put my head around the door and saw Lord Runcie, the former archbishop, who had regaled the family with an amusing story. 'Brian', he said, 'Have you met Terry?'

Terry Waite is a very big man in every way. We shook hands and he suggested we adjourn to his bedroom next door for a chat. I told him that a candle had burned in St Clement Danes for him throughout his captivity, and he replied that we must never spurn little acts like that, for news of them might well get through and engender hope. We talked for a while about silence and prayer, and I was astounded at the fluency and energy of a man who had been chained in solitary confinement for 1,763 days. I was aware that I was keeping him from his family, and stood to say goodbye, when I heard the bells of the village church and remembered that they were ringing for Terry. I told him so as we listened to them ringing out across Wiltshire. When I returned from my Hercules flight, I popped into the church and noticed that he had written his thanks to the bell-ringers in the visitors' book.

My time as Chaplain-in-Chief of the Royal Air Force coincided with a fascinating period in international political activity. The lowering of the Iron Curtain allowed warmth to permeate Eastern Europe and so end the Cold War. There was a rapprochement with South Africa following the endeavours of Nelson Mandela and

The Assistant Chaplains-in-Chief at RAF Gatow, Berlin, March 1993

Desmond Tutu, but the Balkan states were in disarray following the death of Tito. It was a time of opportunity and responsibility, and I made every day count.

As a means of raising the profile of the Chaplains' Branch, I held my quarterly meetings with my Assistant Chaplains-in-Chief at a variety of RAF stations instead of them always being held in my office. One such meeting took place in Berlin, by this time a unified city. We had two free days in the programme; one we spent with a local guide in the city of Potsdam, horrified at the plight of Soviet soldiers still occupying their derelict barracks, and delighted at the sight of Sanssouci Palace, the former summer palace of Frederick the Great, King of Prussia.

On the second day we visited Colditz. I had driven there with my elder son, Mark, almost as soon as the Iron Curtain fell. I must have been one of the first RAF officers to go out of his way to get into Colditz Castle. I was sure that my team would enjoy the experience, too. At the small museum, containing the incredible escape artifacts made by the POWs held in the castle during the war, we were met by a very attractive young lady named Annekaterina (Anna for short). She escorted us to the castle, which housed patients with mental disabilities on the upper floors, and led us into the courtyard. It was instantly recognized from the film, 'The Colditz Story'. The chapel had been untouched throughout the period of Soviet occupation, and was covered with dust and debris, and the tunnel under the floor was still intact. There were empty Spam tins and other war-time memorabilia

Entrance to the French Tunnel 1993

With Staff Chaplain Brian Smith in Colditz

lying about, and it seemed as though the POWs had only just been liberated. As I looked at the broken altar, I heard Anna say softly, 'I would like to restore this as a place of prayer.' So I asked her what would be her first priority, and she said, 'The windows, to keep out the rain'.

Some months later, I returned to Colditz to present a cheque, from my Discretionary Fund, for DM 4,000 to Dr Pohlack, the district Finance Minister, to repair the chapel windows. My Staff Chaplain, Brian Smith, accompanied me, and the chaplain at RAF Gatow, Berlin, came with a cheque from the Station Fund. I wore ceremonial day dress for the occasion, and as we drove through the streets of Colditz, people stood at their doorways waving and cheering. I waved back, somewhat taken by surprise at the reception. As the car stopped outside the museum, a smiling Anna presented me with a large bouquet of flowers. I commented on the enthusiastic welcome from the townsfolk, and she said, 'They probably thought you were the King of Norway; he is visiting Colditz today.'

The Chief of the Air Staff telephoned one day in September 1993, with a request from the Defence Minister of Lithuania that I should advise him about appointing chaplains in their armed forces. It was forbidden under Soviet rule, but for twelve months the republic had been free and independent of the Soviet Union, and they wished to move forward. I arranged a date in November and flew to Vilnius in a Yak 42 of Lithuanian Airlines.

I was met by a friend from the Chief Chaplains' meetings, Monsignor Alfonsas Zvarinskas, who was accompanied by a colonel from the Iron Wolf Brigade of the Lithuanian Army. Alfonsas spoke only Russian and German, but the colonel spoke good English. I assumed that he had been to the UK, but he told me that he had been taught English in the Russian Army, when he was in command of an Intercontinental Ballistic Missile site in the Ural Mountains.

It was a fascinating week, although deep snow covered the entire country, and it was –26 degrees at night. I was based in a comfortable hotel in Vilnius, but spent the week touring the country in an army minibus, with Alfonsas, the Colonel and a young female interpreter from the British Embassy.

We went first to Klaipėda, the northernmost ice-free port in the Baltic states and which had been a forbidden city under the Soviets, for it housed the repair docks of the Baltic fleet. I was met by the Commodore of the port, and taken to a reception, which went on into the late evening. Alfonsas and I stayed overnight with the local parish priest, while the interpreter stayed with a friend and the Colonel went to the barracks. The priest, a Monsignor, spoke a little English, and prepared a meal of pickled fish and cabbage. By the warmth of a single-bar electric fire, we talked long into the night, and Alfonsas told me his story.

During the Soviet era there were Patriots hiding in the forest and when he had taken the Blessed Sacrament to them, he had been followed by the Secret police, but he had managed to shake them off. This happened several times before he was arrested. When he refused to disclose the hiding places, he was taken to the headquarters of the KGB in Kaunus, and after two years solitary confinement, he was sent to the Gulag in Russia for twenty-four years.

The following morning, after I had concelebrated Mass with the two monsignors, despite my explanation that I was an Anglican priest, I paid an office call on the Commodore. During our talk he told me that he had been merely an administrator in the Soviet Navy, but showed me a photograph taken during a NATO conference at which he had been an observer. When he went to chase some coffee which had been ordered, I turned the page of the photo album and saw a list of participants at the conference: he was listed as the Commodore of the Soviet Baltic Fleet—some administrator. We had a convivial lunch on board a research vessel moored nearby.

The following day I drove, with my entourage, to the air force base of Šiauliai in the north of Lithuania. For over an hour we had driven through deep forest and

The Colonel and BHL salute the Lithuanian Patriots at Rainaia with Mgr Svarinskas

everywhere was white with snow. Suddenly, Alfonsas stopped the minibus, and asked us to get out. As we stood in the snow he called us to follow him into the forest. It was like a clip from a film of wartime Nazi execution squads, and I felt a shiver in my spine, which was not caused by the temperature. He halted by a monument deep in the forest at Rainiai, the site of a massacre of 74 'political' prisoners by the Russian KGB in 1941, a few days before the German army occupied Lithuania, and began to explain the atrocities carried out against them. As he described in graphic detail how they were mutilated while still alive, the poor girl translating his words became distressed, and I stopped his flow, saying, 'Enough. I understand, Alfonsas.' She translated for him with a grateful smile at me. 'They kept the engines on the trucks running to drown the screams', he added as a full stop. I was reduced to silence at the horror of this pretty glade, and could only salute their memory, in which the Colonel joined me.

Occupying an entire wall of the Commander's office in Šiauliai was a map ranging from the eastern coast of North America to the Ural Mountains in Russia. I told the Colonel that I would point out my home on the map. As I looked closely, I saw that the names were in the Cyrillic alphabet, but as the characters are similar to Greek I was able to read it. To my astonishment, the only names over the UK were the US

Air Force bases, and not one RAF station. The Colonel pointed out Birmingham, saying that he knew it well. 'There,' I said, 'I knew you had been to the UK, you speak English so well.' 'Oh, no,' he replied, 'Birmingham was the target of my Missile Site.' I looked at him for a moment before we both broke into large smiles.

On the next day, 23rd November, I was in Kaunus to take the salute alongside the Defence Minister at the Armed Forces Day parade. They didn't have much in the way of mechanised weaponry, but as the troops marched past, their pride in a free Lithuania was evident. Although the sun shone, I was grateful for my RAF greatcoat.

After the parade, Alfonsas Zvarinskas and I strolled along the main street and every few yards someone would come up, genuflect, and kiss his hand. I asked him what this was all about, and he merely said, 'Well, they remember how it was.' As we passed a typical city monolithic block, he indicated small, frosted glass windows at pavement level, and said, 'One of these was my cell. This is the KGB building.' As we came to the corner he looked sideways, and seeing that the door was open, he led me up some steps and into the grim building. A janitor told us to go away, but when he saw Alfonsas he went through the (now customary) ritual. 'Your files have gone to Moscow, Monsignor', he told Alfonsas, 'They took away some boxes, the rest are upstairs, hundreds of them.'

We descended a dark staircase into the basement. At the bottom Alfonsas opened a door in the wall, and choked quietly as he explained that he spent forty-eight hours behind this door when he was first captured. He beckoned me to enter; it was really a cupboard with a six-inch wide shelf to prevent you collapsing onto the floor. He shut the door: it was sound-proof and totally black. I was emotional after two minutes, but he had spent two days without food or water in that hell-hole. Then he had been stripped and photographed in the small room ahead of us, the tripod still in place, before spending two years without trial in a solitary cell along the corridor. As we stood in his former cell, he pointed to the frosted-glass window, high beyond reach, which we had seen outside, Then, to my astonishment, he said, 'I could only thank God for his great goodness.' 'Goodness? I said, 'Why do you say that?' 'Because sometimes, if the wind was right, I could hear snatches of Beethoven or Mozart from the Conservatoire next door, and I knew that life was normal outside.' He was a remarkable man.

On the last day of my visit, I went to his home for breakfast. During the meal he went upstairs and returned wearing the striped uniform of the Gulag. I was humbled by the sight; how he must have despised the clothing, but he had kept it as a reminder of man's inhumanity to man. He told me that every day he had kept some bread and water to celebrate Holy Communion for the other prisoners in the cell block, and that his fellow prisoner, Archbishop Slipi, had even trained and ordained priests during the night hours.

At the beginning of October 1994 I made my only visit to Hong Kong, where the Staff Chaplain and I stayed at RAF Sek Kong, near the Chinese border, and then for a few days on Hong Kong Island, before returning home. The following week Joy and I were invited to a reception at No.10 Downing Street. We had met John and Norma Major briefly after Her Majesty The Queen had unveiled the Canadian Memorial in Green Park, but I never for a moment thought he would remember us. However, while we were announced as Archdeacon and Mrs Lucas, he greeted us by our Christian names. It was an enjoyable party, and when I congratulated him on the strength of the G&T, he laughed and asked whether I liked ballet. When I said that I did, he led us over to a small group and said, 'Darcy, here is an admirer.' I was, indeed, an admirer of Darcey Bussell, but to be exposed without warning to the warmth and beauty of the young dancer was unfair, and I could only ask if she was 'resting' at the moment. She said that she was, and then Joy came to my rescue, and asked her if it was painful. Not for the first time, my wife astounded me, for I had no idea what she was talking about, but Darcey clearly did, and they had an animated conversation. It transpired that Joy had read of Darcey's leg injury a few days earlier.

I was invited by the Vicar of Ascension Island to re-dedicate the church following a renovation and a new roof. I was delighted to accept, and as Strike Command had largely paid for the roof, Air Vice Marshal Gordon Ferguson joined me from that Headquarters. While I was there the runway was closed to large aircraft, so I had to fly by Hercules to Recife, on the east coast of Brazil, in order to connect with the RAF Tristar aircraft returning to Brize Norton from the Falklands. I was sitting in the co-pilot's seat and flying at 24,000 feet above the South Atlantic, about half way between Ascension and Brazil, when the Hercules' captain, Flight Lieutenant Nick Stein, whom I had married at Cranwell, asked me if I wished to speak with Joy in Caythorpe, as he was about to phone his wife. The line would be sent through a switchboard in Portishead. He also advised me that the crew would be able to hear our conversation. The line was as clear as if I was calling from Lincoln, and just over £1.00 was charged to my telephone bill.

I delighted in Ascension Island, and when I was invited back in 1995 to cover Holy Week, while the Vicar was away, I took Joy with me. After the Maundy Thursday Eucharist, we had dinner with the Station Commander before walking along the beach to watch giant Green Turtles laying eggs. Every year, these turtles, both male and female, migrate from Brazil to Ascension, swimming a total distance of more than 1,200 miles across the South Atlantic.

A large cross stands on a hill above the capital, Georgetown, and so we drove up a cinder track to the top where I held a Good Friday service for the population of largely St Helenians. There are the remains of 43 volcanoes on Ascension, so, as a geographer, Joy was in her element. We took the car across Donkey Plain to the east side of the island, where there is a tracking station for the Ariane space rocket, but I found the most moving place was a little inlet named 'Comfortless Cove'. There are ancient graves of sailors who had caught the plague, and who were put ashore here to die in isolation.

I heard the Tristar landing during the conclusion of the Easter Eucharist on Holy Saturday evening, but the lovely St Helenian people in the congregation so detained us with their good wishes that we had to drive fast to the airfield, say farewell to the Administrator, and board the aircraft, which immediately taxied out for take-off and the long flight home.

A few weeks later I departed for Johannesburg on a South African Airways Boeing 747. The Government of South Africa had invited me to give the address at the 75th anniversary parade of the South African Air Force. It was the beginning of the busiest week in my life. The High Commission in London had provided a full brief of my programme, and the Staff Chaplain had done his work and provided a list of speeches I was to make and gifts to be exchanged. I was also to address chaplains in training at their equivalent of Cranwell. The subject they wished me to cover was the RAF In-Service Training for chaplains, so I had a short video compiled at Amport House.

Padre Potgeiter, the pilot and BHL about to board the Alouette lll helicopter of No.22 Squadron

Flying past the Table Mountain cable car station

At 0700 local time on a Tuesday morning after an overnight flight, much of which was spent on the flight deck of the 747, Brigadier Chaplain Lucas Potgeiter, the SAAF Chief Chaplain, met me at the aircraft steps, and whisked me away to my VIP Chalet in the grounds of the Officers' Mess at Air Force Base Waterkloof in Johannesburg. I showered and changed into uniform before breakfast, and then a fast car took me to Pretoria to meet Lieutenant General James Kriel, Chief of the South African Air Force. We looked at my visit programme and when he saw that there was no visit to the Bush, he altered it to include a flight to the Botswana border to see big game.

After my return to the Mess to change into casual dress, Lucas and his wife and I departed for a three-hour flight to Cape Town in a small Cesna Citation belonging to No.104 Squadron. Arriving at Ysterplaat Air Base, Cape Town, I was met by the Brigadier and taken to a small reception where the Castle beer flowed freely. I responded to the speech of welcome and exchanged gifts with the brigadier, before being taken away by three of the Cape chaplains and their wives for a night in a splendid restaurant affording a marvellous view of the city centre. At well past midnight they insisted that I see the city from the Table Mountain road. It was a truly wonderful sight, but as I had hardly slept for twenty-four hours, I was glad to see my bed in the Mess.

The next day I inspected the Gate Guardian, a Mk lll Shackleton, and later a Canberra and a Buccaneer—it was the aircraft with which I grew up. I took to the air in an Alouette lll helicopter of No.22 Squadron, for a flight over Simon's Town naval base en route to the Cape of Good Hope, before returning to fly up the cliff face of Table Mountain, followed by a low-level (20 feet) dash across the flat top of the 'Table' before landing at Ysterplaat. The chaplains then met me and took me to the Kanonkop winery in Stellenbosch, before returning for my flight to Johannesburg. I can remember the pilot circling high above the Big Hole Mine at Kimberley for me to take photographs, but I slept for most of the journey.

The annual Memorial Service took place on the Thursday at Air Base Swartkop (Bays Hill) near Pretoria. The service was in three languages—Afrikaans, my address in English and isiZulu—because the first non-statutory members of the SAAF, a group of former ANC fighters, were on parade. Most of the government ministers attended and the large arena on the hill top was full. After lunch I addressed the group of young chaplains in the college and answered their questions about chaplaincy in the RAF.

The flight north to Air Base Hoedspruit on Friday morning was made in a Beechcraft King Air 90, over the dark and forbidding Draken Mountains. As we descended the pilot asked if I could see the runway dead ahead. I could not, for the entire base had been toned down with a green runway and dispersed buildings. The Brigadier Base Commander welcomed me with a reception for his officers and

BHL with the Game Warden looking for Cheetah in the Veldt

their wives, and when I had responded to his welcome, he arranged for me to go into the veldt to track big game.

Lucas Potgeiter and I joined a game warden for a lunch of barbecued waterbuck steaks, before setting off in the back of a pickup truck to find cheetah. They used cheetah to keep down small game on the runways at night, so they knew where they were. The warden pulled up by some scrub and told me to follow carefully in his footsteps as we walked into the veldt, 'because we have had some problems with puff-adder here.' I followed very carefully until he stopped and whispered, 'Cheetah, a hundred yards in front. See them?' I couldn't, until suddenly, a beautiful animal stood up in the bush and yawned as he looked at me. The warden whispered again, 'Keep looking at him and walk slowly backwards to the truck.' I wanted to ask how I could walk backwards and still follow in his footsteps, but I thought better of it, and hoped the puff-adder were not hungry.

As we drove along the track, the cheetah followed just inside the bushes bordering the track, until he loped across in front of us, looked at me again, and wandered off with his mate. We drove deeper into the bush and saw all manner of wild game, and to see the giraffe, buffalo, antelope, rhinoceros and hartebeest in the wild is a totally exhilarating experience.

As darkness fell, the warden took me to a lion farm, and we transferred to a battered old Land Rover. I sat in the front with the driver and a native stood between us with a loaded rifle, and Lucas stood in the back, holding on for dear life. It was cramped in the front, and I had to leave my left leg hanging out of the non-existent door. A hind quarter of waterbuck was loaded beside Lucas, and we drove into the bush looking for lions. The meat was chained to a tree, and then we drove on, flattening small trees in our path. A moment later I saw through the gloom a lion pacing along a hundred yards away to the left, keeping up with us and snarling. 'He's hungry', said the warden.

This meant that my left leg was the nearest piece of meat to a hungry lion, and I tried in vain to get it inside the vehicle. Then the warden lost his presence of mind. He had great difficulty in getting the Land Rover started when we set off; now he switched the engine off. There was a deafening silence; only the constant sound of stealthy rustling from the bush and an occasional howl in the distance broke the stillness. Overhead, the Southern Cross shone brightly among the numberless stars. It was perfect creation.

Then the wretched lion roared about twenty yards away, and my left leg jerked in anticipated pain. The chap with the rifle slammed the bolt and fired off a round from just above my head. The lion sloped away and made a wide circle around the front of the vehicle as another round was rammed up the spout. Then the warden

The Cheetah has found us

switched on a spotlight, and I could see that the lion was trying to lead us away from the lioness and three cubs who were feeding off the chained waterbuck meat. The lion lay down near his brood and watched them until they had eaten enough before eating anything himself. Lucas and I slept in the King Air as it droned back over the Draken Mountains towards Johannesburg.

It was a frantic week, and I enjoyed every minute of it, though I was exhausted by the end of it. The Potgeiter family had been extremely generous and hospitable. If I had a complaint, it was that my visit was a few weeks too early; the country was preparing for the Rugby World Cup.

Early in 1995, Patriarch Alexius II, the 16th Patriarch of Moscow and the spiritual leader of the Russian Orthodox Church, contacted the Archbishop of Canterbury to seek advice on establishing a chaplaincy in the Russian armed forces. It sounds unimaginable, but there it was. As I was the senior of the three Service Archdeacons, the Archbishop asked the Chief of the Air Staff if I could undertake this mission. By this time, the Chief of the Air Staff was becoming used to strange requests for me to offer my services, but this must have capped the lot. As it was going to be a busy weekend I was allocated a VIP aircraft from No.32 Royal Squadron. Thus, one Friday that August, a BAe 125-700 flew Joy and me from the nearest long runway to Caythorpe, which was at RAF Waddington, to Moscow. The crew consisted of two pilots and a corporal stewardess, who served a delightful lunch en route. On landing in Moscow we were met by Air Commodore Philip Wilkinson, the UK Defence Attaché, who took us to the VIP lounge while the aircraft was refuelled and he dealt with our arrival formalities. Then, accompanied by Phil and his wife, Angie, we flew on to St Petersburg, for I was to address a group of Orthodox seminarians on Service chaplaincy there the following morning.

I had asked to visit the Hermitage Museum in the Winter Palace, the former state residence of the Russian emperors. The British Consul had arranged for a guide to show us around after lunch, and having viewed the items on my list, I asked if we could see the recent discoveries of French Impressionist paintings. She said it would take another hour, so I asked the pilot of my aircraft, for I had invited the crew to join us, and he replied that we would depart only when I was ready. So we saw the stunning paintings which the western world had thought lost forever.

We returned to Moscow in the late afternoon for a dinner party hosted by Phil and Angie, and I preached at the Anglican church on the Sunday morning at the request of the chaplain, my old friend from our time in Malta, Fr Chad Coussmaker. On the Monday morning I changed into ceremonial day dress, and set off in an embassy car with a young lady interpreter to meet the Patriarch's

In Russia August 1995. Joy on extreme left and the two pilots behind BHL the stewardess to the right

envoy, the 'Bishop of the Russian Armed Forces and Forces of the Interior' in a large monastery in the suburbs of Moscow.

We were ushered into a large and rather gloomy room in the old monastery building by the bishop's interpreter, a man in a grey suit. He spoke in rapid Russian to my interpreter and she explained that the Bishop was on his way. A minute later a large, bearded bishop of the Russian Orthodox Church filled the doorway and came over with his hand outstretched in welcome. We sat facing each other across a vast table, each with our interpreter beside us. He made a short speech of welcome and invited me to explain chaplaincy in the Royal Air Force, the Army and the Royal Navy. As I was explaining the responsibilities and the various chains of command, I noticed that this monk-bishop had deeply etched laugh-lines at the side of his eyes. So I included some amusing anecdotes about Service chaplaincy. He laughed hugely and enjoyed the stories of how chaplains integrate fully into Service life, bringing with them the love of Christ. He began to ask penetrating questions about pastoral care, the rank structure, how we handled the dual responsibility to church and state, and absorbed my answers like a sponge.

Finally, after over two hours of dialogue, we exchanged gifts, and taking my arm he walked with me back to the courtyard where we had left the car, still asking questions and devouring information. 'Should our priests wear uniform as you do?' he asked. I suggested that in my view it would be wiser at first to adopt the model of our officiating chaplains and wear clerical robes until their presence in the armed forces was accepted. Then, in the fullness of time, an appropriate uniform could be adopted. I refrained from mentioning it, but after seventy years of Political Officers, an Orthodox priest in uniform might not be trusted. As we said goodbye the formal handshake was replaced by a bear-hug of an embrace and much kissing of cheeks. He said I was welcome to bring some of my chaplains to Moscow to stay at the monastery at any time.

In the back of the car I opened a beautifully illustrated book of Russian monastic churches, and read the inscription he had scribbled on the inside cover before he handed it to me. I showed it to the interpreter and she translated it for me. The Bishop had written: 'With love in Christ, and for further cooperation in the military field between Russia and Great Britain. Yours, Savva.' To which I added a quiet, "Amen."

· · · · · · · · · ·

The following article, by The Reverend (Group Captain) Brian McAvoy QHC MBE MA, was published in the Autumn 1995 edition of the RAF Chaplains' Branch Bulletin, and is reproduced here with his permission.

"All is changed, changed utterly, and a terrible beauty is born"

W B Yeats.

Such thoughts, I'm sure, were far from Brian Lucas' mind when he moved into the chair, and office, recently vacated by his name-sake and predecessor in June 1991. Four years later, he is still in the chair (he brought it with him to Innsworth!) but the office has changed, the structure of the Branch has changed, he has changed (more grey hair—see Conference photos) and much that could have been predicted in 1991, wouldn't rate much higher than National Lottery odds now. Any pleasurable anticipation of the position of Chaplain in Chief must have quickly evaporated as one development (change) after another presented themselves to him for consideration and decision. A two-star Head of Branch is not expected to innovate, so extra pressure was also applied to resist the changes. An invidious position indeed!

Not given to self-pity, Brian met all that was thrown at him, and set about achieving the best that he could for his beloved Branch. His years and experience as a chaplain, including a tour next door to his new office gave him the base-line from which to operate. The maxim that "age and treachery will always overcome youth and skill", seen in an 18 Group Squadron Bar somewhere, also played a part!

Most of the detail of this element of the "Life of Brian", both fact and rumour, are known to all of us, and it is not my purpose to relate them here. Enough to say that when courage and spiritual uplift were badly needed, even the consolation of Wales beating Ireland was denied him. And he had to take on a range of stars, civil servants, politicians, and even station chaplains, as he moved forward, within the very tight parameters allowed to him, in attempting to bring to birth the "terrible beauty" which is to be the Chaplains Branch before and beyond the next millennium. He was not alone. Surrounded by well-meaning advisers, if only he could work out what they really did mean, he had the unenviable task of bringing a bunch of healthily cynical, if not exactly rebellious, "seen it all before" chaplains with him. That he has but partially succeeded is much more of a compliment than a criticism. Those of us who have tried to persuade our brother clergy of the merits of a course of action they don't like will fully agree. There were compensations. All right, there are not many Turkish restaurants In Gloucestershire, much less Innsworth, and there was a "punishing" schedule of visits to such places as Greece, Lithuania, USA, Turkey, Russia, South Africa, Benbecula, Hungary, Colditz, easily satisfying his stated interest in travel. There was even a car and mobile phone to make up for the loss of a London "pad", but these, too, were but 'tools of the trade' and, by MT's own admission, an essential part of the equipment for Brian to do the job as it would develop in rural Gloucester.

Collated an Archdeacon, installed a Canon of Lincoln Cathedral, a Companion of the Order of the Bath, an FRSA (you can guess what that is), the headed notepaper became ever more impressive. Only in defence of the Branch and its affairs did Brian ever use his position, and, most importantly, his "common touch" remains a clear and natural characteristic in his walk with kings and the rest of us at every level of rank.

His Celtic roots are hugely important to Brian in his spiritual life. From St Cuthbert in Lindisfarne and St David in his native Wales, the threads and links between the saints of the ancient Celtic church and today are real and integrated into his walk with God. An ascetic he is not, and the old custom of the saints standing up to their necks in cold water reciting psalms holds no attraction for Brian! Enough to observe others, or read about them.

Tales and adventures abound of his travels and contacts. Nobody could be said to have wrung more out of every minute of a career, which reached such illustrious heights, and I'm sure seems all too short.

Well, the terrible beauty has been brought to birth and Brian now leaves his new infant to stand on its own feet and grow. Like all our children, it has its teething problems and growing pains, but it has been given a good start. Thank you, Brian, for being you. We wish you well and God speed in all you set out to do in "retirement"

Brian Eile.

(Brian the Other)

CHAPTER FOURTEEN:

Just a Quiet Country Parish

My last overseas visit as Chaplain-in-Chief came at the very end of my service in the Royal Air Force. On Friday, 25th August 1995, Joy and I flew to Stavanger for the weekend, where I presented a cheque towards the restoration of the chapel used by the British contingent at the NATO Headquarters, Allied Forces North Europe, in Norway. We stayed at the home of the Senior British Officer, Brigadier Gordon Ferguson, who had arranged a programme for us, including an all-rank BBQ and a boat trip along the stunning Lysefjord, returning over the mountains to Stavanger.

The following Monday my successor began his tour of duty. I had completed my tasks as Chaplain-in-Chief of the Royal Air Force. The chaplains were well equipped for their ministry and were supported in their work at the very highest level of the RAF. After all the turbulence of the previous four years, the Branch had emerged with a taut but healthy budget and an appropriate management structure to suit the requirements of government strategy. But I had the greatest satisfaction from fighting off the attack on Amport House, and as a retirement present the chaplains commissioned a watercolour painting of the house and gardens.

Suddenly faced with an empty diary for the first time in my life, I felt very tired. The total reorganization of the management structure of the RAF chaplaincy to comply with Government policies, together with the enormous amount of travelling I had undertaken around the world, had taken its toll, and I spent the next few weeks catching up on my sleep, and watched the aircraft flying overhead from nearby Cranwell.

I had thought that on retirement I might offer myself to work for a children's charity, having cared for adults all my life, but as I sat in my garden in the late summer sunshine, it became clear to me that I would be hopeless for such work. The man who wept at the tales told by the youngsters of the Weston Spirit at

Amport House would not have the objective clarity of purpose for working with disadvantaged young children; I would either become emotional or very angry at their situation. I suppose I was suffering a kind of bereavement; I had really loved the chaplains and their families very much, and I was missing them. What then was I to do in the next phase of my ministry?

One of my last acts as Chaplain-in-Chief had been to appoint myself as a locum for Padre Chris Long at RAF Akrotiri, so, on 23rd November 1995, I flew from RAF Brize Norton in a VC10 bound for Cyprus. I spent the evening of the 22nd in the company of Sir Patrick Moore, who was to be a fellow passenger to Cyprus. We had met some years earlier in RAF Akrotiri and it was excellent to spend some hours with this enthusiastic and kind man.

For just over two weeks I was back in my milieu, but as a civilian priest in black clerical shirt and blazer. Although the Station Commander graciously accommodated me in the VIP bungalow opposite the Officers' Mess, I was happy to be 'Padre Brian', released from the shackles of responsibility. I knew so many people at the school, hospital, and local shops that I felt totally at home. I swiftly fell into the routine of visiting sections, hangars and the hospital in the morning, and visiting other parts of the island in the afternoon, with, of course, visits to the kebab houses at night with friends.

All too soon Monday 11th December saw me in the departure lounge enjoying a Brandy Sour, waiting to board the VC10. I had lunched with the crew in the Mess, and was delighted that my old friend, Group Captain Al Kearney was flying as captain. Al was the Station Commander of RAF Brize Norton and was obliged to fly with the squadrons based there periodically. He told me that I was to join him on the flight deck for the flight home. We were all strapped in for departure when the Flight Engineer found a problem. It was serious enough to prevent the VC10 from departing that day. So, a night out at a kebab house with the crew was mandatory. The following day we were once again all strapped in for departure, and, what joy, we taxied to the holding point at the end of the runway. Again a problem was discovered and we taxied back to the Terminal Building. We enjoyed a quiet night in the bar of the Mess. When the aircraft was unserviceable on the Wednesday morning, I was obliged to book a ticket on the Cyprus Airways 1800 departure from Larnaca Airport, for I was to preach at St Margaret's Church, Westminster, to the Guild of the Nineteen Lubricators on the Friday. Never was the saying, 'If you've time to spare, go by air' more proven, but the interlude had been just what I needed at that time, even though it had shed no light on my future.

During the residential summer sessions of the General Synod of the Church of England held at the University of York in July 1995, I was walking around the lake with David Smith, the Bishop of Bradford, and formerly the Bishop to the Forces, who had become a good friend. He asked what I was going to do in retirement, and when I said that I hadn't a clue, he invited me to join him at Bradford as his Chief of Staff. He was looking for someone to handle the routine running of the Diocese which would give him more time for reflection and dealing with external tasks. He gave me a month to consider it, and I did take much of that time, for I was tempted. He would be a good colleague to work with, but I feared that I would miss having the final decision-making role, which I had come to appreciate. So I declined his generous offer and closed the door on work in diocesan administration.

By way of relaxation, I wrote a 56,000 word novel; a thriller based on Middle Eastern terrorism, which I called 'Sabini'. It involved the unmasking of a terrorist group, which used Aleppo in Syria as a base to assemble a sizeable fleet of assorted purchases of redundant RAF aircraft. I had no intention of becoming a writer of fiction, and when a literary agent I met in the Savage Club had read much of it, he advised me that while the writing was of a good standard, there is a great deal of similar material in the market, and I would have to persevere in order to have it published. It has remained parked on my computer external hard drive ever since.

Another good friend, John Kirkham, the Bishop of Sherborne, phoned one day in September 1995 to ask permission to put my name forward for consideration as the Bishop of Cyprus and the Gulf. In a moment of weakness I agreed, and shortly afterwards Bishop Len Ashton, the former Chaplain-in-Chief, who had been the first Bishop of that Diocese, rang to say how delighted he was that I had agreed. The chaplain from Kyrenia telephoned to say that he and his congregation were behind me. Joy said that she would support me if I wanted to accept the post were it to be offered, but I was not at all sure about it. When we were invited to go for interview by the Vacancy in See Committee, I decided that this was not right for me, and removed my name from the short-list.

All the while, the local benefice of Caythorpe was vacant, and after six months recovering my breath, I telephoned Bill Ind, the Suffragen Bishop of Grantham, to say I was willing to offer my service as Rector of the benefice. He lost no time in coming to Caythorpe to talk it through. I said that I would be willing to do the job for five years, but that I would not wish to live in the Rectory, but remain in my own home. He prepared the ground with Bob Hardy, the Bishop of Lincoln, whom I knew well through my Canonry, and he, in turn, arranged a meeting with the Patron, Mr Julian Fane of Fulbeck Manor. I warmed to Julian, and his wife Julia, at once, and I attended a meeting at the Manor of all the churchwardens of the three parishes in the benefice: Caythorpe, Fulbeck and Carlton Scroop with Normanton. I liked them, and they seemed to like me. At the last minute the Bishop informed me that there was a lady in Fulbeck training to be a deacon, and asked if that would be alright. She attended the meeting, and I discerned that Barbara Hancock would make a good deacon and a useful colleague.

A week later, early in November 1995, just after the actual date of my retirement from the RAF, the Archbishop of Canterbury's Secretary for Appointments, Mr Hector McLean, wrote to me and asked me to travel to Westminster to discuss a senior appointment.

On Monday 13th November, I was taken up to his office in Fielden house, Little College Street, and we discussed my future. I told him about the Benefice of Caythorpe, yet I agreed to make myself available for 'major ministry', and it was revealed later that I was being considered as a candidate for a suffragen bishopric. At a subsequent meeting with Hector's successor, Tony Sadler, he disclosed the actual bishopric. It was an interesting job, but I was becoming increasingly uneasy at the prospect of being consecrated a bishop; it was something I had not sought and did not want. Tony said the appointment would be made by the end of February 1996, and with some reluctance, I agreed to make myself available, and wait.

I took my old friend John Kirkham, the Bishop of Sherborne, to lunch in London to explain how I felt, and to ask for his advice. I told him that, at my ordination, I had only offered myself to God as a priest. *'You did not, you offered yourself for whatever God had in store for you'*, he said, and he was right. I caught myself looking at mitres and purple shirts in the windows of clerical outfitters, imagining myself all decked out as a bishop of the church prancing about the place, and I despised myself for it. The small part of me that was willing to proceed along this path was not my best self. I have enough trouble with my *alter ego* when processing through a church after High Mass, and to keep my feet firmly on the ground I continually recite the Jesus prayer as I process: *'Lord Jesus Christ, Son of the living God, have mercy on me, a sinner.'* Furthermore, I felt unable to support some of the pronouncements coming from the General Synod. The Church of England is moving far away from its ancient place as the one, holy, catholic and apostolic church in England. This was the most miserable period of my life.

Meanwhile, the good people of Caythorpe were without a priest of their own. As I looked out of my study window I could see the spire of the parish church at the top of the village: I was pulled in two directions, and the parish was winning the struggle. Hector McLean had put Bob Hardy, the Bishop of Lincoln, in the picture, and Bob had written to me saying that he understood, and would keep the Caythorpe appointment open until the end of February, but that he would then have to move forward with it. I wrote to Tony Sadler in mid-February and said that as the end of February was nigh, I proposed to contact the Bishop of Grantham to proceed with the induction to the Rectory of Caythorpe. He telephoned me two days later and asked me to hold fire because they were almost there, and a meeting planned for that week, with the Diocesan Bishop concerned, would see the conclusion of the matter. I was to telephone him on the Friday, 1st March, a propitious date for a Welshman.

I rang him on St David's Day to be told that the Bishop was ill and the meeting had to be postponed. It was the sign I had looked for, and I asked him to remove my name from the list. He tried to persuade me not to do that, but I was adamant. Later that morning I wrote to the Bishop of Lincoln and telephoned the Bishop of Grantham. I felt a peace and equanimity that I had not experienced for a long time.

On 5th March the Bishop of Lincoln wrote, '*Dear Brian, From a selfish point of view I am glad things have worked out this way, though I know how unsettling these periods can be.*' On the 8th March the Bishop of Grantham came to see me and I signed the forms of declaration and accepted the appointment of Rector of Caythorpe, Fulbeck and Carlton Scroop with Normanton. He said that I would be a Priest-in-Charge initially, but that the Bishop of Lincoln would institute me as Rector very soon afterwards. In a typical Church of England manner, having accepted the post of Rector of the benefice, that same day the benefice was suspended for a period of five years. I was disappointed that I had been misled, but let it go. In fact, the suspension was lifted after three years, and I was installed as the Rector. It had been agreed that I should continue to live in my own house, and the Rectory would be sold.

On 28th March I was licensed as the Priest-in-Charge of the Caythorpe Benefice in a service at the Parish Church of St Nicholas, Fulbeck. The following Sunday I once again saw reflections in the chalice as I raised it during the Holy Eucharist, but this time they were reflections of my people, not of someone else's flock. I was once more a parish priest, and I rejoiced in it. Taking over a chaplaincy in the RAF involved a formal exchange of signatures on the church inventory and a few days going through the files with your predecessor. In Caythorpe I started with a few names on a piece of paper; no inventory check, and not one file to refer to, and my predecessor had left twelve months earlier.

The main difference between a chaplain and a parish priest is that parishioners have long memories and so there is a considerable inertia when it comes to refreshing the round of services. Whereas in the Royal Air Force the chaplain is regarded as the expert in his field, and his proposals are largely accepted, in a parish there is a great deal of cajoling and persuading to be done, and assurances to be given, before you can change even the hymn books. That apart, people are much the same, and ask to be loved and valued, as you gently bring them closer to their Saviour.

Bishop Bob Hardy had asked me to work to bring the three parishes in the benefice together, but I quickly realized that the people in Caythorpe, Fulbeck, and in Carlton Scroop, valued their own parish church, and related to it as the place where their parents and families had worshipped down the years, in the same way as I felt towards St Theodore's Church in Port Talbot. I decided that instead of attempting to create a uniform single group, it would be better to encourage the three parishes to become more cohesive, while retaining their independence.

I had a good team. Mrs Mary Siddans, a farmer's wife, was a churchwarden at Caythorpe; she knew the village well, and was a totally reliable, strong and loyal support. She was also a Welsh lass and good company. Her colleague as churchwarden was Richard Johnson, who was a bank cashier. Mr Reg Baxter, who lives across the road from the church, has lived in Caythorpe all his life. He, too, was a discreet and loyal friend. He carried out the onerous tasks of winding the tower clock and opening and locking the church every day, year after year. A third member of the Parochial Church Council (PCC), who knew Caythorpe to his fingertips, was Dr Alasdair Fraser Darling, who had been the senior partner in the village medical practice, and a former churchwarden.

In Fulbeck, one churchwarden, Geoff Cottingham, farmed on the estate with his father and his brother, and the other, Tony Robinson, was a retired squadron leader, who had lived in the village for a very long time. Apart from Julian Fane, who owned the estate, and offered me every support, the parish church of St Nicholas was cared for with military precision by a lady I called my 'Sergeant Major'. Mrs May Burrows called a spade a spade, and saw to it that everything was done correctly. In that she had my support, and, in return, I had hers. We worked in total harmony, and I was grateful for her loyalty, attention to detail and willingness to put herself out. When she died, her tasks were taken over by a team of people.

Carlton Scroop and Normanton are two hamlets. Formerly separate parishes, both with a church dedicated to St Nicholas, they were amalgamated and Normanton church was declared redundant, and taken over by the Churches Conservation trust. Malcolm Hage and Denis Oliver were the churchwardens for most of my time as Rector. While Malcolm shared my love of steam locomotives, Denis was a veterinary surgeon, and I joined him on more than one occasion as his guest at the Court Lunch of the Worshipful Company of Farriers, of which Denis is the senior Past Master.

With these folk, and many others around me, too many to mention by name, I began the task of building up the body of Christ in the benefice. At RAF Cranwell, the workshops had made me an attractive metal sign to erect in the front lawn of my married quarter. On my posting to Germany I put it in my garage, and when we bought our house, I brought it to Caythorpe. Now it was erected in our front garden, for my home was also The Rectory, and I had built an extension at the rear of the house large enough to accommodate committee meetings.

One of the first things I did was to appoint what I called the Standing Committee of the PCC; it was made up of the two Churchwardens, the Lay Chairman, the Hon. Treasurer and the Hon Secretary. Such a committee was established for each of the three parishes and we met monthly in the Rectory to take forward items which could not wait for the next meeting of the full Parochial Church Council.

Then I 'refreshed' the Sunday morning service of Sung Eucharist, and harmonised its use across the benefice, and I arranged a service in all three churches every Sunday at some time in the day. The most difficult part of being a country parson is finding where people live in order to visit them in their home. A neighbour, Canon Gordon Mitchell, was very helpful with this as he had been Rector of Fulbeck years earlier, but people had moved since his time; and, apart from the members of the PCC, he couldn't tell me where many of the people in Caythorpe lived. Even when I knew the address, I had to find where the front door was; often it was in an alley or a yard or at the end of a drive.

Joy was my best source of information in this regard, for she had lived in Caythorpe since 1988. Although she had not been involved in village life, she knew the parents of Helen's school friends, and when she resigned as Acting Headteacher of nearby Brant Broughton primary school, she taught part-time in Caythorpe School. When I retired as Rector, I became known by the schoolchildren as '*Mrs Lucas' husband*'. At first, people were at a loss to know how to address me: should it be Archdeacon, Canon, Air Vice Marshal, or Rector? I simplified the whole thing by inviting everyone to call me Brian. And so it was.

Every year for seven years Joy and I hosted a series of buffet supper evenings. We would hold eight parties over a period of three weeks in July and so welcome to our home about 250 parishioners each year. Each party would begin with drinks in the garden before serving the food, so they were great fun, and people enjoyed meeting parishioners from the other two parishes.

The steady round of Sunday services, together with the Holy Day and Wednesday Holy Communion services I had started in the little Lady Chapel, which I had created in the north transept of St Vincent's Church, kept me busy. My training at Oxford and at Llandaff Cathedral taught me that worship is always for the glory of almighty God, and so it has to be well-prepared and of the highest order. I cannot abide clergy fussing about in the chancel and sanctuary before the service begins, when all should be calm and prayerful. When, as the Chaplain-in-Chief, I was the visiting preacher at an RAF church, I was always rather unforgiving to a chaplain who had left worship preparation to the last moment.

The village school was not a Church School, but I found a ready welcome from the Headteacher to take school assembly from time to time each term, and I invited the school to use the Parish Church for its Harvest Festival, Christmas concert and Nativity Play. Similarly, I was invited by the Principal to become a member of the Chaplaincy Support Group at the Agricultural College at Caythorpe Court, which later became a campus of De Montfort University. The students there came to the Parish Church for a very exuberant Carol Service each December.

When I offered a course of confirmation classes, I was delighted to find that a steady stream of older children and adults came forward. I held the children's classes in church, to make them feel used to the building, but the adult groups met in 'The Rectory'. The latter groups were very satisfying, for they required me to brush up on my theology and do some serious reading. In the fullness of time, Barbara Hancock was made a Deacon and became a very useful member of the team; moreover, she became an effective preacher and shared with me the preaching and teaching ministry.

The parochial ministry is similar to military chaplaincy work, except that you have to work harder to be accepted by people outside the church circle; you wear a very different uniform from them, and you don't see your people at their place of work. The only exception to that was when Joy and I took turns in riding in the cab of Julian Fane's huge combiner during the harvest.

The other big difference between a Service chaplain and a parish priest is the amount of time spent on raising money to keep the fabric of the buildings in good repair. In all three of the parishes in my care, I encouraged the people to widen the use of the buildings: we had flower festivals, and concerts by visiting choirs and chamber orchestras, and a concert by a young teenage harpist in the parish, who made her debut at Fulbeck church prior to going on to Chetham's School of Music.

During my time as Rector, the entire nave and chancel of St Vincent's church was redecorated at a substantial cost to the people, and considerable amount of time expended by me on obtaining a faculty for the work, obtaining grants from charitable bodies and tenders from the contractors. Unfortunately, the architect omitted to include the east wall of the nave in the specification, and, as there is underneath the lime-wash a mediaeval 'Doom' painting, a separate faculty was granted only after I had arranged for a specialist conservator from London to examine the painting and give permission to decorate over it. The exercise was repeated at Carlton Scroop, and both churches looked splendid in their cleaned and sparkling interiors. In Fulbeck it was the roof cladding which caused us headaches, and considerable expense.

How much more jolly life is when flags are flown from public buildings. I frequently flew the Red Dragon of Wales at my house in Malta and also in Cyprus; in the Mediterranean flags and bunting are flown at the drop of a hat. When I first saw the proud tower of Fulbeck Church, I decided that it deserved a flag, but it was some years before it came to the top of my list of things to do.

The first thing was for me to climb to the top and assess the possibility. To my joy I discovered metal tethering rings in the four corners of the tower parapet, indicating that there had once been a flag pole. This meant that I didn't require a faculty from the diocese, as I was reinstating a decayed structure. Mr John Hinchliffe, who had relatives buried in the churchyard, offered to pay for the flagpole, and Major General David Toler, a former churchwarden of the parish, said that he would provide the flag. The Earl Marshal laid down in 1938 that the only flag permitted to be flown from church buildings in England is the flag of St George, and David Toler was very happy to provide one of a suitable size. A Fulbeck carpenter and joiner, Nigel Johnson, made the base and he, my son Simon and I hauled the pole to the top of the tower in time for it to be fixed in place for the Queen's Golden Jubilee celebrations at the beginning of June 2002.

With Nigel Johnson and the new flag pole on Fulbeck Tower 2002

249

On Monday 3rd June, everyone gathered on the green in front of the Hare & Hounds, and David Toler, over 80 years old, and I climbed to the top of the tower where I had folded the flag in such a way that it could be 'broken' by a hard tug on the lanyard, and had hauled it to the top of the pole. At 2 o'clock, I gave David the signal to 'break' the flag, and it flew out above the church tower as the bell ringers below us began to ring. There was cheering from the colourful crowd far below, and then I made a rapid descent to stand on the step of the village cross and, after a prayer for her Majesty, the parade of costumed villagers paraded around the village.

Then it was time to dash to Caythorpe where Joy and I were judges for the various competitions on the playing field. As I drove the mile and a half, I could hear church bells ringing across the countryside from village to village, and delighted to live in such a country under such a Queen.

I retained my links with the Royal Air Force, and preached in Lincoln Cathedral on Battle of Britain Sunday, and attended the annual Old Cranwellians Reunion Dinner each year in College Hall, Cranwell. When Chaplain-in-Chief, I had preached somewhere in London and mentioned in my sermon that Service personnel were being 'costed not valued' by the Government. I went on to warn that servicemen are voters too. I was unaware that he was present until General Sir (later Field Marshal Baron) Peter Inge came up to me at luncheon at the London home of Dame Felicity Peake, and asked me for a copy of my sermon. We both felt very strongly that the members of the armed forces were close to exhaustion. When I was Rector of Caythorpe, he became Chief of the Defence Staff, and one day we were fellow guests at a luncheon in the Commandant's residence at Cranwell. After lunch he came up and suggested we had a walk in the garden. I lost no time in asking him why he had come to Cranwell. He smiled at me and said, '*Well...*' I cut in and said, '*If you are costing the joint, desist; hands off my beloved Cranwell.*' I am a firm believer in saying your piece whenever the opportunity arises. Then we turned our conversation to politics and defence matters, until I spotted the Commandant looking anxiously through the window, and we rejoined the party.

In June 1940, the then Prime Minister Sir Winston Churchill gave orders for the formation of a British Corps of at least 5000 Parachute Troops. By 1943, these troops consisted of the 1st and 6th Airborne Divisions, each of which had their own Royal Signals Headquarters and Signal Regiments. The 1st Airborne Division saw plenty of action during Operation Market Garden at Arnhem. That operation was planned at Fulbeck Hall, which was the base of the 1st Airborne Division, under Major-General Roy Urquhart, before they left for the Battle of Arnhem. The Royal Signals Headquarters was based in Caythorpe, with the men billeted here and in the surrounding villages. In June 1965, their successors formed No.216 Parachute Signal Squadron.

Every year the villagers of Caythorpe have commemorated the bravery of those men with an Arnhem Weekend in September, which is attended by the veterans and serving soldiers from the Squadron. Many of the latter parachute into a field to the north of the village on the Saturday morning. As the years pass the number of veterans diminishes, but those who return to Caythorpe don their 'red beret' and march with pride to the church for the memorial service. During my time as Rector the salute was taken in the High Street by Major General Anthony Deane-Drummond CB, DSO, MC and Bar, a retired officer of the Royal Signals, whose career was mostly spent with airborne forces. I consider him a delightful gentleman, in every sense of that word.

Deane-Drummond served in Operation Market Garden as second-in-command of the divisional signals, and was captured at Arnhem, but escaped. He made for the Rhine and successfully swam to the south bank, but was almost immediately taken prisoner. The next day, he managed to escape from a group who were being escorted out of Arnhem, and spent the next eleven days hiding inside a large cupboard in the German Guardroom until he felt safe to move. After leaving his hiding place, Deane-Drummond made contact with the Resistance, and two weeks later he was brought back to British lines as part of Operation Pegasus.

Each year, at the Reunion Dinner held in Caythorpe Court, which was then an Agricultural College, Joy and I had the good fortune to sit either side of him as he presided over the proceedings. One year, in the middle of the meal, he suddenly stood up and pointed to a veteran sitting at one of the tables. 'You!' he called out. And the old man got to his feet and saluted the General, as Tony Deane-Drummond motioned him to go towards the door. Then, excusing himself to Joy, Tony left the top table and met up with the veteran near the door and embraced him for some minutes. Then, turning to the assembly, he explained that this man had been his driver in his escape towards the Rhine. '*I last saw him on the river bank; we said goodbye and we jumped into the Rhine. I have not seen him to this day, and assumed he hadn't made it.*' Tears shone in many eyes at the revelation, and I found that I had an eyelash in my eye, for I had to wipe it several times.

The north aisle of St Vincent's church is known as the Arnhem Aisle, as it has a carpet specially woven with the arms of the Airborne Signals, and a stained glass window commemorating the link with the village. When the Squadron became part of 16 Assault Brigade and had to move barracks, I was asked to accept a Memorial Stone which had been brought 8,000 miles from the Falklands. Inscribed on the plaque are the names of members of the regiment, who gave their lives in the Falklands War. I suggested that it would be most appropriate near the village War Memorial just outside the churchyard gate.

I employed my old custom of loitering with intent; alongside the young people who sat on the village green in Caythorpe drinking lager, and with those who frequented the three pubs in the village. It was a matter of sadness to me when one of the pubs, 'The Eight Bells', closed and became a private house. That pub was the only one to have a name related to the village of Caythorpe, for it is rare in a small village to have a ring of eight bells in the church tower. Not long after the Queen's Jubilee, the bell frame in Caythorpe became unsafe and the bells could no longer be rung. I required £15,000 to repair the frame and refurbish the eight bells, and when I mentioned this to a friend I had made in the village he said at once, *'I'll give you a cheque for that; although I don't attend church I like to hear the bells.'* It meant that, together with some money we had collected for the purpose, we were not only able to repair and re-hang the bells, but we also restored the organ in the church.

John and Ruth Watson were members of the PCC but their greatest contribution to the church came about almost by accident. John is a retired engineer and a good worker with wood. He began to make delightful little 'Holding Crosses' which fit into the palm of your hand. Apart from postage, they never charged for them, but recipients were asked to make a donation to church funds. As they gained in popularity the money came in steadily and was held in a separate fund. Once an amount of several hundred pounds was amassed, the three of us would meet to decide on an object for the money. It had to be something to enhance the spirituality of the church, so it could not be spent on repairs to the fabric. In this way we bought a new nave altar, new chairs for the chancel and for the Lady Chapel. The crosses also funded a complete set of new hymn books and three altar frontals for the high altar; and the list is still ongoing.

St Vincent's church has a double nave, so the addition of a north aisle by Sir Gilbert Scot in about 1860 gave it an eccentric aspect, and this was made worse by a Victorian double-decker reading desk jutting into the chancel arch. I obtained permission from the diocese to remove this in order to open up the chancel. Happily it had been placed on top of the paving stones, so the Sunday after I pulled it out, no-one noticed the improved space at the early Communion service.

Although I adore the architecture of our fine old churches, I have come to the conclusion that in most cases ancient church buildings work against the conduct of modern liturgical worship. They are generally too big, too cold, too dark, lack toilets, and are not attractive to new converts. They do have an aura of spirituality from centuries of devout prayer, but that doesn't seem to cut much ice these days. For most of my ministry in the Royal Air Force I had used redundant buildings as churches. These ranged from old gymnasia to former messes, and they worked very well. When divided by screens, they were small enough to fill on a Sunday morning, they were inexpensive to heat and light, there were toilet facilities, and, above all else, they were multi-purpose.

The parish churches of the land are, indeed, glorious examples of fine architecture, but the cost of maintenance in accordance with their listed status is draining the finances of the parishes, and robbing the church of money needed to provide clergy to preach the gospel. The church building stands in the parish which cannot afford a priest. It begs the question 'What is the purpose of the Christian Church?' In the meantime, the fewer number of clergy are spending time encouraging the people to prop up the estate, time which should be spent on evangelism.

Without any doubt, the project that continues to give me the greatest pleasure is my decision to floodlight the Parish Church of St Vincent in Caythorpe to celebrate the end of the second millennium. The Parochial Church Council were lukewarm about the idea as it required a faculty from the Diocese and money was, as always, in short supply, but I was determined that it was going to happen. I obtained a quotation from a local lighting engineer which was affordable with a grant offered from the Church Floodlighting Fund. So I persuaded the PCC that it was a good idea. The small investment was repaid within a year by allowing parishioners to pay a modest sum to have the church floodlit for significant family events.

I held a short service in the church at midnight on 31st December 1999, and as the year 2000 was ushered in, I switched on the floodlights, and the congregation spilled into the churchyard to see the effect. The warm Ancaster stone glowed in the light, and the spire shone in the night sky. It looked glorious, and I still have the same frisson of excitement when I see the church lit at night.

For my family, the 1990s was a decade of academic achievement. Mark was awarded a BSc degree in Business Information Systems at Sheffield Hallam University, Simon had a BA in Humanities from Manchester Metropolitan, Helen gained a BA in Physical Education and Geography at St John's University College, York, and later obtained an MSc degree from the University of Lincoln. Meanwhile, Joy added to her long-held Fellowship of the Royal Geographical Society the award of a Master of Education degree at the University of Hull; so I am now married to a Fellow and a Master.

The five years I had promised to the Bishop of Lincoln became over seven, and I decided that it was time to conclude my parochial ministry for no other reason than I wanted to spend more time in my study. I had made the decision two years earlier and had informed the Bishop of Lincoln, so that he would have time to appoint a successor in time for a smooth handover when the time came. It was to no avail, so I put all the parish files, which I had created from scratch, into a large stack of archive boxes and took them to the Rural Dean for him to use during the interregnum.

CHAPTER FIFTEEN:

The Grand Finale

Having agreed with the Bishop of Lincoln to serve as Rector of Caythorpe for five years, I went on to complete seven and a half before I retired at the end of August 2003. I preached at a Sunday Choral Evensong in St Vincent's church, which was followed by wine and nibbles, when the people of Caythorpe presented me with a very generous gift. The PCC later presented me with a framed cartoon by the Grantham artist Terry Shelbourne, which was titled, 'Just a quiet country parish'. It depicts me dressed in swirling robes and flanked by a Colonel (David Ronald, the PCC Lay Chairman) and a Royal Navy officer (Roger Welby-Everard, the PCC Treasurer) saluting to my right, and a cartoon of Joy at the organ to my left. A flight of Red Arrows aircraft fly about my head. The people of Fulbeck and Carlton Scroop made separate and generous presentations in their own churches. The kindness of people was overwhelming.

A week later I set off in my car for the Benedictine Abbey of Bec-Hellouin in Normandy. I had arranged to spend a week in silence with the monks in an attempt to reflect on how I would exercise my ministry in retirement, before continuing south through the Dordogne to the coast near the Spanish border during the following three weeks. I knew that I wanted to spend more time in my study with my library, but any retirement has to be structured. For the previous six years I had been making annual journeys to all parts of France recording and photographing the great Gothic cathedrals, so I knew that idleness would not raise its head.

It was during an afternoon visit to nearby Lisieux Cathedral that I first noticed a shadow in my left eye. Two days later, I recognized it as a detachment in the retina, and I offered my apologies to the Abbot of Bec and quickly returned home. Within twenty-four hours I was admitted to the Queen's medical centre in Nottingham for a retinal repair.

Laon Cathedral. The north side of the nave

What a difference fifteen years had made in medical science. I was prepared for the trauma of my right eye in Germany, but not a bit of it. Two days later I was discharged, and two weeks later I was once more able to drive. In fact, it healed too quickly and tore again, requiring another few days in hospital, and this time I returned home with a gas bubble injected into the eye to slow the healing process. I had to keep my head down and it was like looking into a bowl of water. However, after three weeks the bowl 'dried up', and I was soon back in the car and resuming my journey to France with my photographic equipment and recording materials. My *modus operandi* is to photograph and describe first the exterior of a cathedral and then the interior; on my first visit this takes about five hours and even longer if there is mediaeval glass to photograph.

My study of French cathedrals has continued in the seven years since I retired, and I have written up fifty-one of them, with the intention of publishing an illustrated book at some stage. As each building demands about five to eight thousand words, it will be a substantial tome when complete. The man who read many of my essays on various cathedrals, and offered encouragement and constant, wise advice was Bernard Kaukas, a celebrated architect and a dear friend in the Savage Club, who has visited our home in Caythorpe. On 9th November 2007, following the opening by HM The Queen of the new St Pancras Station, Simon Jenkins wrote in 'The Guardian' newspaper, '*For years the fate of St Pancras rested with one man—British Rail's environment director, Bernard Kaukas, who battled to win £3m from his board to prevent the collapse of the roof. His love of the place, again unsung, almost certainly saved St Pancras from demolition.'*

Another friend in the Savage Club is Eddie Bell, the Chairman and Publisher of Harper Collins before he established his own agency. Not only is he acknowledged in Margaret Thatcher's memoirs and John Major's autobiography, but he once told me of his invitation by telephone to go to Moscow where he was asked in person by President Gorbachev to publish his memoir, a commission which he readily accepted. He tried to find a publisher for my book, but without success; he thought it was due to its narrow focus. Yet, in several cathedrals, I have talked to British visitors who had little idea of what they saw before them, and who borrowed my notes and found them fascinating and helpful, so there could well be a market for the book. In the meantime, it is a good excuse for a holiday in France, and on entering one of the great cathedrals now, I greet it like an old familiar friend.

I have found that the best part of a holiday is the planning. This can take several weeks and at least a ream of computer printer paper, because I print my chosen itinerary and, having printed it, I change my mind, and print the revision. And so it goes on. But it's fun. I once printed a twenty-four day route only to reverse it entirely, and found that going the other way round was much more satisfactory.

Bourges Cathedral from the south-east

257

I always take my own duck down pillows. I cannot get on with the nylon variety of continental squares, bolsters and the like. They also form good and safe padding for fragile glassware and electrical items in the suitcase. '*Glassware?*' I hear you cry. Certainly. Having unpacked, there is nothing finer than to sit down on the balcony of your hotel, looking out over the Mediterranean (always pay the extra for a sea-view) as the day draws to a close, and pour a libation of a G&T or a single malt. But all you can find in your room is a plastic tumbler in the bathroom or an uncertain glass in the minibar. You can do better than that. Always abscond from home with a good lead crystal spirit glass or two. Another must for me is my iPod, for I also like music while sitting on the balcony with the same libation, or it might well be the second one by now. It beats bells out of watching Canal+ TV. Don't forget to take with you a comfortable folding chair for a reflective rest from the driving seat at some panoramic view. I've also found it of use in some hotel rooms.

You invariably take too much clothing, so once you've packed, take out a third of the clothing and put it back in the wardrobe. You won't miss it, unless you put back all your shirts. I throw a blazer in the back of the car if the journey is to last three or four weeks, on the basis that the longer you are away, the greater become the odds that you'll be invited to some function and a blazer will always see you through. Besides, it hides the cases of wine on the way home.

Toward the end of my time as Chaplain-in-Chief, a fine bass singer in the choir of St Clement Danes, Kenneth Jones, invited me to attend a Savage Club House Dinner as his guest. Ken is a great character, with the stature of Mr Pickwick, and he has been a welcome visitor to my home when he came as a guest speaker at the annual St Vincent's Dinner. Early in 1947, after singing for Lord Mountbatten at the Viceroy's Palace, he left the Press Club in Delhi at the same moment as a white-suited Indian gentleman, and they walked together as Ken tried to persuade him of the folly of partition. That is the kind of behaviour which comes naturally to a Savage. The next morning's newspaper portrayed a photograph of the gentleman in the white suit on the front page: he was Private Secretary to Jinnah, the leader of the All-India Muslim League until Pakistan's independence in 1947 and Pakistan's first Governor-General. Other speakers at the annual St Vincent Dinner have been the actor David Howe, who sometimes played the Vicar in 'Last of the Summer Wine', and Julian Baker, Professor of Horn at the Royal College of Music, who related anecdotes from his time with the Hallé Orchestra under Sir John Barbirolli.

The Savage Club was founded in 1857 by George Augustus Sala, as a Bohemian club for gentlemen involved in art, music, literature and drama, and 'who enjoy good conversation and the sale of excisable liquor.' Later, the disciplines of science and law were added to the categories of membership. The Club was founded at the Crown Tavern, Vinegar Yard, Drury Lane, but throughout the Second World War it was established at No.1 Carlton House Terrace in St James's. When they were not

Ken Jones the Bass in the Savage Club

stuck in the BBC's Light Entertainment Department in Bangor, it was here that Ted Kavanagh, Tommy Handley and the rest of the ITMA team (many of whom were Savages) wrote some of the scripts of their wartime radio broadcasts. For the last decade or so it has been with the National Liberal Club at No.1 Whitehall Place, Westminster.

I enjoyed the Savage Club evening as Ken's guest enormously. The following year I accepted another invitation from Ken, but when he asked me a third time I declined to trespass further on his generosity, and asked if I could apply for election as a member. He nominated me and the operatic bass, Lynton Black, seconded my nomination, and I was elected in 1996 as a Savage.

Another Savage who visited us in Caythorpe was the actor Martin Benson. His first film role was in 1948 when he was thirty. In a typical piece of understatement he told me that, before that, he was fully occupied between Dunkirk in 1940 and GHQ Cairo in 1946. After the war, he posted himself to Alexandria, found an empty building and with the help of his sergeant, later the well-known actor Arthur Lowe, he converted it into a theatre. Still a serving officer, he ran it as a repertory company. He came to Caythorpe to give me advice about the reredos in St Vincent's church; it was (and still is) in need of expert cleaning. While in *The King & I* at Drury Lane Martin had time between matinee and evening performances, and with his dressing room a second home, he began to paint, and had pictures in the RA Summer Exhibitions in the 1950s.

A practising Jew, Martin was a brilliant raconteur and his Jewish stories, told after dinner at the Savage, had everyone helpless with laughter. Martin Benson's film roles included parts in The Sea Wolves (1980), The Pure Hell of St. Trinian's, and Doctor at Large to name but a few. He was Ramos in Cleopatra (1963), Mr Solo in the James Bond film Goldfinger (1964) and Maurice in A Shot in the Dark, the 1964 Pink Panther film. But he was known more famously for his role as Kralahome, the King's Vizier, with Yul Brynner as the King, in the 1956 film of Rodgers and Hammerstein's *The King and I*.

Stanley Unwin, one of the most unassuming men I have ever met became a particular friend in the Savage Club. He had been a BBC Outside Broadcast sound engineer and used to entertain the broadcasters in the OB Van with bursts of Unwinese. This was heard by a producer who saw that this was genuine entertainment and so 'Professor' Stanley Unwin was born. We would enjoy long conversations when he came into the Savage for what he called 'a tilty-elbow.' He sent me a recording of his story of the Nativity in Unwinese, which is very moving as well as hilarious. 'Deep joy'.

My First Savage Club House Dinner, 1999. The menu card drawn by John Worsley, who created 'Albert RN'.

At the heart of the Club's life is the House Dinner, when Savages and their guests gather to relax in good company. This tradition goes back to the very early days of the Club, for Savages have always enjoyed wining and dining together, and today it occurs about twice a month. A member of the Club is chosen by the Honorary Secretary to chair each dinner, and then he chooses his menu and arranges for one of the art members to draw a menu card for the occasion featuring the chairman. Menu cards of the past are displayed around the Clubroom, and those by famous artists become very collectable. On the night of the dinner, we meet in the bar for a livener after the journey to the Club, and then climb the elegant stairs of the National Liberal Club to the David Lloyd George room, where we keep our Steinway Concert Grand piano.

There is an unwritten rule that there are no speeches at a House Dinner, which is an admirable arrangement. After dinner the Club Pianist leads the assembly of men in singing Edwardian choruses, which always ends with '*If you were the only girl in the world.*' It sounds bizarre in the cold light of day, but at the time it engenders a feeling of well-being and contentment. Then members entertain their guests with an array of talent which could not be afforded if fees were charged. There is an amazing range of performances, from dazzling piano pieces to operatic arias, via magic and dramatic recitation to horn quintets and jazz. I remember travelling on the last train from Kings Cross, after a memorable House Dinner with Eric Midwinter in the Chair, when a lady next to me asked where I had been. I replied, '*I have been in the company of gods!*' She moved to another seat.

Just over a year after my election to membership, Richard Baker, a member of the General Committee, and another welcome visitor to Caythorpe, invited me to lunch and asked me to consider becoming the Club's Honorary Secretary. At its founding, Sala had styled himself '*Hon Sec, pro tem.*' Ever since, the Club has been administered by a Hon. Sec., elected from its membership, and this was the position I was asked to consider. I protested my youth as a member, but that was deemed irrelevant; they wanted someone who would run the club with a firm hand. So I accepted the position on the basis that I would travel to the Club for one day a week, and that my out-of-pocket expenses would be paid.

In London's famous old clubs, the Secretary runs the club as a Chief Executive on behalf of the Finance and General Purposes Committee; in this the Savage was no exception. I was regarded as the Chief Executive, and as long as the Club functioned well, I was expected to get on with it. I began with an examination of the Club Rules. There were some anomalies and rules which I thought were due for revision. I enlisted the aid of John Braun, a Savage who had been responsible for drafting the first Consumer Protection Programme for the then European Economic Community prior to his retirement, and who had a keen eye for the correct terminology of law-making. In short, he was invaluable, and our proposals for changes in the Club Rules were accepted by membership at the Annual General Meeting.

As I became more and more involved in the lives of the members, I found a great store of caring and gentle men from all walks of life. It is the mix of disciplines which makes the Savage such an entertaining club: artists, musicians, actors, writers, professors, doctors, legal luminaries, solemn or reverent characters, kind or quirky ones, the conversation at the bar is as cerebral as it is amusing. The unofficial motto is 'Leave your halo in the hall.' In 2007 the club celebrated its first 150 years. In a letter of congratulation, HRH The Prince Philip, Duke of Edinburgh, himself a member of the Club, wrote: '*I am sure that the founders of the Club would have been delighted to know that their initiative had survived and flourished for such a long time. They obviously hit on the right formula, and I have no doubt that it will continue to attract enthusiastic members for many years to come.*'

To celebrate the 150th anniversary I arranged for the Post office to issue a 'smiler' stamp, which was bought by a large number of Savages. I tried to have a railway engine named '*Savage Club*' to no avail, despite a nice letter from the General Manager of GNER. I fared no better with my idea of tying a Club bow tie around the bust of former Savage Sir Henry Wood on the Last Night of the Proms, although the leader of the 'Promenaders' was sympathetic to my cause.

Why do we call ourselves Savages? Nobody knows for certain; co-founder Dr. G L M Strauss said that it was to honour Richard Savage, an eighteenth century poet. Richard was a bohemian all right, but pretty minor as poets go. Another view was taken by Stephen Fiske who, in 1916, wrote that the Club was named to immortalize the tragic end of Henry Savage, a poor 'penny-a-liner', found dead in Covent Garden; starved, alas, in the midst of plenty. It might have been this story which gave rise to the Savage Club Benevolent Fund, which, while it is quite independent of the Club, looks after Savages who suffer sickness or fall on hard times, often between periods of work in the uncertain world of the arts.

We employ a full-time Assistant Secretary, Susan Habacon, who works in the club office every morning, and a full-time Club Steward, Michael Leonard, a gentle Irishman with whom I often clashed over Rugby. It soon became apparent that my dear friend Richard Baker had been economical with the truth when he told me that a day a week would suffice. When preparing for the 2003 Licensing Act, I was working about five hours a day, either in the office or on the computer at home. I retired from the Rectory of the Caythorpe Benefice in August 2003 and so I was able to devote much more time to the Club.

The Savage is a member of the Association of London Clubs (ALC) which is an association open to the club secretaries of London's Private Member Clubs. By this time I had been elected as a member of the Executive Committee of the ALC, and working in concert with my brother and sister secretaries, the workload generated by the 2003 Act became bearable. Even so, it required me to be in London almost every day while the necessary preparations were under way. When the Secretary of the Oriental Club was Chairman of the ALC, he invited me to become the Honorary Chaplain to the Association, a post I still enjoy.

In 1998 the opera singer, Lynton Black, suggested a Club Carol Service at St Clement Danes. The Committee agreed to it, and I was asked to arrange it with the church for December. The result was an outstanding success and has been repeated each year since. In December 2000, I accepted with alacrity the suggestion from the timpanist Stephen Henderson that I might wish the choir to be joined by the Savage Club Brass Ensemble, which later adopted the old Savage musical title, Philsavonia. St Clement Danes is a big church, but each year, at 6 o'clock on the first Monday in December, it is filled with Savages and their guests for one of the finest carol services in London.

The increased work load, which demanded so much more of my time looking at my computer monitor, was in danger of having an adverse affect on my eyesight, and so, with great reluctance, I stood down as Hon Sec at the AGM in 2008, but I continue to offer candid advice freely to my successor in the Club Bar.

Meanwhile, I was still involved in the life of the Royal Air Force as Honorary Chaplain to the Bomber Command and the Coastal Command Associations. It was the latter which brought me to preach again at Westminster Abbey in 2004. The occasion was the Dedication of a Tribute to those who served in Coastal Command and its successor formations. The Tribute took the form of a bas-relief sculpture sited in the South Cloister of the Abbey, and was the result of an enormous amount of hard work by the Maritime Air Trust under its President, Air Chief Marshal Sir John Barraclough, KCB CBE DFC AFC. It was Sir John who asked me to preach at the Service of Thanksgiving following the unveiling of the Tribute by Her Majesty the Queen. We had lunch together several times, for he was determined that I should have every piece of information at my fingertips.

On Tuesday 16th March the Abbey was full of veterans of Coastal Command and the High Commissioners and Ambassadors of our allies. The Dean presented me to Her Majesty as she arrived in the South Cloister for the Dedication and unveiling, then we all processed into the Abbey for the service. As the service began I glanced across the sanctuary and was looking directly at Her Majesty The Queen, His Royal Highness The Prince Philip, Duke of Edinburgh, and His Royal Highness Prince Michael of Kent. At first I smiled, which The Queen returned, but then it was difficult to know where to look to avoid embarrassment.

I was verged to the pulpit for this my third sermon in the Abbey, and again I was taken aback at the size of the church. I have preached at Canterbury, Guildford, Lincoln, Liverpool, Norwich and Truro Cathedrals, and at York Minster, all of which afford a view of the entire congregation before you. But at Westminster Abbey you behold a vast concourse of people from the pulpit and then, through the choir screen, you can see a miniscule part of the large congregation gathered in the nave, which is following the service on TV screens. Undeterred, I saw very many of my friends in the Transept seats, and Joy in the Chapter Stall at the east end of the choir, and I began to enjoy the experience. In order to give an example of the work of maritime aircrews I told the story of the Shackleton crew arriving in the Mess at St Mawgan during the Open Day, which I describe in chapter four of this book. I was told by a verger afterwards that Her Majesty was highly amused by the anecdote.

Travellers in an Antique Land

In November 2005, I joined my son Mark in a holiday in Syria. Joy had given me an eight-day trip to Syria as a birthday present some years before, and I had since wanted to spend longer in the country. I arranged a twelve-day itinerary with Bales Worldwide Tailor Made Holidays. I specified the places we wished to visit, using only 5-star hotels, and an air-conditioned chauffeur driven car. We flew to Damascus and were met by Hussein, our excellent English-speaking chauffeur and guide. We stayed in the Cham Palace Hotel in Damascus for a few days before heading north to Hama.

On the way north, we made a short detour to visit the town of Maaloula, 4,000ft high in the mountains to the west of the motorway north to Homs. Here, in the Greek Catholic Monastery of St Sergius, built about 320 AD, I enjoyed one of the highlights of our journey. Maaloula is an Armenian town; three quarters of the population are Christian and the language is Aramaic. The young lady showing us around the church of St Sergius was a Christian, and I asked her to speak in Aramaic, as it was the language which Christ spoke. She said softly in Arabic, '*I will pray with you in Aramaic.*' Hussein, a devout Moslem, interpreted the Arabic for us and bowed his head. From the rhythm of her speech, I recognized the prayer, even in Aramaic. When she finished, I asked Hussein to ask her what she had said. It was indeed the Lord's Prayer—in the very language in which Christ first taught it to the disciples on the hillside, and in a church built about 300 years after his death and resurrection.

In Aleppo we stayed for four days in an old Syrian hotel in the Armenian district. We delighted in Aleppo, and gave Hussein some time off while we walked everywhere. In a passage in the fantastic Citadel Mark and I were approached by two young ladies in their twenties who asked us, in fluent English, about research possibilities in Bio-technology in British universities. We talked for ten minutes or so, then shook hands and they went on their way, their long flowing robes giving them an elegance all their own. I tried to imagine two English girls approaching a couple of Syrians in the Tower of London and conducting a similar conversation in Arabic, but it seemed too surreal.

We spent a night in Deir Ezzor, arriving after dark. When I drew my bedroom curtains the following morning I was greeted with a magnificent view of the slow-moving Euphrates curving below the hotel, and already people were at work in

The River Euphrates from my hotel room in Deir Ezzor

the fields on the opposite bank. That day we travelled due south along the west bank of the river, with the desert at a height of thirty metres to our right and never more than a kilometre from the flood plain. We were making for Mari, a few miles from the Syrian border with Iraq. As we left Deir Ezzor Hussein said, '*We've picked up a tail*.' A black Mercedes was right behind us. Once out of the town, Hussein accelerated until the desert was flashing by. I glanced over my shoulder, but the Mercedes was sticking to us. An hour later we came upon an army checkpoint and were flagged down, but the Mercedes flashed its headlights, and we were instantly waved on. This happened again as we came within a few miles of the Abu Kamal border crossing with Iraq. Hussein thought our 'tail' was from the Security Forces.

The Mercedes followed us off the road and, past an army patrol, into the entrance of the archaeological site of Mari. The two men came over to shake hands, '*Welcome to Syria, Mr Lucas*,' said the elder of them with a warm smile. They knew my name! The younger one was speaking in rapid Arabic into a mobile phone and I saw that he was armed. I felt strangely reassured by their presence, and said as much to Hussein. He agreed that it was good for tourism that Syria took care of its visitors.

The sun was even hotter at noon as we left the ancient city site of Dura Europos, just north of Mari. Hussein, eased our car along the rough track and turned north on to the highway from Baghdad to Damascus. The black Mercedes followed right behind us until we reached the town of Deir Ezzor, where, with a flash of the headlights, they turned off the road. In the centre of the town is the junction with the desert road to Palmyra, and so, turning west, we left the mighty Euphrates.

The desert seems endless and empty, but three hours after leaving Deir Ezzor we saw the trees of the oasis of Palmyra emerge as a green smudge on the horizon. I had been to Palmyra during my previous visit to Syria, but I hadn't gone up to the old Arab Fort above the ruins of the ancient city. Hussein drove up the winding track to the Arab Castle on the hill to the north, where we saw the sun set across the desert to the west. As the shadows crept across the low sandy hills, and the ancient world of Palmyra spread out below us turned first pink and then a kind of deep blue, before being snuffed out by the onset of night, I considered that it was one of the timeless experiences of mankind. The Bedouin of today, soldiers and airmen of two World Wars, the crusaders of old, and the disciples of Christ had all witnessed the same 'lights out' as they turned into their tents for protection from the night.

Two days later we visited Bosra, just six miles from the Jordanian border. On our return, we joined the Amman to Damascus motorway, and sped north. Soon, the Golan Heights became visible on the horizon to the west, and I was reminded how Syria was caught up in religious tension on all sides. Sitting in the back of the car as it threaded its way through the traffic, I reflected that the young skilled eye surgeon, who was propelled into the Presidential Palace on the death of his father, cannot find life easy as he tries to develop commerce with the west and at the same

Mark and Hussein in the Syrian Desert

time be faithful to the cultural and religious demands of his people. The Syrians are friendly and courteous people, but they are also proud and independent; they are still people of the desert at heart.

Toward the end of our holiday in Syria I noticed a slight haziness in the vision of my left eye, but put it down to desert heat haze. On my return to Caythorpe it was not so evident, but by the beginning of 2006 it was clear that all was not well with my left eye. Too late it was diagnosed as Age-Related Macular Degeneration (AMD) which had turned 'wet'. I saw the consultant in Lincoln Hospital who affirmed that it had gone too far and so nothing could be done to save the sight in that eye. There is still peripheral vision in that eye, so I can drive and live an almost normal life.

· · · · · · · · · ·

When I retired from the full-time priestly ministry, Joy and I searched the surrounding towns and villages for a spiritual home. It is traditional for a priest to move away from his former parish on retirement in order to allow his successor a free rein, but in my case my home had been established in Caythorpe since 1988. I therefore gave the bishop an undertaking that I would worship elsewhere. After a few weeks, we discovered the parish of St Mary, Stamford, an elegant market town about forty minutes drive south along the A1. There are two churches in the benefice: St Martin Stamford Baron, with the Cecil Chapel and close ties with Burghley House, and St Mary the Virgin, where, at 11.00 each Sunday, High Mass is sung. It reminds me of my youth in St Theodore's Church, Port Talbot, with three ministers in vestments at the altar, incense and a very high musical tradition under the direction of the organist Fergus Black.

When we first attended this church the Rector was Fr Michael Thompson, who had been a priest in Port Talbot some years after my time there. He made us most welcome, and when he moved on to another parish, he telephoned me and asked if Joy and I were going to attend his last Mass in Stamford on Michaelmas Day, and, if so, would we also be at the 'bunfight' after the Mass. I said that we would be there, and then he asked me if I would say a few words, about the interregnum and to reassure the people. I agreed to do this most willingly, and began to give some thought to my little speech at the 'bunfight'.

We arrived in good time, but the church was already full, and Joy managed to find a seat at the back, while I went into the Sacristy to put on my cassock and join the other clergy. The Sacristy was packed: the Bishop of Grantham was already robed, so was the Rural Dean, the other clergy and the acolytes. I was able to change in a corner, and so I missed the seating announcement. I asked Canon Donald Gray if he knew where I was to sit, and he asked a churchwarden, '*Where is the Preacher sitting?'* I protested that I was not the preacher, just attending. *'Oh yes you are,'* he said, and showed me the order of service. At once the procession formed and the service started.

It was a priest's worst nightmare. As we were processing down the aisle I was trying to put some thoughts together: I must mention Michaelmas, Fr Michael, and the interregnum. When I found my seat in the sanctuary I jotted three things on the back of my service sheet: *'In No Strange Land'* by Francis Thompson, with the lines, *'The angels keep their ancient places—Turn but a stone and start a wing!'* that would be a prompt for Michaelmas; *'Wherever the Catholic sun doth shine, There's always laughter and good red wine. At least I've always found it so. Benedicamus Domino!'* by Hilaire Belloc, was my prompt for Fr Michael; and I also wrote the words, *'More than one way to bath the baby',* the keyword of a joke which would lead into some remarks about the interregnum. That was all I had for my sermon, and too soon I found myself in the pulpit looking down at a packed church.

Afterward, I could not remember a word of it, but Joy said it was very good, and the Bishop complimented me on the time I must have spent preparing it. Only Donald Gray knew the truth, and he just winked at me. I joined the rota of retired clergy to keep the services going throughout the interregnum and ever since Fr Michael Ruff was appointed as the Priest-in-Charge, I have remained a regular celebrant and preacher in the benefice.

My love of flying is undiminished, and in August 2001 Joy gave me the treat of a flight in a North American Havard T6 from Tollerton Airfield near Nottingham. My pilot was Professor Brian Salter, Professor of Politics at Kings College London, and he allowed me to take the controls of this venerable wartime trainer, which I wanted to fly in South Africa but time didn't permit it. More recently, in 2008, Air Vice Marshal Paul Robinson, a friend from his time at Cranwell, took me flying in the Grob Tutor from Cranwell, and allowed me to fly the aircraft from Sutterton back over Sleaford.

For the rest, my time is fully occupied as the Honorary President of No.3 Welsh Wing, Air Training Corps; the President of the Sleaford and District Aviation Society (SDLAS); Governor of a local High School; the Honorary Chaplain of the Bomber Command Association, of the Coastal Command and Maritime Air Association, and also of the Association of London Clubs. When I am not attending to these organizations or writing sermons, I am either driving through the length and breadth of France with my cameras, or constructing a model railway layout at home.

My duties in No.3 Welsh Wing require me to wear RAF uniform once more when, at the request of Wing Commander Bob Wilson, the Wing's Commanding Officer, I take the salute at parades or present awards or a Sword of Honour on

Inspecting No.334 (Neath) Squadron ATC

behalf of the Commandant Air Cadets. As the Wing covers a huge part of Wales from Cowbridge in the south to Aberystwyth in the north, the annual Dining-in Night is held in Tenby, when my job is to entertain them after dinner. I do it willingly, for about a hundred ATC officers and their guests fill the Giltar Hotel each April and I am always impressed at the time and energy these men and women give freely to the young people of their towns and villages.

Similarly, in my role as a school governor, I look forward to my visits as the link governor with the English Department, for it gives me the opportunity to speak to the young people of their hopes, fears and aspirations.

The great joy of age is grandchildren. Mark and Susan have two daughters, Scarlett who is now nine, and Lola who is six; the girls look forward to their stay with us during holidays, and we delight in having them. Simon and Kirsty have our only grandson, Dylan, and baby Evelyn whom we have yet to greet as they live in Arizona. Helen and John have a two-year old daughter, Beth, who is delightful and energetic company. In 2008 they all came to stay for Christmas, and the house was filled with laughter and scintillating repartee, as my wine store emptied.

Well, my tale is told. That young boy, who dabbled in amateur dramatics at school, has appeared on life's stage and played his part. How well it was received is not for me to say, but, on reflection, I do not think I would have changed any of the scenes very much. Ever since my boyhood, when my gang of six friends emerged gasping for air from the small garden shed at my home, I have discovered that I thrive on leadership roles. I have discerned that true leadership requires self-confidence, and I had this in spades from my parent's encouragement as a lad. It also requires the most effective leader to lead from the front, and not to be afraid about making a few mistakes along the way. The greater the pressure through the defence cuts in the 1990s, the more determined I became to fight for my beloved chaplains. I have always been happy to poke my head above the parapet, whether as Chairman of the Conservative Association at university, resulting in a break with the Party, or in my preaching, I believe firmly in telling it as it is. That might be why I was so well-suited to life in the RAF, for of the three armed forces the Royal Air Force is the most meritocratic; the fact that I was never happier than when performing loops and stall turns in the air probably helped.

The RAF and P&O cruising have certainly provided many opportunities for me to indulge my delight in new horizons, not only in exploring different cultures, but also, at times, by extending my priesthood to its limit. My faith and trust in God is far more profound now than when I first believed, for I have been used by him in so many ways. But to be used you have to be available, hence my ministry of loitering with intent in crew rooms, hangars and wherever people congregate. When I was a young priest in Llandaff Cathedral, and first saw the faces of the congregation reflected in the chalice at the Holy Eucharist, I could never have imagined the variety of reflections I would see in the future. Many of the faces are now reflected in a higher glory as they have died to this life; others have become life-long friends; all of them are remembered with tenderness.

Dylan Thomas, in his poem 'Fern Hill', wrote that even when he was a young lad, time was rushing inexorably towards his death. That is true, but it doesn't concern me at all, for I am too busy to think about it. I prefer his line in another poem which avers, '*The ball I threw while playing in the park has not yet reached the ground.*' That's a much better view: while the ball is in the air, there is still time to do things. I see no prospect of boredom in old age; probably there will be some infirmity, which has to be faced with equanimity and serenity. But for the present, I am content.

· · · · · · · · · ·

"*The ball I threw while playing in the park
Has not yet reached the ground.*"
From, "*Should lanterns shine.*" by the late Brother Savage Dylan Thomas (1914–1953).

INDEX

271